JACOBEAN DRAMA

Jacobean Drama

A Critical Study of the Professional Drama, 1600–25

David Farley-Hills
Professor of English
University College of Swansea

St. Martin's Press   New York

First published in the United States of America in 1988

Printed in Hong Kong

ISBN 0–312–01274–8

Library of Congress Cataloging-in-Publication Data
Farley-Hills, David.
Jacobean drama.
Bibliography: p.
Includes index.
1. English drama—17th century—History and
criticism.   I. Title.
PR651.F35   1988   822'.3'09   87–28909
ISBN 0–312–01274–8

Contents

Acknowledgements

I should like to thank especially Mrs Rita Williams and Miss Gabriella Scascia for their help in preparing the typescript and my daughter, Sandra, for her help in typing some of the original foul papers.

1
Introduction: Jacobean Professional Theatre and Shakespeare

The twenty-five years of Jacobean professional theatre were the most brilliant and dynamic the world has seen. The twenty-five years were not literally all Jacobean: James I came to the throne in 1603 and died in 1625 and although he must take some small credit for the chief glory of his reign, the date that matters for theatre history takes us back to 1599 with the re-opening of the 'private' theatre of Paul's boys, followed in the following year by the opening of the revamped Blackfriars theatre. Both were small halls (Paul's nothing much more than a large room) but their opening brought forth an avalanche of play-writing that established a new generation of writers for the stage, the most important of whom, Jonson, Chapman, Marston, Middleton challenged the dominance of the one major figure surviving from the earlier decade: William Shakespeare. The rivalry, the competing for markets, the clash of attitudes towards theatre that meet in response and counter-response well illustrate the Chapmanesque contention that 'all things by strife engender'. In the centre of this vital turmoil, the boisterous Jonson, stirring up antagonisms, setting new artistic standards as well as a new awareness of the power and responsibility of the dramatist, forced an essentially commercial theatre to become fully conscious of its public function as a platform for ideas and of the play as a literary form.

The period has come to be thought of as the age of Shakespeare and Shakespeare's response to the new challenge was one of extraordinary inventiveness. But to see Shakespeare isolated in a nimbus of excellence is both to grossly underestimate his major colleagues and rivals and to fail to understand those theatrical forces that shaped Shakespeare's greatest work. The neglect of the other major playwrights of the day by the modern professional theatre (give or take the occasional performances of a handful of Jonson's

1

plays and little else) is an absurdity and a particular disgrace for publicly subsidised theatre. For Shakespeare's plays are one important, but only one, part of that astonishing flowering of theatrical talent that was a result of the coincidence of a number of key developments: the evolution of play traditions from both medieval and classical past and of staging from the more immediate Tudor past that gave an opulent variety of choice of methods and approaches to the playwright and the presenter; the stability of a permanent location for the stage (increasingly 'stages' as the theatres multiplied) able to develop a professional expertise that had reasonable chances of offering financial reward; a censorship that prevented plays from becoming too topical and too particular; the interest of mixed audiences, containing both those who insisted on the theatre being lively and those who insisted on the theatre being serious, with the essential requirement of being willing to pay for what they wanted. Not all the plays satisfied both elements of their audiences all the time, but the best did.

Jacobean theatre was first and foremost entertainment. All theatre is of course essentially entertainment, however committed to external causes it appears to be; it is play-acting, playing the game of being the big world outside, acting out patterns of interpretations of the big world. Like all play, it does you good (in a number of senses) and it does society good by articulating communal responses. The great strength of the Jacobean professional theatre is that it rarely loses sight of its entertaining role and interprets that role with seriousness. There were some Jacobean playwrights, Jonson above all, who chafed at the role that linked him with the mountebank and the juggler (though in *Volpone*, *The Alchemist* and *Bartholomew Fair* he comes brilliantly and explicitly to terms with the relationship), but Jonson was fortunate in not being able to escape the conditions imposed on him by his theatre and it is no coincidence that his best work is for the popular theatre.

The Jacobeans were not very good, on the whole, at entertaining themselves, certainly they were not as good as we are. This is understandable: life was grim for most of them for most of the time—drudgery, disease, poverty, malnutrition, early death constantly threatened, and their religion, with the prevailing emphasis on original sin and man's innate depravity, encouraged them to take a painful view of the world. Spare time was spent more usefully in prayer than in amusement: the churches were habitually packed on Sundays and the sermon was attended more assiduously by most men than the play. In these circumstances entertainment might be (and sometimes was) tempted to become escape, but it was also equally tempted to take on the admonitory role of the theatre's older sister and erstwhile nurse, the Church. Entertainment then became not mere escape, but a recreation (in both senses) of shared beliefs. Not surprisingly much Jacobean drama is an expression of deeply held religious beliefs, though these beliefs are not often paraded or made too explicit and because, since the Reformation, religious belief was a highly controversial matter there are wide differences in the doctrinal assumptions of different playwrights, from the stark Calvinism of 'City' playwrights like Middleton and Webster to the secular Anglicanism of the bishop's son, John Fletcher. Class differences play a part here: 'City' meant 'bourgeois', but the other of the two poles between which the field of professional drama was held was the Court, whose shade the more gentlemanly playwright (or the more sycophantic) sought. The differences between Court and City, Calvinist and Anglican, rarely became explicit or overt in the drama, partly because this was a theatre of professional entertainment from which it did not pay to alienate the best customers, and partly because of a ferocious, if inconsistent, government censorship which aimed to keep the stage out of overt political (which also meant religious) controversy. The differences therefore remain mostly implicit or are usually dealt with (in the case of Court versus City) in a bantering manner, but the influence of religious and political ideas remains important, especially in the first decade of the seventeenth century.

Because Jacobean professional theatre had to pay its way, it had to pay close attention to what its audiences wanted to hear and what they would tolerate. There is no doubt that one of the things even the stinkard would expect of his theatre was moral and religious doctrine, for this had been the case since time immemorial. No satisfactory entertainment would be entirely without it and the Jacobean's favourite reading (to judge from the statistics of publication) was religious controversy. There was, however, as one might expect, a wide range of audience expectation and this was to some extent reflected in differences between the audiences of the different theatres throughout the Jacobean period. It is of course extremely difficult to know what the average Jacobean spectator wanted to hear, or even to identify who the average spectator was. Our best evidence is in the surviving texts we are trying to illuminate, the plays themselves, but the majority have failed to survive. Even among those that have survived it is impossible from the plays alone to judge how much a brilliant eccentricity would be valued above an adequate orthodoxy. All one can say about the Jacobean audience is that it seems to have crossed class barriers so that in the big open-air theatres at least, like the Globe and the Fortune, one could expect to find a wide spectrum of London life from illiterate pot-boy to wealthy gentry. The more expensive covered theatres, Paul's and Blackfriars in the early years of the century, the Phoenix (or Cockpit) and others later, were no doubt too expensive for the rabble rout, for by the time of Fletcher's *Wit Without Money* (c.1616) and Jonson's *Bartholomew Fair* (1614)[1] it cost a half-crown to go into the best seats—thirty times the cost of standing room at the Globe at the turn of the century. Even in the early days of the new Paul's and Blackfriars the entry cost sixpence and it seems obvious that (with an estimated wage of around seven shillings a week for a workman in 1601[2]) the poorer sort could not afford the entrance fee. Although the audience of the 'private' theatres, so-called, was therefore made of the better-off, it would be wrong to think of it as homogeneous. The gentry-city jokes of Dekker and Webster's *Westward Ho* and *Northward Ho*, which were mostly at the expense of the gentry, suggest a mixed bourgeois, courtly audience at Paul's in 1604–5 with even a preponderance of City people. Paul's was in the City centre and was very small (about 100 seats) so that it would presumably not take much to fill it with tradesfolk, who were often in a better position to afford regular play-going than the gentry. It may not be a coincidence that the principal playwright of Paul's, John Marston, shows a Calvinistic bias in the plays he wrote for that theatre (for the City was more inclined that way than the Court) while his later plays (for the Blackfriars) show a marked easing in the Puritanical outlook of the earlier plays. The City playwright Middleton also began his career here with comedies centring on financial trickery; his Calvinistic ironies show no favours.

Blackfriars was a larger theatre (some 700 seats perhaps); closer to Westminster and on the western edge of the City, it may have had a greater proportion of gentry in the audience. The recurring controversy over the obstruction caused by the coaches of the fashionable, which had prevented Burbage exploiting Blackfriars for his own company, suggests that courtly customers were an important part of the audience. This courtliness again appears in the repertoire, which favoured the more gentlemanly attitudes of establishment Anglicanism, not only witnessing Marston's conversion to a softer line, but applauding Chapman's brilliant mythologising and the secular romanticism of Beaumont and Fletcher. When the middle-class social realism, popular with Paul's audience, is represented at Blackfriars—as in *Eastward Ho* (1605) or Beaumont's *The Knight of the Burning Pestle* (1607)—it is the tradesfolk who have to take the brunt of the ridicule.

Even in the popular theatre a difference can be detected between those like the Curtain, the Fortune and the Red Bull on the north side of the City and those like the Globe on the South Bank. The Globe was in easy reach by water of the fashionable western suburbs where Stow describes 'a continual new building of divers fair houses' in 1598,[3] and its audience was almost certainly a mixture of gentry and City, so that in a play like *Hamlet* Shakespeare could write a popular play that would also please the wiser sort (as Gabriel Harvey remarked[4]) while Henslowe's plays for the the Fortune and the Red Bull are on the whole a good deal less sophisticated and avant-garde. The location of theatres has not been given enough attention by scholars. It would be quite wrong, however, to exaggerate the differences between the theatres in this period. Plays were sometimes transferred from one theatre to another: Middleton's *A Trick to Catch the Old One* (c.1605), for instance, was first performed at Paul's and then transferred to Blackfriars, where its demonstration of the defeat of the money-grabbing Hoards and the usurer Dampit, that must have satisfied the moral conscience of the City, would no doubt delight the land-owning and money-borrowing gentry. Transfers too were not unknown between 'private' and 'public' theatre. Webster's adaptation of Marston's *The Malcontent* for the Globe demonstrates that not much of the text needed to be altered for the open-air theatre, though Webster's Induction has to reassure its audience (in the person of Henry Condell) that it is going to be subject to 'neither satire nor moral, but the mean passage of a history'. Satire is no doubt what a Globe audience might have reason to fear from the 'eyrie of children' rather than its own staple fare of Shakespearean 'history'. It is possible that the differences between the 'Tragedy of King Lear' (Folio) and the 'True Chronicle History . . . of King Lear' (Quarto) can be accounted for as adaptations for a Court and Globe audience. Exchanges between 'private' and 'public' theatres became frequent after Shakespeare's company took over Blackfriars in 1608.

In some ways the Webster Induction to *Malcontent* emphasises the different expectations of the two kinds of audience. That difference is partly the result of the very different stage conditions. The 'private' companies were boys' companies, exclusively acted by children, whereas the 'public' theatres had male adult players. There were also big differences between acting in small covered theatres and on the larger open-air stages. The Globe and Fortune would naturally favour the big gesture, the 'private' theatres greater intimacy. Boy actors would in any case be much less capable of the grand effect and it is not at all surprising that their talents were exploited in the direction of mimicry and comic deflation. One of the ways that the adult companies defended themselves from the economic threat posed by their smaller rivals was to exploit their capacity for tragedy, and it can be no coincidence that the Globe staged *Hamlet, Macbeth, Othello, Sejanus* over the years that in the 'private' theatres are most notable for satirical comedies. That the covered theatres did pose a serious threat to the adult companies for a time is clear from the famous passage in the Folio version of *Hamlet* where Rosencrantz describes how the boy players 'carry it away' (II. ii. 326–64). The difference in theatrical conditions between the two types of theatre at this period leads to a marked difference in the playwrights' approach to theatre. Whereas the adult companies tend to affective theatre, in which the audience is encouraged to share in the feelings of the characters and the assumption is therefore that the characters are 'real' and have a life of their own (Hamlet himself is a pre-eminent example), the boys' theatres favour a detached relationship between audience and character (what Brechtian jargon now calls 'alienation') in which character is seen primarily as a device for thematic patterning. Hence the boys' companies produced a theatre of ideas. Jonson is the supreme example of this detachment. The more critical, aloof attitudes of the gentlemanly audiences of the 'private' theatres is well caught in a remark by The Prologue in the Induction to John Day's *The Isle of Gulls* (written for Blackfriars in 1606) where one of the audience threatens to hiss the play if it lacks bawdy and the Prologue comments: 'You should not deal gentleman-like with us else'. The public audience was presumably better-behaved, more caught up in the action. After around 1608, when Shakespeare's company took over the Blackfriars theatre, there is a rapid decline in the importance of the boys' troops and the distinction between the two attitudes to theatre fades. Of course the two opposed views are constantly influencing each other; Shakespeare's *Troilus and*

Cressida, for instance, shows many of the qualities of 'alienating' theatre.

Because the conditions of the boys' theatres favoured a drama of ideas there is a marked tendency for the theatre scripts for the 'private' theatres to be much more literary. The difference in survival rate between scripts in the two kinds of theatre is largely explained by this. Of the hundreds of plays written for Henslowe's theatres (as recorded in the *Diary*) very few survive, only something like 5 per cent of the output of popular playwrights like Dekker and Heywood survive and often those plays that do survive were written for 'private' theatres. The bulk of the work of such playwrights was what we might call 'disposable' theatre. We can conclude from the *Diary* that John Day wrote or had a hand in twenty-two plays for Henslowe between 1598 and 1603, only one of which survives; of the six of Day's plays or collaborations that survive, three are of his rare incursions into 'private' theatre. The same is true of the major dramatists; much of the work for the popular theatre of Jonson and Chapman has been lost whereas nearly all their work for the elite theatre has survived. This is no coincidence. Jonson preserved carefully those plays to be thought of as 'literary' and their publication was intended primarily for the reader, for whom Jonson had a higher respect than for his audiences. It is currently fashionable to emphasise that the professional theatre of the Jacobeans was an acting rather than a closet theatre, which is true, but misleading as far as the surviving texts are concerned. Nearly all of the texts that have come down to us (and it is often the reason why they have come down to us) are specifically addressed to readers and were intended to be mulled over in the study by discerning literati. Though many derive from acting copy their very publication is an appeal to be assessed as literature by a reading public. As in so many things Shakespeare is something of an exception to the generalisation that those texts that survive are those for which the primacy of literary value (that is, readability) is tacitly asserted. Even so, Hamlet's advice to the players to respect the author's text (III.ii.39) may be a sign of Shakespeare's increasing concern with literariness as the Globe begins to move up market.

At the beginning of the period with which we are concerned Shakespeare was established as by far the most successful of all the commercial playwrights. Until Paul's theatre had re-opened in 1599 there had in effect been only two London theatre companies for a

number of years, Henslowe's Admiral's Men at the Rose,
transferring in 1600 to the new Fortune Theatre, and Shakespeare's
Chamberlain's Men at Burbage's playhouse, the Theatre,
transferring in 1599 to the newly built Globe. During this time
Shakespeare had maintained his pre-eminence (and founded his
fortune) on a series of English history plays and on a type of
romantic comedy that was essentially an affective drama, in which
the stage, through the exercise of the audience's imagination, was to
become the places it represented: where the audience is exhorted to
'Think, when we talk of horses, that you see them / Printing their
proud hoofs i' the receiving earth'. It is at this period that
Shakespeare's genius for life-like characterisation, the necessary
basis for affective theatre, is most conspicuous. The formula of
life-like people in exotic situations gave his insular audience
imaginative space to disport themselves, encouraged the vicarious
pleasures of time warp and place warp, while at the same time
vitalising communal prejudices that renewed the audience's pride
in themselves as favoured by Providence—for this was Kent (or
Surrey) and Christendom.

As the new century dawned, Shakespeare had to face a challenge
which was also an opportunity. The boys' theatres for a time took
custom away from the public theatre (as Rosencrantz tells us) but
they opened up a new market, made up not only of 'the wiser sort',
but (of more immediate importance) of those who could afford to
pay more. Shakespeare was not slow to grasp the point and *Hamlet*
might be seen as his first counter-attack in regaining lost ground.
The Globe in any case, as I have said, was in a good position to
attract the courtier, and from *Hamlet* onwards Shakespeare's plays
reflect this attempt to appeal to a more sophisticated audience as
well as to capitalise on the advantages the adult theatre had over the
boys' companies (as for instance in the staging of tragedy). But this
implied taking on board some of the new freight. One has only to
compare the last of Shakespeare's old-style comedies, *Twelfth
Night* (written for Queen Elizabeth, Christmas 1600) with his next
comedy (if it is a comedy), *Troilus and Cressida*, to see the great
change that had come about—it can be no coincidence that the
light-hearted fantasy of *Twelfth Night* now gives way to a cruelly
satiric account of the Trojan war, just at the time when Marston and
Jonson had established the new fashion for satire in the boys'
theatres. If (as one version of the *Troilus* Quarto of 1609 tells us) the
play was 'acted . . . at the Globe' it shows Shakespeare's company

taking the battle boldly into enemy territory, all the more remarkable because Heywood's older-style chronicle play on the Trojan war, *The Iron Age*, had not long since been staged, most likely by Worcester's men at the Rose. Nor is *Troilus* the only Shakespearean venture in this new direction: it is one of three 'dark' comedies, that have a more markedly sardonic tone than anything that had gone before. *Measure for Measure* (1604), for instance, not only reflects the sordid, cynical world of the fashionable satiric comedies of Marston and Middleton in the 'private' theatres, but quite unlike Shakespeare's earlier comedies foregrounds philosophical debate (on justice) that would seem to have the wiser sort in mind (including in this case King James). It is interesting to remark that just at the time Chapman, Jonson and Marston were getting themselves into hot water with the Court, Shakespeare was assiduously courting Court favour—*Macbeth*, for instance, dates from around 1605. Shakespeare's tragedy too, from *Hamlet* onwards, is substantially a new departure, not only challenging the boys on ground they were ill-equipped to fight on, but in *Lear*, even more than *Hamlet*, entering profoundly into philosophical debate and in *Coriolanus* challenging the neo-classicism of Jonson and Chapman, and triumphing.

In these years the deftest craftsman of the Elizabethan theatre became an artist of universal import. The process by which he steals his rivals' clothes and then turns them into something entirely his own can sometimes be seen in considerable detail. It is obvious in the least successful of Shakespeare's responses, *Troilus*, where the sneering Thersites can hardly have been conceived independently of such classic snarlers in Jonson's 'comicall satyre' as Asper and Macilente of *Every Man Out of His Humour*, and where abstruse and wordy debate on 'honour' and 'value' have left modern criticism much to ponder on, but seem to have failed to impress the Globe—if we are to interpret the address to the reader of the 1609 Quarto as indicating that it was not applauded when produced there (it was, says the address 'never stal'd with the stage, never clapper-clawd[6] with the palms of the vulgar'). It is less obvious in a play like *All's Well That Ends Well*,[7] which must date from shortly after *Troilus* (to judge by the *Troilus* allusions still buzzing in Shakespeare's head). *All's Well* has puzzled critics, because it uses Shakespearean romantic material (a story of love overcoming unlikely obstacles) in a most unromantic and un-Shakespearean manner. But its theme is the power of love to transform. The play tells how the heroine,

Helena, a poor physician's daughter, urged by her love of the Countess of Rossillion's son, Bertram, follows him first to the French court and from there to Florence to win him. With the approval of the Countess, Helena proceeds to the French King, who is dying of an incurable sickness. She cures him with a remedy bequeathed to her by her father and as a reward the King promises to grant her a wish. She chooses Bertram from the courtiers and the King agrees he should marry her. Very reluctantly Bertram agrees, but immediately after the marriage escapes to Florence where a war is being waged against the Sienese. He proclaims himself a follower of Mars, rather than Venus: 'This very day / Great Mars, I put myself into thy file . . . a lover of thy drum, hater of love' (III.iii.8–11). He has refused to consummate the marriage, telling Helena she will not have him as a husband until she has won the ring he wears on his finger from him and has conceived his child. She achieves these impossible conditions by exchanging roles with a girl in Florence, the chaste Diana, whom Bertram is trying to seduce. She persuades Diana to agree to sleep with Bertram in exchange for his ring and then, unbeknown to Bertram, substitutes herself for Diana in Bertram's bed. The impossible conditions are thus fulfilled.

In spite of the fairy tale quality of the plot the play has little of the atmosphere of fairy tale. Bertram is presented not as an aristocratic prize worth the capture, but as an immature boy (the word is used of him by both his mother and the King), who prefers the company of the braggart fop Parolles to Helena and who chooses war rather than marriage. The confrontation between the male world of war and the female world of love, expressed later and at length in *Othello* and *Antony and Cleopatra* as a confrontation of equal values, is here presented as a confrontation between the negative, empty world of male heroics and the irresistible and positive force of female sexuality. In *Troilus* both love and war had been treated dismissively, now war is mocked in terms of a children's squabble over a drum, while the Countess, Helena, Diana and her widowed mother demonstrate the steady and irresistible strength of feminine purpose. We hear something of Bertram's exploits on the field of battle where it is reported 'the French count has done most honourable service' (II.v.4), but what we actually see is Parolles, having foolishly boasted he will recover a lost drum, being scared out of his wits into treachery, in an ambush arranged by his own side to test his valour. In this farcical ambush the French officers pretend to be Russians and invent a nursery pseudo-Russian as part of their pretence. The nonsense words remind us that Parolles himself is all words—like his name—and suggest a contrast between the male world of empty boasting (at the sign of the drum) and the female world of purposeful endeavour. The empty wordiness of the world of men is further reinforced by the presence in the household of the Countess of Rossillion of the Fool, Lavatch, whose unfunny and ineffectual presence contrasts in its fatuity with the dignified Countess from whose house the action issues and to which it returns. It is she who is the tutelary Venus.

Helena is the emissary of this goddess, curing the King's sickness by a power that is not her own (II.i.150–3). The illness too involves a loss of potency, as Lafew suggests in one of the many ingenious sexual allusions that bedeck the play (II.i.74–7). In the same way Helena brings Bertram back from his attempt to escape his sexual responsibilities to what he describes as 'the dark house and the detested wife' (II.iii.288). A dark house love is, for it contains the mysteries into which Bertram is finally initiated at night in bed with Helena and under a vow of silence (IV.ii.58). Bertram is thus brought back to his mother's house to acknowledge the power of a natural force that he has not been able to resist.

Puzzlement over this play would have been considerably less if it had been seen in the context of the contemporary theatre. For the theme of the power of love to restore to life is the central subject of Chapman's major series of comedies beginning with *The Gentleman Usher* for the Blackfriars theatre in 1602, to be followed by *Monsieur D'Olive* and *The Widows' Tears*. Chapman in these plays explores the neo-platonic theme of the power of God's love to transform experience. Like *All's Well*, each of these Chapman comedies begins in a world where love is rejected and each enacts the process by which love can once again revitalise. Like Shakespeare's play, the Chapman comedies present their mythic subject through social settings where mystery is played down and the tone of witty worldliness predominates (this is particularly true of the sardonic *Widows' Tears*).

The Gentleman Usher marks a distinct change in direction, not only for Chapman, but for early Jacobean comedy. At the height of the fashion for satiric realism, which he had himself done much to initiate in earlier comedies, Chapman turned in his final comedies to romantic themes presented as myth. At this time Chapman was one of Shakespeare's most successful rivals—perhaps the most successful—as a writer for the public stage. He had (it seems) been given the privilege of inaugurating Henslowe's new Fortune Theatre with his play *All Fools* in 1600[8] and Henslowe was not the man to take business decisions lightly. Chapman's modern reputation as a scholarly pedant is totally out of keeping with the evidence of the popularity of his plays on the Elizabethan popular stage. Shakespeare undoubtedly would have found this move towards romantic plots congenial, for he was never fully at home in satire and he must have been only too willing to follow the new trend of his rival.

That *All's Well* is Chapmanesque in its language was remarked long ago by Tillyard in his discussion of the so-called 'problem' plays of Shakespeare,[9] but the combination of mythic subject (the triumph of love over impediment) and realistic treatment is of the essence of Chapman's method in these late comedies. The tone combines worldly cynicism with otherworldly miracle. In both *All's Well* and *Gentleman Usher* the miraculous is presented through the cure of an apparently incurable illness, and in both plays the curing is presented as the result of divine intervention. In Chapman's play, indeed, there are no less than three cures, though only one (that of Strozza in the sub-plot) is obtained directly through divine intervention. Chapman is concerned to contrast the miraculous cure of Strozza with the natural cure effected by the physician Benevenius of the lovers Margaret and Vincentio, in order to illustrate in the two plots the power of love as it is manifested both by direct divine power and in nature. Shakespeare, with dramatic economy, brings the themes together by having his heroine, Helena, both the agent of the divine cure and the romantic heroine, whose overcoming of the impediments to love illustrates the triumph of love at the natural level. Helena thus combines the roles of Strozza's wife, Cynanche, whose Christian teachings lead to Strozza's miraculous cure, and Margaret, whose faithfulness overcomes the threat of her seduction by her lover's father, the Duke Alphonso.

With equal economy Shakespeare combines in Bertram the role of romantic lover (Vincentio) and principal impediment to that love (Alphonso). Just as Alphonso is cured of his destructive attempt to thwart his son's love of Margaret, so Bertram's early irresponsibility and immaturity have to be overcome before he can be freed to take on his role of lover and husband of the heroine. Shakespeare's treatment of Bertram's negative role (emphasised above all in his friendship for the empty Parolles, whose role as braggart soldier helps Shakespeare deflate the masculine world of war) is also peculiarly Chapmanesque. Alphonso too is defined by the company he keeps, in his case the vicious Medice, much as Bertram's friendship for Parolles helps him guide us away from any sympathy we might have with Bertram's plight as reluctant husband. Even more tellingly Shakespeare adopts—very unusually for him—the characteristic Chapman association of comedy and evil in this play. Parolles's evil nature is presented in terms of the ridiculous, much as Medice's inadequacy is revealed through such absurdities as his incompetence in trying to recite the masque speech that has been prepared for him to speak at the Duke Alphonso's entertainment. Chapman's expressly comic figures, Bassiolo (the gentleman usher of the title) and Pogio (Strozza's nephew) both have the role of stumbling on truth unawares in their folly: 'cold wisdom waiting on superfluous folly', the telling phrase in which Helena describes Parolles, fits Bassiolo to a T. Shakespeare's clown in this play, too, is not by accident the least funny, the least likeable, of his clowns, for he too represents that male irresponsibility that Shakespeare demonstrates in the play as the negative to the feminine saving power of love (like Bertram, Lavatch is willing to change sexual partners at the drop of a glove and treats love and sexuality as a mere entertainment).

This is not the place to attempt to chart the ways in which Shakespeare's practice as a playwright was changed and enriched by the influence of his contemporaries. My purpose has been to give one brief example to show why Shakespeare's career cannot be seen in isolation, but as one of several outstanding examples of the richness and variety of a theatre in which for too long Shakespeare's name has been a shadow inhibiting a proper understanding of his great contemporaries and so, ironically enough, preventing an adequate assessment of the master himself. There are signs of change: a new theatre has opened at Stratford-upon-Avon, dedicated to the production of early drama other than Shakespeare, a new Fortune theatre is promised in Somerset and there is the prospect of a new Globe at Southwark in London where currently the enterprising Bear Garden Theatre is one of the few places where some of England's finest drama can be seen. It has been something of a scandal that plays like the Chapman comedies, the brilliant range of Middleton's comedies, the best of Marston, Heywood, Dekker, Beaumont and Fletcher have remained largely unplayed in modern times and if this book can do even a little to achieve a better perspective on this splendid theatre it will have served a useful purpose. Meanwhile the world of scholarship can hardly be exonerated, not only from having encouraged the study of Shakespeare in isolation from his peers, but also from its failure to provide adequate texts for many of these major plays. The situation again is gradually improving but the critical commentator is still too often forced to use inadequate nineteenth-century editions (of much of Middleton, for instance).

2
Journeymen and Gentlemen

An account of some of the lesser playwrights of our period will give some idea of the range and vitality of the drama at this time and help to provide us with some measure of the greatness of those outstanding men whose work requires more detailed treatment. Two hardly deserve the title of 'lesser' men, for they stand out above the rest in merit and in the vast quality of their output: these are Thomas Dekker and Thomas Heywood. Both were very much professionals of the popular theatre, though both contributed work for the 'private' stages at different periods of their careers. Heywood himself tells us he could claim responsibility for some 220 plays 'in which I have had either an active hand, or at the least a main figure';[1] of these only about twenty survive. Dekker's output seems to have been equally extensive, with a not dissimilar survival rate. The fact that comparatively few of their plays survive (in contrast to the very high survival rate of the major figures) is partly the result of accidents like the burning down in 1617 of the Cockpit Theatre, Drury Lane, by a City mob, which 'burnt their [the actors'] play-books and did what other mischief they could'.[2] Heywood must have lost a considerable number of plays in the conflagration. That so much failed to survive must also be a reflection of the playwrights' attitude to their plays as for the contemporary stage, not monuments to posterity; Heywood is explicit: 'my plays are not exposed to the world in volumes, to bear the title of works (as others)'.[3] The more literary writers like Jonson and Chapman on the contrary write as much for posterity as for a particular audience.

Another contrast with the more literary men of the theatre is that both Dekker and Heywood are conservative in their stage techniques rather than innovatory, though both (inevitably) have to adapt to the surges of fashion over the years. Both men are of Jonson's generation (born in the early 1570s), but write for the most part as if the Jonsonian revolution had never happened. Both share those optimistic, humane assumptions of the earlier generation and are reluctant to shed the stage techniques that accompany them. Dekker, in the early play *Old Fortunatus*, is old-fashioned enough to write an old-style morality play, while Heywood's fondness for clowning in the midst of seriousness and a non-satirical treatment of the actual links him to such earlier figures as Robert Greene. But there are important differences between the two men: Dekker's optimism, for instance, is temperamental, whereas Heywood's is habitual.

Though essentially a popular playwright until mid-career, Heywood (unlike Jonson and Chapman) was a university man. By temperament, however, he is very much a man of the people. Several of the plays that survive from his career in the popular theatre, such as *The Wise Woman of Hogsdon* (c.1604), *The Fair Maide of the Exchange* (c.1602) and the second part of *If You Know Not Me You Know Nobodie* (1605) are comedies of London life, though treated in a romanticising way quite unlike the satirical City comedies of the period. These plays would be written for the Earl of Worcester's men (later Queen Anne's men) at the Curtain Theatre until 1604 and then at the Red Bull, where Heywood held a similar position to Shakespeare in his company, as actor-sharer of the company. Both these theatres were to the north of the City and must have had a predominantly bourgeois audience—certainly this is the impression that the plays themselves give. The second part of *If You Know Not Me*, for instance (which incidentally bears no significant relationship to the first part), unashamedly cashes in on London pride by telling the story of the building of the Royal Exchange by the entrepreneur capitalist Sir Thomas Gresham. With a reprint of the 1560s 'Agas' map the reader can still follow Queen Elizabeth's progress across London from Somerset House to Bishopsgate (Scene 13) in considerable detail. The play is both a celebration of the London of his City audience and its mercantile values, and a nostalgic evocation of the great Queen's mythic golden reign; a characteristic Heywood combination of hard fact and appeal to collective sentiment. The overwhelming impression given by Heywood's drama is of the desire to please his audience by flattering their prejudices; by skilfully balancing the familiar and the unusual he manages both to reassure and entertain: a favourite recurring motto is *'Aut prodesse solent aut delectare'*—they usually give benefit or delight.[4] Of all the Jacobean dramatists Heywood is the least seriously concerned with moral and religious doctrine and he is quite capable in a play like *The Wise Woman of Hogsdon* of depicting the immoral with sympathy. The wise woman, the character around whom the comedy revolves, is not only the benevolent matchmaker who presides over the play's sexual pairing, but is also fortune-teller, bawd and midwife who disposes of the bastard children by abandoning them at rich men's doors, 'such as are able to keep them' (874–5).[5] There are some fine vignettes of London life in the play, such as the scene where the wise woman shows how she has acquired a reputation for skill in medicine by getting the patients to diagnose their own illnesses (II.i.). Yet for all the realism of these scenes Heywood is concerned to present his London at some remove from his audiences's own experience by placing his story in an earlier generation before St. Paul's had lost its steeple in the storm of 1561 (l.1941), and perhaps even suggesting a late medieval period if we are to credit the implication that the heroine's father fought in France and Spain with John of Gaunt (ll.1647–8). The first part of *If You Know Not Me* is an example of the kind of epic theatre Shakespeare had made popular in his Henry VI sequence. It deals with the reign of Mary Tudor and the perilous survival of Princess Elizabeth. The play is of course both patriotic and adulatory of the Virgin Queen, but Heywood's tolerance is such that the arch-enemy, Philip of Spain, is sympathetically presented as both fair-minded and humane.

Heywood's refusal to be doctrinaire is as much a strength as a weakness, for it gives him the rare ability for his generation of presenting things more as they are than as they are required to be. T. S. Eliot refuses the term 'realist' for Heywood and perhaps rightly,[6] but his drama is the closest to the realistic that Jacobean drama ever gets. However, because Heywood's principal concern is, as I have said, with satisfying his audience, he has an eclectic readiness to use whatever techniques are likely to fulfil this end. His finest play, the tragedy *A Woman Killed With Kindness* (1603),[7] illustrates this well. In one of the most effective scenes of the play, the scene where the honest serving man Nicholas reveals to his master, Frankford, that Frankford's wife and the man he has befriended, Wendoll, are having an affair under his own roof (Scene 8), the scene opens with wholly convincing realism. The serving men of the household are clearing away the remains of the gentlefolks' dinner (the stage directions are very explicit: 'one with voider and a wooden knife to take away all, another the salt and bread, another the tablecloth and napkins. . . .'). Frankford enters 'as it were brushing the crumbs from his clothes with a napkin'. Nicholas approaches his master with some trepidation, but with the conviction that it is his duty to tell him of his wife's conduct with Wendoll, and there follows an exchange between master and servant which is totally convincing in terms of both character and situation. Frankford is both incredulous and suspicious, angry with his servant yet increasingly persuaded by him, while Nicholas is torn between his love and duty to his master and the fear that he is over-stepping the bounds of dutifulness and causing pain. Heywood is superbly professional in his pacing of scenes in the theatre and this scene is an excellent example. Nicholas goes out, leaving Frankford to agonise over what he has just heard. His wife and his guests, Wendoll and another, return to the tidied room to play cards. At this point Heywood shifts theatrical modes. The card talk is allegorised with extensive use of the 'aside' from Frankford and Nicholas to reflect suspicion towards wife and guest. Though this part of the scene needs careful handling in production the transition from realistic to symbolic mode can (as I have witnessed) be made perfectly acceptable on stage because the scene is still viable at the literal level. Heywood is responding to that characteristically Jacobean feeling that the actual world conceals layers of hidden meanings. The next scene of the play (Scene 9) exploits this feeling in a somewhat different fashion, less for psychological purposes than moral. Here we are concerned with the sub-plot in which Sir Charles Mountford has been beggared by a lawsuit with Anne Frankford's brother, Sir Francis Acton. Susan Mountford, Sir Charles's sister, comes to her uncle and former friends to beg assistance, only to be rejected by each in turn. Verisimilitude is not totally discarded, but the effect has some of the formality of morality drama. Heywood's emphasis remains, however, strictly secular.

Heywood's eclecticism is as evident in his career as a whole as in this particular play, although the special ordinariness, which makes his contribution to the Jacobean theatre so distinctive, and so valuable, always remains characteristic. This is true even when the subject is exotic, as with *The Iron Age, Part I* (c.1600), a wholly successful chronicle play of the Trojan war[8] (and a better play, incidentally, than Shakespeare's play on the same subject—as contemporaries seem to have thought), or the somewhat fantastic adventure story of the two parts of *The Fair Maid of the West*. Perhaps this sense of what is normal is most remarkable in the nearest thing Heywood gets to classical tragedy, *The Rape of Lucrece* (c.1607), remarkable because the subject is itself one of human nature pushed to extremes. *The Rape*, contemporary as it is with *Coriolanus* and a number of other attempts at a stricter classical tragedy, is perhaps the Red Bull's attempt to keep up with the new fashion. Far from being a misconceived attempt to write in an alien manner, as Grivelet argues,[9] *The Rape of Lucrece* is a largely successful tragedy in ways characteristic of Heywood. Like most of his plays that survive it is skilfully plotted and paced. Emphasis is placed on the political theme of the rise and fall of Tarquinius while the rape (off stage) and suicide of Lucrece is treated as one episode illustrating the depravity of the Tarquinii. By concentrating on the politics Heywood is both able to fill the play with incident that propels the action forward and to avoid over-indulging in the sensationalism of the Lucrece episode. The humour, both low life and the more carefully handled antic disposition assumed by Brutus and Valerius (who sings where it is unsafe to be found discussing state affairs), also helps prevent a descent into 'senecal' melodrama. Heywood was not to be seduced by neo-classical notions of unity of tone. His handling of the Lucrece episode avoids the kind of tortuous ethical interpretations found in Middleton's treatment of the story and presents Lucrece as the good Elizabethan wife nobly choosing suicide in defence of her own and her husband's honour.

The Rape of Lucrece was a popular play, written for the Red Bull audience, but sufficiently acceptable to an elite audience to be performed before the Court in January 1611/12 by the combined companies of the King's and Queen's men. The fact that it achieved five editions by 1638 suggests too that it was read with some avidity, although in the address to the reader Heywood with characteristic modesty disclaims any original intention of having it printed. As he advanced in years, in fact, Heywood moved up-market. On the opening of the Cockpit in Drury Lane (an elite theatre) in 1616 Heywood became its principal dramatist, and in the later part of James's reign we find him adapting Plautus in such highly actable plays for the 'private' theatre as *The English Traveller* and *The Captives*. Heywood's later reputation has not, on the whole, done justice to his outstanding talents.

Dekker's career is a much sadder tale of a steady decline in his own time of a reputation which reached an early peak, after a period with Henslowe, in a number of collaborations for the boys' companies at the beginning of James's reign. By temperament Dekker, like Heywood, is a popular playwright, especially in that his plays are primarily designed to engage his audience's feelings rather than their intellects. Because he was by nature an optimist and disposed to look on human nature kindly, those feelings are usually—and sometimes stiflingly—good-humoured and benevolent. Dekker had no such firm base in the theatre as Heywood's additional (and perhaps more lucrative) roles of actor and financial sharer in his company. In attempting to earn his bread by pen alone Dekker tried for a time to keep abreast of the new theatrical fashions of Jonsonian satire, but in doing so he worked against his own grain. It may be too that Dekker had aspirations to be remembered as more than a theatrical journeyman. He had quite early in his career been well received in high places, for the *Pleasant Comedie of Old Fortunatus* was proposed (as we know from Henslowe's diary) 'for the court' and presented before the Queen on 27 December 1599. In his most ambitious play, *The Whore of Babylon* (1606) he announces 'we present / Matters above the vulgar argument' and in the address to the reader describes his work as a 'dramatical poem', a term that Jonson had used to describe *Sejanus*, with the same implication that this was a serious work that would repay the reader's careful attention. Dekker's address indeed goes on to complain of the distortions inherent in stage representation, with the implication that the plays are better read than acted.

The *Whore of Babylon*, however, was written for a popular playhouse (the Fortune), as was most of Dekker's works, and it suggests some tension between the playwright and his audience. It also, more damagingly and unlike Jonson, implies a disparity between Dekker's literary aspirations and his popular talent. When in the prologue he appeals to his audience to be guided by 'Your judgement, not your passions', he would forgo his best gifts as an affective dramatist. There is indeed a central contradiction in Dekker's stance as playwright. His most successful and by far the most appealing play is *The Shoemakers' Holiday*, written—like most of the dozens of early plays in which he had a hand—for Henslowe and played for the first time in 1599. Like Heywood's *If You Know Not Me, Part II*, Dekker's play is brilliantly calculated to appeal to a City audience, showing as much devotion to the King (presumably Henry VIII) as sly disapprobation of the aristocracy. It presents a picture of bourgeois triumph (like Heywood's play) in showing the rise of Simon Eyre, the shoemaker, to the dignity of Lord Mayor of London. Eyre is depicted as eccentric, generous, energetic, kindly, above all concerned for the welfare of his dependants. He is the model of patriarchy that the average Elizabethan saw as the ideal pattern for society; indeed the play could be said to be built on metaphors of fatherhood in which Simon is to his dependants as King is to his people and as God is to King and people, and the play ends on an explicit interlinking of these expressions of paternity as the King benevolently grants his subject-children their requests, to a chorus of 'God save your Majesty', 'Jesus blesse your grace'. In this relationship the aristocracy are given no special place, though an indulgent use is made of hierarchy by having the aristocratic hero Lacy marry the bourgeoise Rose, a former Lord Mayor's daughter.

Dekker in this play is constructing a peculiarly middle-class myth of unlimited free enterprise within a framework of complete social stability. The contradictions inherent in the myth are resolved (as such insuperable contradictions must be) in a laughter that implies good feeling and a universal goodwill among men. To create this mythic world he moves back in time sufficiently to blur his audiences' memories (as Heywood was to do in *If You Not Know Me*) but—again like Heywood—stays close enough to his own times to allow for vivid illustration in terms of a real London world that his audience can readily recognise and identify with. Simon himself embodies this world with complete success: he is both larger than life and yet convincingly lifelike, both a suitable embodiment of mercantile vitality and a real-life figure who complains that his wife's maid farts in her sleep (I.iv.33) and who can indulge in some shady dealings when there's something to be gained by it (as in the transaction with the Dutch captain [II.iii.]). In the later plays this fusion of symbol and substance is less satisfactorily achieved. In the satires that follow *Shoemakers' Holiday*, *Satiromastix* and the two plays written with Webster, *Westward Ho* and *Northward Ho* (discussed elsewhere) the satiric purpose is partially obscured by the narrative vehicle that carries it.

More successful are the pictures of contemporary life in *The Honest Whore* and *The Roaring Girl* (collaborations with Middleton, except for the second part of *Honest Whore*). The scene of *Honest Whore* is nominally set in Italy, though it is an Italy that boasts both a Bedlam madhouse and a Bridewell prison. In these popular plays (for the Fortune theatre) Dekker once more shows the talent for engaging audience sympathy for his characters that is so marked a feature of *Shoemakers' Holiday*—Moll the Roaring Girl, though more Middleton's perhaps than Dekker's, is a good example, as is the touching scene of *I Honest Whore* (II.i.) where Bellafronte the prostitute is allowed to break through her conventional role to reveal her love for Hippolito. Like the *Ho* plays, however, these later comedies suffer from two besetting sins: a tendency towards opaqueness of plot that makes following the details of the story tortuously difficult, and a tendency to sentimentality which is indulged to the detriment of dramatic tension. The opacity is considerably eased on stage, as was apparent in the successful production of *Roaring Girl* at Stratford in 1983 with Helen Mirren in the title role. None the less, Dekker's liking for three distinct and nearly equal actions (in both parts of *Honest Whore*, in *Roaring Girl*, and in the later *If This be not a Good Play the Devil is in it*, 1611) means that too little opportunity is allowed for the audience to identify with and respond to the characters. At times, too, it makes the action difficult to follow (the best-worst example of this is the complex financial chicanery of the Barterville plot of *If This be not*). Dekker's sentimentality is evidenced in the very title of *The Honest Whore*, which concerns itself first with the conversion of the prostitute Bellafronte to virtue and then (in Part II) with the ill treatment accorded to her by her husband Matteo. I have argued at length elsewhere that it is characteristic of Dekker to resolve tensions too readily through the arbitrary interventions of the good.[11] In *II Honest Whore*, for instance, benevolent intervention controls the events: the converted whore Bellafronte acquires a benevolent father, Friscobaldi (absent from the first part) who in the disguise of the serving man Pacheco guides his daughter to success in saving her husband and marriage. The disguised Lodovico has a not dissimilar role in intervening first to help the henpecked Candido and then his friend Hippolito, while—as in the first part—the play ends with the appearance of the Duke of Milan to preside over the play's reconciliations. The ending of the play, in which first Friscobaldi forgives his son-in-law and then blesses the marriage ('A Father's everlasting blessing fall upon both your heads' [II.ii.476]) and then the Duke endorses the blessing, as with *Shoemakers' Holiday*, links parental benevolence of family and state.

The figure of the benevolent father is not arbitrarily chosen by Dekker: it is essentially an expression of a Christian conviction that permeates all his work. For the triumph of good is not just a cliché with Dekker (though often too easily asserted). His humane religiosity becomes explicit in the two allegorical plays that come in a period of decline in the quantity and quality of his work: *The Whore of Babylon* (1606) and *If This be not a Good Play, the Devil is in it* (1611). The *Whore of Babylon* seems to have been Dekker's attempt to stem the tide of failure by producing something spectacular and considered for the Fortune. That it was not a success we can tell from its 'Address to the Reader' and from its almost immediate appearance in print for its only seventeenth-century printing. A passage in the Address prefacing *If This be not a Good Play* suggests (as Hoy remarks[12]) that the failure of the earlier play had led to a rupture with the Prince's Men at the Fortune theatre, who seemingly had rejected the new play, which was accordingly first performed by the Queen's Men (Heywood's company) at the Red Bull. It was also (apparently) a failure. Dekker had already, after 1606, turned largely from play-writing to the writing of tracts, but by 1613 his ability to support himself with his pen ended in the ignominy of a debtor's prison (not for the first time) where he languished 'almost seven years together'.[13]

It is not difficult to see why both these religious plays failed to please their Jacobean audiences. Both attempt to resurrect an old-fashioned allegorical mode in which the emphasis is placed on representing abstraction and little attempt is made, especially in *Whore of Babylon*, to embody the abstractions in plausible, life-like character. It was the mode of the old morality play that Dekker had revived with some success in *Old Fortunatus* in the 1590s. But by 1606 the fashion was for surface realism. Though both Middleton and Jonson might be thought of as allegorical (as I have argued) their allegories are as concerned to offer a coherent and plausible picture of the world that embodies their truths as in the coherence of the truths themselves. In both playwrights there is a brilliant embodiment of the abstract patterning in the clothes and costumes of the contemporary world. Dekker's fervent piety had become impatient of the garments and was anxious to show truth naked. Had he had a philosophical mind this might have had an interesting outcome, but his strength as a dramatist lay in his ability to depict people sympathetically and he forfeited this for commonplace ideas. *The Whore of Babylon* is in essence a psychomachia in which the forces of light (represented by Titania the Fairie Queen, that is Queen Elizabeth) and of darkness (represented by the Whore of Babylon, that is, the Pope of Rome and such henchmen as Philip II of Spain) struggle for the soul of England (Fairie Land). It was perhaps intended as a rejoinder to the first part of Heywood's spectacularly successful chronicle play for the rival Red Bull theatre, *If You Know Not Me*, which also has Queen Elizabeth as its heroine. While Heywood chose the form of the chronicle play, with the historical figures caught up in the web of the particular, Dekker's characters are mere pawns in a chess game whose outcome is never uncertain. There are occasional excursions into the more familiar Dekkerian territory of the streets of London, as in the scenes in which Plain Dealing reports to Titania on the (not entirely happy) state of the nation, but it is all at second hand and merely reminds us tantalisingly of the rich and varied life that Dekker has excluded from his stage epic. The theme that runs through the play, the treachery of Papists like Campion (Campeius in the play) and Dr Parry (Paridel), was a topical one of the year after the Gunpowder Plot against James I, but such topicality is largely undermined by the archaic mode of presentation, which removes the action irremediably from any kind of actuality. *The Whore of Babylon* is not an entirely unimpressive play, thanks to the sustained dignity of its language, but the reader has only to consider its inappropriateness for stage revival to see how far short it comes of the highest standards of Jacobean theatre.

If This be not a Good Play is both a worse and a better play than *Whore of Babylon*. It lacks the latter's high seriousness and global scope, but it is sufficiently close in some of its scenes to the earlier comedies of intrigue to have retained some of the old vitality. The play is schematically constructed to illustrate the work of the devil among three estates of the realm: clergy, king and commerce. There is a good deal of topical reference in all this to current grievances such as the King's granting of monopolies and the plight of the soldier in time of peace. In the opening scene we are introduced into hell, where a dissatisfied Charon insists that the diabolical community show more enterprise in capturing souls. In response Pluto, King of the Underworld, sends the devil Ruffman to Naples to subvert the Court, Shacklesoul to a Naples monastery to undermine its discipline and Lurchall to the office of the corrupt financier Barterville. Dekker's favourite three simultaneous actions are initiated with the inevitable consequence that the play fails to produce a central focus. But at least the allegorical scheme allows the abstractions of evil to become absorbed—through disguise—into the human world of Naples, and much of the action therefore is concerned with what Dekker represents best, the bustling and quirky world of human intercourse. Dekker's handling of the allegory unfortunately proves somewhat inconsistent: Ruffman and Shacklesoul find themselves in communities that are remarkable for their virtue: we find Alphonso, King of Naples, for instance, newly enthroned, issuing enlightened laws to grateful subjects. These pious intentions immediately collapse without a struggle, but the threat has come from without and the allegory implies a natural goodness in man, an impression reinforced by Alphonso's virtuous uncle and the sub-prior of the monastery, who refuse to be corrupted by evil. Lurchall's experience in commerce, however, is different. In Barterville he meets someone who is more than a match for him in evil, though Dekker fails to exploit the ironic potential of this situation in the way Jonson does in *The Devil is an Ass*. The inconsistency of approach derives from Dekker's habitual optimism, which can conceive of a particular example of human depravity in the merchant (who joins the likes of Guy Fawkes and the regicide Ravaillac in hell in the final scene) but who thinks of people as naturally good unless perverted by diabolic trickery. Once the devils are exposed Alphonso returns to the paths of virtue as quickly and painlessly as he left them and is duly rewarded with the hand of the beautiful Erminhild, whom in his wickedness he had spurned. The allegory of evil thus turns out to be somewhat uncertainly based, the presence of the devils suggesting more that man is a victim of evil than himself responsible for it in the world. This, joined with the over-schematic handling of the action, tends to deprive the characters of any inner life and of intrinsic interest. Most of the characters—Alphonso is the clearest example—seem mere puppets controlled by external forces. Dekker has deprived himself of his greatest asset as a playwright, his ability to depict affective character.

After *If This be not a Good Play* there is a long silence. A few tracts appeared from prison, but no plays. The childlike faith that in all Dekker's work seems to struggle for release from the opacity of its material deserved him a better fate. But the remaining ten years or so of his life (he died in 1632) are not all gloom. The one unaided play of these late years that has survived, *Match Me in London* (c.1621), is a colourless play in the alien manner of John Fletcher, but in one or two late collaborations, notably his sympathetic portrait of the witch in his collaboration with Ford and Rowley, *The Witch of Edmonton*, the characteristic humanity of the man survives.

Of the other professional dramatists of the period much less needs to be said. A few, such as John Day, Henry Chettle, Antony

Munday, Samuel and William Rowley, William Haughton, George
Wilkins, Gervase Markham, were seemingly as prolific (in their
collaborations especially) as Dekker, though very little of their work
survives. Others, such as Wentworth Smith, Richard Hathwaye,
William Rankins, Robert Wilson, are even more shadowy, surviving
fortuitously for the most part by courtesy of Henslowe's account
book. As well as these professional hacks there are the more
occasional contributors—sometimes a player like Robert Armin,
'Shakespeare's fool', or the leading boy player turned adult actor,
Nathan Field, would add to their company's repertoire; sometimes
poets of note in other spheres would contribute: so Michael Drayton
was for a time employed as a Henslowe hack; Samuel Daniel, more
interested in closet drama, contributed one play, the enigmatic and
dull, neo-classical, *Philotas*, to the public stage (Blackfriars); and
another poet, Barnabe Barnes, wrote one play for the public theatre
(Globe) that has survived. Other writers for the public stage had
more famous careers elsewhere, such as the extraordinary Lording
Barry who, having failed as a theatrical entrepreneur, turned
successful pirate, but *en route* managed to write the very
entertaining imitation of Middleton, *Ram Alley*. Sometimes
theatrical offerings would come from amateurs of the theatre,
gentlemen like Cyril Tourneur, whose one surviving play *The
Atheist's Tragedy* has had rather more attention than it deserves. It
was not, however, until Charles I's reign that the gentleman
playwright truly came into his own; through most of our period the
profession of playwright, however lucrative it became for the few
successful, remained largely a beggarly affair and many of its
representatives might justifiably be described in Jonson's pregnant
phrases: 'Sharpham, Day and Dicker were all rogues . . . that
Markham was not of the number of the faithful . . . but a base
fellow, that such were Day and Middleton.'[14]

Heywood can ruefully note towards the end of his life that for all
their literary successes the playwrights achieved no social standing:

> Mellifluous Shakespeare, whose inchanting quill
> Commanded mirth or passion, was but Will;
> And famous Jonson, though his learned pen
> Be dipt in Castaly, is still but Ben.
> Fletcher add Webster, of that learned packe
> None of the mean'st, yet neither was but Jacke.[15]

John Day, mentioned twice in these Jonsonian gibes, is one of the more interesting of these minor figures. It seems likely that he was the John Day who was charged with the manslaughter of the talented Henry Porter, author of the *Two Angry Women of Abington*, in June 1599, so illustrating the seamier side of the playwright's lifestyle (Jonson too, or course, had been guilty of the manslaughter of a fellow actor). Day seems (to judge from Henslowe's accounts again) to have been a prolific author of plays for the public theatres, though the only examples of these that survive is the collaboration with Henry Chettle, *The Blind Beggar of Bednal Green* (1600) and *The Travels of Three English Brothers* with William Rowley and George Wilkins (1606/7). For a short time Day also wrote for the private theatres: *Law Tricks* (1604) and *Isle of Gulls* (1606) for Blackfriars, and *Humour out of Breath* (1607/8) for the short-lived Whitefriars Theatre. His attitude to his role of playwright is best illustrated from the Induction to *Isle of Gulls* where his spokesman, the Prologue, tells the audience that his author was not present at the performance because he was busy on his next play 'to get him a handsome suite against summer' (l.23).[17] Day was, however, a university man of considerable talent and his unpretentious view of his role was a matter of deliberate choice. Occasional jibes at Jonson's exalted view of the dramatist's role punctuate *Isle of Gulls*[18] and it is clear that Jonson's exalted view of his art was not for him. Day, then, is unashamedly an entertainer and little else. Nothing could illustrate this better than his adaptation of the story of King Basilius and the wooing of his daughters from Sidney's *Arcadia* for *Isle of Gulls*. Sidney's curious and improbable account of the wooing of Pamela and Philoclea (here called Hippolita and Violetta) by Musidorus and Pyrocles (here, Demetrius and Lisander), the latter in feminine disguise as Zelmane, an Amazon, with both the King and Queen falling in love with Pyrocles–Zelmane in his different manifestations, is changed by Day from pastoral romance to theatrical farce: Sidney's exquisite pastoral princesses become worldly-wise husseys exchanging bawdy jokes as they anticipate the sexual pleasures of marriage (III.ii.). Day's sensitivity to consumer demand also requires him to venture some satire and Burns makes a good case, in his introduction, for seeing Bacilius as a satiric portrait of James I.[19] Certainly the play ran into considerable trouble, for in March 1606 Sir Edward Hoby reveals in a letter that 'Sundry were committed to Bridewell' after a performance at Blackfriars.[20] The performance, we learn from the same letter, involved an impersonation of two nations: presumably the Scots were being mocked as they had been in *Eastward Ho*. There is also the more general satire, of equal appeal to an audience of the gentry, against the upstart court favourite, here represented by the villain Dametas 'a little hillock made great with others ruines' (I.ii.25). In general, Day's play gives the impression of trying to please his audience at the expense of all other considerations and it does so by appealing to an element of seedy dissipation while ignoring the intellectual seriousness that Jonson, Chapman and Marston considered them worthy of.

It is something of a surprise to turn to the later play, *Humour out of Breath*,[21] and find a strain of poetic delicacy of which only very occasional glimpses are found in *Isle of Gulls*. The opening act in particular weaves a web of lyricism that is almost Shakespearean, except that it lacks the master's robustness. Florimel's praise of music (I.i.) and Aspero's prose discourse on dreams (I.ii.) are splendid bravura moments in a play that also can boast of such sprightly dialogue as that between Florimel and Aspero at the beginning of Act III. But Day's poetic talents are more lyrical than dramatic: he lacks the Shakespearean ability to mould words to character and the play disappointingly degenerates from poetic romance to a farcical intrigue that reaches the height of inanity in the scene where Aspero escapes prison by playing blind man's buff with his jailor (IV.i.). Day's only wholly successful work is significantly one that could never have appeared on stage, the series of verse dialogues that were seemingly extracted from earlier plays and published in 1640 as *The Parliament of Bees*.

If Day's career presents us with a delicate poetic talent overlaid by the coarse exigencies of vulgar entertainment, William Rowley's considerable contribution to Jacobean theatre must be seen as all overlaying.[22] He is the journeyman of the theatre *par excellence*, a comic actor whose principal claim to fame is that Middleton thought him a worthy collaborator not only for *A Fair Quarrel* and *The Spanish Gypsy*, but for his finest tragedy, *The Changeling*. Rowley's other collaborations include *The Travels of Three English Brothers* (with Day and Wilkins), *The Witch of Edmonton* (with Ford and Dekker) and *Fortune by Land and Sea* (with Heywood). His four surviving unaided plays, of uncertain date, *All's Lost By Lust, A Match at Midnight, A Shoemaker a Gentleman* and *A Woman Never Vext* represent the lowest common denominator of Jacobean popular theatre. Middleton obviously saw in Rowley a poor man's Dekker, for he uses Rowley's cheerful optimism much as he had used Dekker's in *Roaring Girl* to provide tonal and dramatic contrast to his own searing vision of human depravity. Rowley can convey none of the benevolent energy that informs Dekker's work; his language is commonly prosaic and his characterisation subservient to the vagaries of plot. He wrote his earliest surviving work for Queen Anne's men at the Red Bull, and later for Prince Charles' men, also at the Red Bull, where he was the principal comic actor. Chambers dates *A Shoemaker a Gentleman* tentatively in 1608. It continues the tradition of 'romantic histories' made popular by Greene and continued through Dekker's *Shoemakers' Holiday* to Heywood. It out-Dekkers Dekker by depicting no less than both the King's sons (the play is set in Roman Britain) joining the gentle craft. It also manages to encompass the Roman persecution of the Christians and somewhat surprisingly depicts St. Winifried sympathetically for choosing a life of Christian celibacy. As part of that fondness for the matter of Rome that characterises the stage about this time it neither approaches (even at a distance) the romantic poetry of *Cymbeline* nor the historical seriousness of Heywood's *Lucrece*—both plays of about the same date.

A Woman Never Vext also perhaps dates from around the same time and shows Rowley again recreating a romantic past—this time a version of 'Merrie England'—in the manner of Dekker and Heywood. It follows Heywood's *If You Know Not Me, Part II* in celebrating the building of a famous London monument, in this case a charity house for the poor by the Sheriff of London, Stephen Foster. Like Heywood's play it concerns itself greatly with buying and selling and the celebration of mercantile values, but fails to be inhibited, as Heywood is, by probabilities of character. It is a play much given to simple binary oppositions of a kind that might delight the structural analyst. Stephen Foster miraculously changes from spendthrift rogue to charitable businessman, while his brother obligingly moves in the opposite direction, and as if this is not enough the ladies of their choice set up their own binary opposition by representing a woman always and a woman never vexed. Such mechanical ingenuity destroys any chance of character or event having any real interest, and we are hardly astonished at the end of the proceedings to find goodness and financial success equally triumphant. It is sometimes asserted (as by Harbage) that the 'private' theatres excelled in bawdy, but it is quite clear from Rowley's plays that bawdy was by no means a monopoly of the better sort; the main difference is that here the sexual innuendo is more obvious and less funny than it usually is in the elite theatres.

At the other end of the dramatic spectrum are those gentlemen playwrights who were willing to dabble a little in professional theatre without (one must assume) taking it entirely seriously. Of these perhaps the best known is Cyril Tourneur, whose one surviving play (the title of one other is known) *The Atheist's Tragedy* has received far more attention than better plays of the period, simply because of a worthless late attribution of the much superior *Revenger's Tragedy* to the same author. Little is known of Tourneur's life or connections with the theatre. He seems to have been a gentlemanly hanger-on of the powerful Vere and Cecil families and to have turned to the stage briefly after the death of Sir Francis Vere in 1609.[23] *The Atheist's Tragedy* was published in 1611 and is described on the title page as 'as in divers places it hath often been acted' which suggests the work of a freelance playwright, though the lost *The Nobleman* (c.1612) is known to have been acted by Shakespeare's company at Court.[24] The play itself is a rather wordy morality play tracing the downfall of the machiavel D'Amville, whose somewhat lurid atheism is alluded to in the play's title. D'Amville is presented as a philosophical libertine of a kind later to become the hero of Restoration comedies, who denies God and argues (like Shakespeare's Edmund) a doctrine of naturalism that would allow men the sexual freedom of the animal world. The hero of the play, Charlemont, in contrast, is the noble Christian, who is saved from martyrdom at D'Amville's hands, by a benevolent providence, as he comes to understand at the close of the play that revenge is the Lord's:

> Only to Heaven I attribute the work
> Whose gracious motives made me still forbear
> To be mine own revenger. Now I see
> That patience is the honest man's revenge.

(V.ii.275–8)[25]

The morality is orthodox Anglican and the irony, which is a feature of the D'Amville scenes (as for instance when God's thunder accompanies D'Amville's boastful atheism—II.iv.139), is presented at D'Amville's expense. This is markedly unlike the pervasive Middletonian irony of *Revenger's Tragedy* where the revenging heroes are enmeshed unwittingly in the evil web they design for their oppressors. Middleton's irony sardonically applies to all in this mad world, it does not differentiate as in Tourneur's play between the aberrant villain and the common decency. In this as in other things—such as, for instance, the hero's uncertainty about his father's ghost—Tourneur follows, at a long distance, a Shakespearean pattern, a pattern whose subtleties of language and thought are largely beyond the playwright's reach. The reasonable competence of this play, however, is some measure of the viability of those dramatic forms the master playwrights of the period had evolved. Many more examples could be given of minor playwrights competently imitating their masters, but it is time now to turn to the masters themselves and show the wealth, the vigour and the variety of these astonishingly productive years on the English stage.

3

Ben Jonson

Ben Jonson has as much right as his namesake, Samuel Johnson, to be called a great Cham of literature. His personality dominates the Jacobean literary world and the course taken by serious theatre in the first decade of the seventeenth century stems, in no small measure, from his hectoring. At the outset of his career as a dramatist Jonson found the professional theatre essentially a theatre of entertainment presided over by the master entertainer William Shakespeare. Jonson changed the emphasis with his insistence on the moral responsibility of the poet, a responsibility that was also a sacred duty. He thus introduced the high ideals of Elizabethan aristocratic literature into the popular theatre. If the message needed to be changed, so accordingly did the medium, and with equal energy Jonson set about demolishing the romantic vehicles of Shakespearean comic fantasy and replacing them with a neo-classical 'realism' dedicated to the idol of contemporary relevance: satire was to replace romance, realism to replace fantasy, people were to be seen as they were through an appropriately realistic medium: 'deeds and language such as men would choose / When they would show an image of the times'.

But as with so many men of strong convictions and forceful energy, the practical energy tended to distort the doctrine. For all his clean-cut dogmatism Jonson is essentially a man, and a dramatist, of contradictions and by that token a comic writer *par excellence*. As a man he combined a swashbuckling ruthlessness with pious rationality; hot-tempered, quarrelsome, violent, abusive, rebellious, he could equally be cool in utterance, magnanimous, conservative, conformist, even sycophantic when great men were concerned. His plays (though, strangely, not his non-dramatic poetry) are a product of these contradictions. As a playwright he wrote for audiences he purported to despise and wrote his best plays for the 'public' audiences he said he despised most.

He dedicates his drama to the aristocratic ideals of restraint, decorum, order, while indulging in savage lampoon and grotesque fantasy. Wedded to neo-classical designs are the gargoyles and

32

grotesques of a sensibility that owes as much to the gothic as to the classical past—in this he is a true Elizabethan. There is as much of the medieval peasant in his make-up as of the Renaissance gentleman.

Of his twenty or so extant plays only four or five could be described as totally successful, but these are of such merit that in comic satire he has no rival on the English stage. Compared to Shakespeare, even to Chapman, his range is narrow and his success within that range even narrower. His greatest plays, *Volpone*, *Alchemist, Bartholomew Fair* and the best of the others, *Every Man In His Humour, The Devil is an Ass* (the exception here is *Epicoene*) were written for the adult players of the public theatre (Shakespeare's company) and are unmistakably marked with a personal stamp that made them unlike anything else of the period, in spite of the fact that there were imitations and sympathetic collaborators. This suggests direct personal involvement that is itself rare within the habitual detachment of commercial theatre. Of the other major dramatists of the period only Marlowe shows a similar personal engagement and it is with Marlowe that comparisons are most fruitful. But whereas Marlowe used the stage to express open rebellion and founded his best work in tragedy, Jonson's rebelliousness is often itself the subject of attack and analysis, though he is never fully conscious of the personal war he is fighting in his plays. They are therefore more complexly related to his personality and his ideas than are Marlowe's.

It is no coincidence that Jonson's greatest plays are comic. Comedy is built out of incompatibilities in the truths of human existence that cannot be resolved logically, where resolution involves reconciliation through the acceptance and accommodation of tension rather than (as in tragedy) its elimination through the defeat of one force by another. Jonson was constantly striving for tragic resolution, but never satisfactorily achieved it, and in his greatest play, *Volpone*, he achieves the paradoxical feat of writing a comedy with a tragic ending. But true tragedy, involving the defeat of the comic daemon that provides his drama with its dynamic, eludes him, because the triumph of the orderly stifles the very sources of Jonson's creativity. Such a process can be clearly seen in a comparison of the tragedy *Sejanus* (1603), with the comedy that followed it, *Volpone*.

The two plays have much in common. Both concern the nefarious activities of a man of rank in collaboration with a less subtle and

ultimately outwitted henchman. Both the Emperor Tiberius and
Volpone play a clever, subtle game of letting fools and knaves hang
themselves with their own rope; both ditch their confederates when
they cease to be useful. One surprising difference between the plays
is that whereas the Godfather figure of the tragedy is left firmly in
command at the end, Volpone, in the comedy, is dealt with harshly
in a judgement scene befitting tragedy. In retrospect it is the tragedy
that makes us laugh, for the message would seem to be the cynical
one: the bigger the rogue the more likely he is to succeed. The
laughter here is the echo of an artistic failure, however, for the
theme is not the incongruities of evil, but its defeat in Sejanus's fall.
The crucial difference between the two plays is in the tensions they
generate. Volpone and his parasite Mosca are at the heart of the
play's dynamic. Volpone's inventiveness and unsentimental clear-
sightedness are relished as the real virtues they are, even against the
logic of the action. As Volpone jumps out of bed, his sides splitting
with laughter at his successful attempt to pull the wool over the
cadaverous eyes of the miser Corbaccio, we can have nothing but
admiration for the satiric justice of Volpone's insight:

> O, I shall burst:
> Let out my sides, let out my sides
>
> .   .   .   .   .   .
>
> O, but thy working, and thy placing it!
> I cannot hold; good rascall, let me kisse thee:
> I never knew thee, in so rare a humour
>
> .   .   .   .   .   .
>
> So many cares, so many maladies,
> So many feares attending on old age,
> Yea, death so often call'd on, as no wish
> Can be more frequent with 'hem, their limbs faint,
> Their senses dull, their seeing, hearing, going,
> All dead before them; yea, their very teeth,
> Their instruments of eating, fayling them:
> Yet this is reckon'd life!

(I.iv.132–3, 136–8, 144–51)[1]

Here is Jonson in all his contradictory variety: Volpone has the comic
exuberance, the inventiveness, of the comic master himself. Of
course, overtly Jonson is repudiating his hero here, the central irony

is that this acute analysis of human greed is *pre-eminently* true of Volpone himself. But that truth lies at the surface of things. The dramatic truth is more profound; for here Volpone is the daemon of comedy, a manifestation of the author's creative self, the disruptive, iconoclastic energy that will not be deceived by formulae or the encrustations of thought on the live beat of things. Were Volpone merely out-misering his victims he would be nothing, but the sheer delight in absurdity that leads him eventually, as he says 'to make a snare for mine own neck! and run / My head into it, wilfully,! with laughter!', gives him a transcending inconsistency that makes him as apt a representative of his master's talents as Prospero is of Shakespeare's. That the normative, neo-classical Jonson is aware of the logical problems his creature creates is clear not only from Jonson's agonising (in the address to the Universities prefacing the play) over the non-comic ending—an arbitrary force had to be exerted to quell this vitality at the end of the play—but in the periodic attempts throughout the play to blacken Volpone's reputation beyond sympathy through the introduction of Volpone's band of 'children', Nano, Androgyno and Castrone, and by the scene in which Volpone attempts to rape the innocent Celia. These scenes signally fail to stem the comic tide; on the contrary they clarify the amoral nature of the comic vitality. The attempted rape of Celia shows more clearly than any other scene how Jonson's conscious will fails to control the comic exuberance (in the address he protests too much, 'it was done off industrie'). Volpone works himself into fantasies of luxury as he tries to convince Celia of the pleasures of copulation until, this failing, he decides to force the issue. At this point Bonario, having been placed by Mosca to overhear the seduction, rushes into the room with the words:

> Forbeare, foule ravisher, libidinous swine,
> Free the forc'd lady or thou dy'st, impostor . . .

The melodramatic infelicities of Bonario's language here have frequently been remarked; they are all the more notable from a poet whose non-dramatic poetry so often exhibits an exquisite refinement in tonal nuance. Bonario's language is unintentionally comic because it does not resolve the problem of Volpone's comic amorality but tries to thrust it aside, leaving two opposing interpretations of the single event in comic juxtaposition. Dramatically the scene is more akin to a moment of discovery in a

Feydeau farce than the solemn reassertion of order it is clearly
intended to be.

Volpone is a great comic play partly because Jonson has not full
control over his subject. His attempt to beat down the irrepressible
itself adds to the comic tension. In *Sejanus*, however, the same comic
thrusts are stifled at birth. Jonson the pedant here set himself the
task of writing a neo-classical tragedy with all the solemnity of tone
and dignity of character that that demanded. Tiberius and Sejanus
are, however, as essentially comic figures as Volpone and Mosca,
for they represent an amoral vitality against which the forces of
order can oppose merely rhetoric in such persons as the ineffectual
Silius and the woeful Arruntius. There are moments when the comic
potential is almost realised. At the beginning of Act V Sejanus,
secure, as he wrongly believes, in the power he derives from the
Emperor Tiberius, relishes it with a comic exuberance remarkably
like that of Mosca celebrating the delight in his own cleverness in
Volpone (III.i.1–33).

> Swell, swell my joyes: and faint not to declare
> Your selves, as ample, as your causes are,
> I did not live, till now; this my first hower:
> Wherein I see my thoughts reach'd by my power.
> But this, and gripe my wishes. Great, and high,
> The world knowes only two, that's Rome, and I.
> My roofe receives me not; 'tis aire I tread:
> And, at each step, I feele my advanced head
> Knocke out a starre in heav'n!

> *(Sejanus* V.i.1–9)

There is an important difference between the imagery of the two
passages however. Mosca expresses his delight in the natural if
somewhat ominous imagery of blossoming and natural fecundity—
the bud, the snake, the insect—whereas Sejanus's imagery is
intrinsically absurd, the imagery of a man who has grown too big for
his boots. For whereas in *Volpone* the comic vitality is constantly
being reinforced and harnessed in the service of the articulation of
an alternative value-system, in *Sejanus* the comic vitality is itself
being mocked and repudiated—though there is nothing of
comparable value to replace it. Exactly the same happens in the
depiction of Tiberius, who is most subtly conceived as a wily rogue

with a genius for not saying what he means. The comic potential of this, again, has to be suppressed in the interest of tragic decorum. The 'industrious' Jonson triumphs and the play accordingly sinks, though it is the kind of impressive failure (especially in its depiction of the rogue Emperor and his zany) that only a major dramatist could achieve.

Jonson's successes are in those plays where the creative vitality—the sense of comic contradiction and absurdity—is held in balanced tension with the urge to explain and justify. In *The Alchemist* and *Bartholomew Fair* this equilibrium is completely achieved, through Jonson's insight that there is something inhuman in perfection. In *Volpone* the playwright had failed to give adequate recognition to the sources of his own vitality and his attempt to deny this vitality is itself the cause of a comic tension that is unique to that play. Neither *Alchemist* nor *Bartholomew Fair* have quite the same comic power, but both are more satisfying works of comic artifice. The wilful ending of *Volpone* is abandoned in these later plays and the comic vitality acknowledged—wryly and equivocally in *Alchemist*, through Lovewit's acceptance of the rogue Face back into his household, with more tolerance in *Bartholomew Fair*, which spells out the Christian message of humility on which the change had taken place: 'why beholdest thou the mote that is in thy brother's eye?'.

Jonson does not abandon the special role of the artist to 'instruct to life', but he tempers this with a new understanding that life itself as we know it exhibits its dynamic in contradiction. We are still asked to condemn the magnificently incurable sensualist Sir Epicure in *Alchemist*, but we are now to some extent enjoined to laugh with Face as he cheats his way into his master's good graces. In *Bartholomew Fair* the condemnation of excess in the extraordinary tutelary goddess of the Fair, Ursula the Pigwife, is tempered by the more unequivocal dismissal of the kill-joy Zeal-of-the-Land Busy whose Puritanical fanaticism is seen as as much an example of human self-indulgence as Ursula's panderings to the needs of the flesh. Here we are all of us so much of the flesh, fleshly, that no one can afford to be over-condemnatory. Certainly not the official representative of law and order, Judge Overdo, who is reminded in the Fair that his first name is Adam. *Bartholomew Fair* can almost be read as an allegory of Jonson's struggles with his own comic daemon: the perverse energy in the gigantic Ursula and in the hectic competitiveness of the Fair are accepted as the *sine qua non* of being human, the truculent negativity of Busy's reproving satire is itself repudiated as sterile and vain, while the special claims of poetic authority (foreshadowed in the posturings of Overdo as well as in the Induction and in the puppet show) are seen to be no better than they should be. Within the Fair Ursula's earthiness presides, but we get glimpses too of a transcendent order in such as Grace Welborne and in the spirit of loving tolerance with which the grossness is finally assessed. Nor is it coincidence that Jonson uses his play to discuss the nature of his art as a game of illusion, not only in the Induction, but in the scene where the puppet-master Leather-head confronts Jonson's other self in the person of the pedantic Busy. *Bartholomew Fair* is an extraordinary achievement. Discarding anything that can seriously be regarded as plot or story-line, Jonson harks back to the old allegorical drama to image the fallen world, the 'feir feld ful of folk' from which the only escape is in the search for a Grace that is finally won by a scapegrace.

In *Bartholomew Fair* a perfect balance is found between the comic exuberance that images the chaos of the fallen world and the framework of judgement which enables us to make meaning out of the chaos. In his less adroit plays there is a constant tendency for this balance to be lost, either (as in *Every Man Out of His Humour*) because the comic exuberance escapes control, or (as in *Cynthia's Revels*) because Jonson insists on imposing a control that defies the logic of his comic argument—as we have seen in *Volpone*. Both Jonson's first successful play, *Every Man In His Humour* (1598) and the most successful of his elite theatre plays, *Epicoene* (1609) show some lack of comic balance.

Every Man In His Humour was Jonson's first major stage triumph. It was staged by Shakespeare's Chamberlain's Men, with Shakespeare in the cast, in 1598, in a version published in 1600, in which the setting is Florence. Later, perhaps in 1605 in preparation for a court performance, Jonson changed the setting to London to bring it into line with the fashion for City comedies then at its height. Substantial revisions of the text accompanied the change of setting and some of these show Jonson shifting his comic ground. The new version (published in the 1616 Folio) is preceded by the famous prologue, which is primarily intended to justify the play after the event in terms of neo-classical orthodoxy and (splendid polemic though it is) should not be taken too seriously as an account of the play in either version. Jonson's claim, for instance, to be concerned with ordinary men rather than 'monsters' is an attempt to persuade his reader (and presumably his Court audience) to see the characters in contrast to the exotic splendours of Shakespearean characterisation. Here as elsewhere, however, Jonson thinks of character primarily in terms of thematic function and the characters are first and foremost representations of the ideas out of which the comedy is patterned. The play has, indeed, its share of Jonsonian monsters in such caricatures of gentility as Stephen, with his aspirations to hawk and hunt and swear fashionable oaths, Matthew with his aspirations to poetry, Bobadill's obsession with an imaginary valour, or, more pathologically, Kitely's obsessive jealousy. These idiotic and ill—as always in Jonsonian comedy—are morality epitomes, not portraits of London life (hence the easy translation from Florence to London). But the morality tradition here is exploited for social satire, not for moral judgement; this is comedy of manners more than morals.

As in later plays, Jonson guides his audience to right judgement by employing a puppet-master (like Face and Volpone, Leather-head and the poet himself in the *Bartholomew Fair* Induction). The puppet-master is both a guide (if sometimes himself in error) to right judgement and the ring-master of the entertainment: and as ring-master he is himself often implicated in the deceptions that are to be analysed, for the entertainer is necessarily a mountebank and illusionist, a seller of imaginary goods. In writing *Volpone* Jonson had come close to understanding the equivocal nature of the comedian's art. In the figure of Lorenzo Junior (of the first version of *Every Man In His Humour*) Jonson had invented a figure at times uncomfortably close to a non-comic authorial viewpoint and therefore without the inherent contradictions and insights of the comic guide. Lorenzo Junior's comic role is to some extent undermined by that very authorial rigidity that it is the function of the comic mode to overcome. In the beginning of the play we find Lorenzo's friend Prospero (Wellbred) sending a letter to invite him to meet the gull Matheo (Matthew) and Bobadilla (Bobadill) to laugh at their stupidity, 'a world of good jests'. Like other 'control' figures in the play such as Musco (the intriguer) and Doctor Clement, the voice of authority, Lorenzo and Prospero are in search of 'a good subject for more mirth' (Q.IV.iii.59).

In both the Italian and the English version of the play Lorenzo's (Edward's) father intercepts Prospero's (Wellbred's) letter and is displeased with the frivolity of its tone as well as the uncomplimentary references to himself. We see Edward's search for mirth initially therefore from a perspective of hostile criticism which is itself undercut by our perception of the father's inflexibility (we are in the familiar world of latin comedy, of trickster sons and blocking fathers). But there is a marked difference in the content of the letter in Jonson's two versions. In the first (Italian) version Prospero's stress is on his friend's dedication to poetry, whereas in the second version this emphasis disappears and the implications are more morally equivocal as Wellbred, for instance, suggests his friend might join him in womanising and mockingly declares he would use Old Knowell's apricots for enticing young women into the orchard garden. The change is interesting, for it shows Jonson deliberately moving his hero away from trustworthy guide to a more equivocal stance as master of comic ceremonies. The shift is later and more spectacularly reinforced at the end of the play where an eloquent speech in defence of poetry (Q.V.iii.312ff.) spoken by Lorenzo Junior is excised from the Folio version. Instead Justice Clement is given a few lines in defence of the poet in response to Old Knowell's scorn for the literary (V.v.37–45). Edward Knowell in the later and more familiar version of the play thus loses something of his status as authorial spokesman and becomes more obviously a source of mirth in others.

The values of the first version, in which intelligence, good taste and a sense of humour (represented in Lorenzo Junior, Prospero and Doctor Clement) are opposed to stupidity, vulgarity and solemnity, become transformed into a playing with comic disruption, in which 'correct' and 'incorrect' values are not so easy to distinguish. The shift is interesting in suggesting that just after *Volpone* was finished (and around the time the merry *Eastward Ho* was being written with Chapman and Marston) Jonson was already moving away from his concern 'to inform men in the best reason of living'[2] towards the humble view of the compromised author implied by *Alchemist* and *Bartholomew Fair*.

The shift towards comic humility becomes in *Epicoene* a shift towards comic irresponsibility. In *Every Man In His Humour* in both versions, the privilege accorded Edward Knowell's viewpoint is on the whole acceptable. His exuberance and easy-going laughter is certainly preferable to the rigidities of his father or the idiocies of the gulls, and we do not begrudge him his reward of Mistress Bridget and the three thousand pounds dowry (F.V.iii.93). With the gentlemanly heroes of *Epicoene*, however, it is not too easy to be tolerant, although the authorial voice asks us to be. The main plot centres on the gulling of Morose, a man who has a pathological hatred for noise, by his nephew Sir Dauphine Eugenie. Here again is the contrast between inflexible age and lively youth—Morose learns that vitality cannot be manipulated to order. The lesson is the lesson of all comedy, that cakes and ale will go on being served in spite of virtue. Where doubt begins to creep in, however, is over the nature of Jonson's comic agents, the courtly friends, Sir Dauphine Eugenie, Clerimont and Truewit. Hearing that Morose has decided to marry in order to disinherit him, Sir Dauphine hits on the ingenious device of dressing up a young lad as the bride-to-be, and issues strict instructions that he should remain demure and reticent until after the wedding, but that he should become voluble and noisy once the wedding has taken place, until, as duly happens, Morose wishes to be saved from the marriage and the sex of the bride can be revealed in return for a restoration of the inheritance. Sir Dauphine triumphs in his deceptions, defeats the beseiged Morose and carries off the loot. As comic rogues Sir Dauphine and his friends fulfil a similar function to Dol-Common, Face and Subtle in *Alchemist* and to Volpone and Mosca in *Volpone*. Jonson's treatment of Sir Dauphine, however, is very different from these 'popular' theatre rogues, who are eventually placed firmly in a framework of moral order. Jonson in those plays is willing to limit strictly the supply of cakes and ale.

In *Epicoene*, however, Eugenie's triumph goes unqualified. In this Eugenie is more like Lorenzo Junior, but without his moral acceptability. In the elite play Jonson has allowed (one suspects) his respect for youthful gentility to over-ride his respect for order. Such concessions to a no doubt youthful audience might well help to explain why he writes better for the popular audience, where such special pleading is less of a temptation. The ultimate effect of this imbalance between vitality and judgement in the play is a reduction of the comic tension: the sense of contradiction which is so conspicuous a feature of the great plays is lost as orderliness gives way to an irresponsible and somewhat tasteless exuberance.

Jonson wrote one further comedy shortly after *Bartholomew Fair*, *The Devil is an Ass* (1616) and then after a considerable gap *The Staple of News* (1626), *The New Inn* (1629) and *The Magnetic Lady* (1632). These later plays are generally and rightly considered a falling off of Jonson's comic powers, though by how much is a matter of some dispute. They mark a return to a more forthright satire, but they suffer from a problem encountered in earlier plays, a tendency for the satiric caricature to distort beyond the limits of mimetic tolerance. The problem is already marked in early plays such as

Every Man Out of His Humour and *Cynthia's Revels* but is countered in
the middle plays by a more complex and humane view of the satiric
target—humankind itself. Caricature to be effective must find a
viable tension between verisimilitude and abstraction. A successful
portrait must be both like enough to its target to afford recognition
and different enough to suggest general statement: the right balance
has to be struck between the particular and the general, exuberance
and patterning. In *The New Inn* (to take that as our example) this
relationship is unbalanced, the distortion of the caricature so severe
that it is difficult to detect any verisimilitude in the satiric targets.
Jonson, unusually, chooses as his main plot a romantic story of
disguise and discovery which relates oddly and unsuccessfully to
the satiric tone of the play, for romantic fantasy is enabled by
drawing the audience into its imaginative world not (as satire
requires) by holding it aloof from that world. A good case has been
made for the coherence of the play at a symbolic level in which the
main plot represents the unreality of the courtly world of the Stuart
Court and the drunken nonsense of the Inn's frequenters
downstairs represents the chaotic reality of a world without ideals.[3]
Symbols need more, however, than coherent patterning to make
them work; they must be able to engage us at the representational
level, so that we recognise their relationship to the felt life about us.
This Jonson significantly fails to achieve, even more in the low-life
scenes than in the courtly fantasy.

The *Devil is an Ass* is quite another matter. Here too we are in a
world of comic fantasy, but where the inhabitants are easily related
to the world of the audience's experience. Meercraft the 'projector'
and his dupe Fitzdottrel present the contemporary scandal of bogus
speculation. More clearly than in any of his other plays—even than
Volpone—Jonson shows us the mad Middletonian world of getting
and spending in which all genuinely human values are subsumed.
So scandalous has the situation become that the devil's emissary,
Pug, finds himself constantly out-manoeuvred in his devilry by the
very people he comes to plague. All this might suggest the
Middletonian theme of the inescapable depravity of human nature,
were it not both for the action of the main plot, in which Wittipol,
having apparently succeeded in seducing Fitzdottrel's wife, is
persuaded by her to forgo his conquest, and by the boisterous mood
of comic inventiveness in which Jonson presents his tale. The
wooing of Mrs Fitzdottrel is taken (significantly) from Boccaccio's
Decameron (5th story, Day three), Jonson borrows not only details of

the wooing from Boccaccio, but some of the verve and panache of the Italian master. He changes the ending of Boccaccio's tale, however, where the lady and her lover come to know the ultimate terms of love ('gli ultimi termini conobber d'amore'). Wittipol, on the contrary, is made by Mrs Fitzdottrel and his friend Manly to recognise the selfishness of his demands and agrees 'to love goodness . . . more/Then I did Beauty' (IV.vi.37–8). Not only is the possibility of human virtue asserted, but more importantly the greed of Meercraft and Fitzdottrel are shown up as the essentially absurd things they are. The play has led us from the crude inadequacies of absolute evil, through the disruptive but equally absurd antics of the world's dealings to a glimpse at the ideal world of virtue triumphant in which Pug, Meercraft and Fitzdottrel are seen as mere excrescences on the face of truth. Nowhere has Jonson made clearer his assumption that the comic images the fallen world, nowhere more convincingly has he shown his belief in the possibility of transcending the limits of that world. *The Devil is an Ass* lacks the subtle sense of the interplay of good and evil, comic and non-comic in the actual world that is the mark of the best of his plays; to some extent it falls back on that earlier and simpler position in which the good (and non-comic) is opposed absolutely to the evil (and comic). In this sense the play is Jonson's true dramatic swansong, for it ends by repudiating that comic muse in which his contradictory talents so triumphantly found their expression.

4

John Marston

Marston's short career as a dramatist, between 1598, when he wrote *Histriomastix* for a private performance at the law school of the Temple, and 1605, when he wrote the tragedy *Sophonisba*, illustrates both the pressures and the opportunities of this most exciting period of English theatre. Exclusively a man of the private theatres—first Paul's then Blackfriars—artistically he is his own man but influenced by both the dominating figures of the day, the overwhelmingly successful, practical man of the theatre, Shakespeare, at the Globe and the neo-classical gadfly, Ben Jonson. He made, within this powerful field of force, distinctive dramatic patterns of his own, which is considerable commendation. He was caught between the theatre of entertainment that Shakespeare so spectacularly transcended and the more learned, didactic drama that Jonson, if fitfully, succeeded in creating. The impulses of the showman led him to both entertainment and outrage, and often, entertainment by outrage. The more learned tendencies of the scholar of Brasenose College, Oxford who was later to become vicar of Christchurch in Hampshire, help to explain an unusual viewpoint that is conservative and sometimes curiously at odds with the flashiness of its vehicles.

Marston was every bit as much a man of the theatre as Shakespeare, indeed he seems to have been a principal in the revival of the boy's theatre of Paul's when it re-opened with a performance of his new play *Antonio and Mellida* in October 1599. Apparently he was the architect of the new stage and of those modifications that had been necessary to the theatre[1] of which John Lyly had earlier had charge. It was certainly a very different theatre from the one Shakespeare's company had had built in the same year over the river in Southwark and with a very different audience, as I have already argued. The size of the theatre, seating perhaps no more than one hundred people,[2] meant that a profit could only be made by charging high prices and this ensured that the audience was exclusive, the privileged playgoers of London—the educated, the fashionable, the leisured. In any case Marston's interest in the

theatre was probably not primarily financial, for he became a
relatively rich man on his father's death in November of that same
year, 1599. It was the theatre itself that excited Marston, hence the
resigned remark in his father's will: 'I hoped he would have profited
by them [his law books] in the study of the law, but man proposeth
and God disposeth.' The theatre was the ideal place to make a
speech, to be theatrical, and all Marston's plays are virtuoso feats of
theatre. This theatricality had already been displayed in his non-
dramatic ventures, for his very first publication, a mildly
pornographic poem *The Metamorphosis of Pygmalion's Image*, had so
clearly drawn unfavourable attention that he promptly turned tack,
attempted to repudiate the erotic by pretending it was meant
ironically and by splashing out in yet more outrageous fashion in a
series of snarling satires whose tone so dismayed the authorities
that they, along with others of their kind, as well as the lubricious
Pygmalion, were condemned to be burnt in June 1599. *The Scourge of
Villanie* had made its mark in other ways, for it went through three
editions before it was stopped.[3] That it was the tone rather than
what was said that gave offence is suggested by the general
orthodoxy in the subjects chosen for attack and the essential
orthodoxy of the sentiments which encompasses, for instance, such
pious (and Calvinistic) moralising as this:

> . . . it is a sacred cure
> To salve the soules dread wounds; Omnipotent
> That Nature is, that cures the impotent,
> Even in a moment; Sure Grace is infus'd
> By divine favour, not by actions us'd,
> Which is a permanent as heavens blisse
> To them that have it, then no habite is.
> To morrow, nay to day, it may be got:
> So please that gracious Power clense thy spot.

(*Scourge*, IV, 114–22)

It is thoroughly characteristic of Marston, however, that this
unexceptionable piety should be presented by a swashbuckling
persona he nicknames 'Kinsayder' (seemingly meaning dog-
gelder[4]—punning on 'Mar-Stone') and in a style of aggressive
roughness that earned him the name 'Furor Poeticus' in the
Cambridge play *The Return from Parnassus* of 1601, where he is

described as 'a ruffian in his style'. Throughout these satires Marston is acting a part and it is futile to hunt out the poet from the role. The tone of aggressive display dominates; a tone to be repeated frequently later by satiric characters in the plays. Marston is at least as concerned to shock and so amuse, as he is, for all the occasional solemnity, to reform. The reformer, indeed, frequently gets bawled out by his own rhetoric. The style or rather styles, for the tones vary, take on a life of their own, sometimes even in opposition to meaning, as Jonson shrewdly understood in having Crispinus spew up the indigestible words that he supposed to be choking him (*Poetaster*, V.iii.465–530); verbal indigestibility is a feature of some of the plays as well as of the satires. In an address to rhyme in the second Book of the satires Marston invites poetic style to join his thoughts, adding that if it will not oblige he will do just as well without it:

> If not? No title of my sence let change
> To wrest some forced rime, but freely range.
>
> ('Ad Rithmum', ll.35–6)

Rhyme is to be treated like an actor's cloak to be discarded, if a bit of theatre can be made out of pretending to do so. Marston has, of course, no intention of abandoning rhyme or any other rhetorical device that is found useful. At his best in *Scourge of Villanie* (as in the fourth satire of Book I, 'Cras') he achieves forceful and lucid satire, where the couplets are very effectively handled; at other times, as in the third satire, which like several others, takes its lead from Juvenal, the language is crabbed and the impression given by the account of sexual depravity is of literary self-indulgence rather than of a genuine *indignation* in responding to the actual conditions of Elizabethan society.

　　The Scourge of Villanie was Marston's last attempt at non-dramatic verse, but he had already tried his hand at the stage, for his first play *Histriomastix* was written for a private performance during the Middle Temple's Christmas revels of 1598.[5] The idea once scouted, that he turned his attention to the stage because of the banning of his satires, therefore seems unlikely, though no doubt the closing off of that medium of expression would add further incentive to turn to the theatre. *Histriomastix* in any case is very competent apprentice work that throws much light on Marston's later development as a playwright.

The Inns of Court audience was an undergraduate audience and, as such audiences still are mostly, no doubt cautious, conservative and serious—for taste aspires to the adult world the young men would challenge. Marston's play takes the form of an old-fashioned morality play with each of the six acts presided over by an abstract genius, Peace, Plenty, Pride, Envy, War and Poverty. The theme is a pious one and takes causal form: peace generates luxury, which in turn generates pride leading to envy and so strife, which destroys wealth and brings poverty, so that people long again for peace. The cyclic nature of the thesis however is overborne by the conclusion, which sees Peace returned to her dominance, offering her throne to Astraea the classical symbol of civilisation, and the play ends with no less a figure than Queen Elizabeth blessing the new reign:

> All sing Paeans to her sacred worth,
> Which none but Angels tongues can warble forth:
> Yet Sing, for though we cannot light the Sunne,
> Yet utmost might hath kinde acceptance wonne.[6]

The allegory intends us, of course, to regard Peace, Astraea and Queen Elizabeth as synonymous.[7] For all its incidental concern for political matters, the conflict of class interest which is stirred up by envy, for instance ('Let's pluck downe the Church, and set up an Ale-hose . . . weele pluck downe all the noble houses in the land e're we have done' say the rabble[8]) the play's concerns are essentially religious. God wills man's tribulations in the process of the triumph of His kingdom. Marston's spokesman in the play, Chrisoganus, points to the providential theme in exhorting Mavortius, a backsliding scholar, to learn the virtue of patience in adversity:

> Thou wants a Solon to consort with thee,
> To prove affliction is the perfect way
> That leads to Jove's tribunal dignity; . . .[9]

Chrisoganus, as George Geckle points out, means 'golden born'[10] and would seem to be a masculine equivalent of Spenser's Chrysogonee, who in Book III of the *Faerie Queene* is represented as the mother of Belphoebe (symbolising the chaste virtue of the Virgin

Queen) and herself of divine origin. The complex of ideas is meant to suggest that the scholar Chrisoganus-Marston has the divine light that will lead him and us to the sacred truths that it is the artist's function to reveal.

It is for this reason that the play is called *Histriomastix or the Player Whipt*, for the play sets out to contrast the true nature of the artist's high calling, with the prostitution of art perpetrated by the mercenary players, led by the hack poet Post-hast. A proper understanding of the use and misuse of the arts is central to the preparation for the coming of Astraea, the Goddess of the arts. Characteristically Marston uses his play to discuss the role of the playwright, an artistic self-consciousness that is evident in all his plays. The balance between display and self-display is often precarious in Marston, as it was to become increasingly in the next generation. In this early play, the balance is justly kept, the playwright's art is seen as a vehicle for truth and Post-hast and his journey-man players are mocked for their trivialising and commercialising of the artist's role into mere entertainment: a temptation that Marston himself was not always able to resist.

Because the balance between vehicle and tenor is right in this play the embodiment of the ideas in the scenes that illustrate the breakdown of order and its restoration is vivid and convincing. Marston shows that enviable ability he shares with his contemporaries to convey the sense of actuality in the spoken word, as here where the players are discussing stage preparations:

> CLOUT. But how shall we doe for a Prologue for Lords?
> POST-HAST. I'le do it extempore.
> BELCH. O might we heere a spurt if need require.
> POST-HAST. *Why lords we are here to show you what we are,*
> *Lords we are heere although our clothes be bare,*
> *Instead of flowers, in season, ye shall gather Rime and Reason?*
> I never pleas'd my self better, it comes off with such suavity.
> GULCH. Well fellows, I never heard happier stuff,
> Heer's no new luxurie or blandishment,
> But plenty of old England's mothers' words.[11]

This is written in the light of Shakespeare's mechanicals and it is nothing if not theatrical. It brings the drama away from abstraction towards the life of its audience. Like Shakespeare's Pyramus and Thisbe too, it flatters the audience by appealing to their superior taste. Marston is always aware of his audience, as he is indeed in his theme of the follies of war, a fashionable repudiation of the jingoism of the Shakespeare of *Henry V* on the popular stage (though, as always, Shakespeare also gives us more than a hint of the other side of the story). The audience of this play, like Marston's later audiences, are the young gentlemen-about-town who would expect the sophisticated ideas that Geckle has demonstrated in the play and would enjoy the satire on the rabble rout. In its appeal it is a foretaste of much that is to come from Marston's pen: it subordinates both plot and character to ideas and it shows Marston's great ability to express ideas in dramatically effective ways. It is also typical of that characteristic Jacobean religiosity and contempt for the world from which so much of the tragedy and satire of the new reign comes to be generated.

Later, as a professional playwright, the early sense of the high calling of his art is apt to desert Marston; indeed there are times, even in his best plays, where the ideas serve the theatricality rather than the other way round, so that we sometimes feel unsure of the seriousness of the commitment to the worthy themes that are adumbrated.

The ambiguities characteristic of his first professional play *Antonio and Mellida*, however, are those deliberate ambiguities calculated to please a sophisticated and fashionable audience. For the opening of his new theatre Marston chose to write an Italianate play, the interpretation of whose ambiguities of tone requires some knowledge of the tradition from which it stems. The exact relationship of the play to Italian Senecanism becomes clearer if we take *Antonio and Mellida* in conjunction with its sequel *Antonio's Revenge*, which Marston had at least already conceived of as he was writing the first part, for the Induction promises that the characters of Antonio and Feliche 'should receive more exact accomplishment in a second part'[12] (a promise, incidentally only partly fulfilled). The two plays were advertised in the Stationers' Register in 1601 as Parts I and II 'of the play called Antonio and Melida' and then published in the following year; the publication bears the signs of careful supervision by the author.[13] Modern commentators find the linkage curious and incongruous on the assumption that one is comedy and the other tragedy.[14] But in the Italianate Senecan tradition, with which a fashionable Elizabethan audience would have been familiar, *Antonio and Mellida*, with its tragic opening and its uncertain outcome until the very end, belongs not to comedy (which concerned itself with people of an inferior social class) but with what Giraldi Cinthio called 'mixed tragedy' or 'tragedia di lieto fin'—tragedy with a happy ending.[15] Marlowe had led the way here in the 'tragic glass' of Part I of *Tamburlaine*. Giraldi Cinthio had himself in his later plays written mixed tragedies which were as much in the Senecan manner as such earlier Senecan horrors as *Orbecche*.[16] *Antonio and Mellida* is as much a 'Senecan' play as such Romantic 'mixed tragedies' as Giraldi's *Arrenopia*, in which, incidentally, a complementary disguise to Antonio's dressing as an Amazon warrior is represented in the Amazonian heroine fighting a fierce duel (disguised as a man) with the villain Omosio. A feature of the Senecan tradition is its particular concern with inspiring 'surprise' or 'wonder' (*admiratio*) in its audience, and Marston does this with a series of spectacular and Cinthio-like 'reversals' like those in the last scene where Andrugio offers his head to Piero to be followed shortly after by Antonio's miraculous appearance from his coffin. Marston goes out of his way to stress the Italianate nature of his drama both by the frequent quotation from Seneca's plays as well as the use of other Senecan texts. Further, in the love scene between Antonio and Mellida and occasionally elsewhere, he has the lovers break into Italian to express their joy at meeting. It is true that the comic element in the play is largely foreign to Italian Senecanism,[17] but Marston shows himself a true follower of the Italian tradition in feeling free to adapt their manner to English taste, for Giraldi insisted on the right of the playwright to adapt ancient practice to new situations.[18] The title page of *Antonio and Mellida* (presumably authorised by Marston) calls the play a 'history', so the distinction that Marston wishes to make is not between comedy and tragedy but between tragedy that is 'imagined' (*tragedia finta*) and the tragedy that is based on actual events.

Marston's originality in *Antonio and Mellida* does not stop at his inclusion of the comic. He develops the effect of *admiratio* (surprise, or astonishment) into what might be called a Mannerist principle, keeping his audience uncertain even to the end about the precise nature of the response expected of them. John Donne's poetry at this period, especially in the 'Songs and Sonets', with their constant surprising turns of tone and meaning, perhaps sets the pace among the *cognoscenti* for this fashionable Mannerism at the end of the 1590s, and Marston exploits it to the full in *Antonio and Mellida* and at a variety of levels. A tone of uncertainty is introduced immediately with an Induction where the discussion of the boy players centres on their uncertainty about the manner in which they are expected to interpret their parts, and there is much stress on the ambiguities of the characters themselves. The boy playing Antonio, for instance, is puzzled that he must play 'two parts in one', the 'true person' of Antonio but also 'his feigned presence of an Amazon, calling himself Florizel and I know not what. I a voice to play a lady! I shall ne'er do it.' The ironic layers proliferate as Marston exploits the increased detachment of effect that can be gained by the use of boy players. Another of the players must act two parts because of the need for doubling (Induc.21) and again this emphasises the ambiguities inherent in relating the stage to life.

Marston deliberately exploits the artificiality of the relationship of stage to life throughout the play, stressing as much the dissimilarities as the likeness. He employs a variety of means: the language veers alarmingly from resonant appeal to the emotions to comic parody, as in the scene, for instance, where Mellida, distraught by Antonio's supposed death, is courted by the foppish rival Matzagente and Galeatzo (II.i.183–202):

GALEATZO. Hark thee; I pray thee taint not thy sweet ear
    With that sot's gabble; by thy beauteous cheek,
    He is the flagging'st bulrush that e'er droop'd
    With each slight mist of rain. But with pleas'd eye
    Smile on my courtship.
MELLIDA. What said you, sir? Alas my thought was fix'd
    Upon another object. Good, for-bear;
    I shall but weep. Ay me, what boots a tear!
    Come, come let's dance. O music, thou distill'st
    More sweetness in us than this jarring world;
    Both time and measure from thy strains do breathe,
    Whilst from the channel of this dirt doth flow
    Nothing but timeless grief, unmeasured woe.
ANTONIO [*in disguise as an Amazon*]. O how impatience cramps my
    cracked veins,
    And cruddles thick my blood with boiling rage.
    O eyes, why leap you not like thunderbolts
    Or cannon bullets in my rivals' face?
    Ohimè infelice misero, o lamentevol fato.
                             [*Falls to the ground*]
ALBERTO. What means the lady fall upon the ground?
ROSSALINE. Belike the falling sickness.

Here we move from the bawdy absurdities of Matzagente as a flagging bulrush[19] to Mellida's affecting sententiousness and then to Antonio's melodramatic outburst and Rossaline's bawdy punning. The element of discontinuity in the language is strongly reinforced by the situation on stage in which each character expresses his or her own private experience largely unrelated to the thoughts and feelings of the others. Mellida is not even listening to Galeatzo's address to her and asks inconsequentially for music to fill up the gap between his meaning and her thoughts. Antonio's response (his true identity disguised from the other characters) is contained in an 'aside' which switches for no apparent reason from English to Italian and is punctuated by the physical dislocation of the stage business of his fall, and this in turn proves incomprehensible to another courtier, Alberto, who asks, confusedly 'What means the lady fall upon the ground?' Rossaline's bawdy reply again suddenly changes the tone from the absurd to the obscene. The switch to comedy as a means of emphasising dislocation explains the suddenness of the comic ending that has often been regarded as a weakness of the play.[20] It is also characteristic of the chief fool of the play Balurdo, whose name, Hunter reminds us, signifies 'fool' according to Florio.[21] One of Balurdo's follies is that his senses literally become confused with one another as when he asks a painter to paint him a song. The effect of this technique of juxtaposition is not unlike the witty discontinuities of Magritte's painting, but it is of course equally a feature of the 'metaphysical wit' of the contemporary poets.

Another kind of distraction represented in this passage and equally important to the play as a whole is in the sudden changes that come over the characters. Piero's change of heart at the end of the play is one example as is his lapse into absurdity on hearing of Mellida's defection (III.ii.175–6) or such inconsistencies as Feliche's sudden change from resigned stoic ('I envy none', III.ii.46) to his envious reply to Castillo, who succeeds in persuading him of his success with women, 'Fut! methinks I am as like a man' (III.ii.70). Antonio's absurd jealousy in the quoted scene is another example, for it undermines his status as romantic hero. The overall purpose of these inconsistencies has nothing to do with the kind of enveloping parody that Professor Foakes detects in this play and in *Antonio's Revenge*,[22] indeed the dislocations would cease to be effective if a consistent tone of parody were adopted, nor are the dislocations simply there for theatrical effect, though they make for effective theatre. The function is to illustrate the theme this play has in common with *Histriomastix* and the verse satires, the essential incoherence, the vanity and instability of man's life, a theme which gives point to Mellida's remarks on the contrast between the orderly world which music envisions and the jarring world of disorder which promises only 'grief' and 'woe' to us earthly creatures ('this dirt').[23] Like Jonson, Marston sees the function of art to point the way towards a divine perfection that it alone of earthly things can adumbrate. That man can only obtain glimpses of this truth is illustrated in the play by the fleetingness with which the theme finds expression, notably in the scene (IV.i.) where Antonio meets again with his father, in such sententious utterances as Antonio's 'Hell is beneath; yet heaven is overall' (l.29) or in Andrugio's Senecan stoicism:

> he's a king,
> A true right king, that dares do aught save wrong,
> Fears nothing mortal but to be unjust
> . . . .
> Who sits upon Jove's footstool, as I do,
> Adoring, not affecting, majesty . . .

> (ll.53–5,61–2)

None of the characters represent these truths, the assurance of a Chrisoganus is denied us here in a world where reality is merely glimpsed. The play itself is primarily concerned with representing the shadows not the substance. In spite of the Prologue's flippancy the play has a seriousness of purpose beyond mere theatricality.

Antonio's Revenge declares its serious purpose immediately in the Prologue:[24]

> If any spirit breathes within this round
> Uncapable of weighty passion . . .
> . . . .
> Who winks and shuts his apprehension up
> From common sense of what men were, and are,
> Who would not know what men must be—let such
> Hurry amain from our black-visaged shows.

It is ironic, in view of this clear declaration of intent, that the play has so often been castigated for its air of unreality. For here Marston sets

out to demonstrate one of the basic truths of Elizabethan
Christianity that, in the words of an Elizabethan translation of a
medieval text: 'our Lord God formed man of the slime of the earth,
which is more vile than the rest of the elements'.[25] The Augustinian
theme of human nastiness and the vanity of the world, re-stated by
Luther, endorsed by Calvin, pervades the late sixteenth and early
seventeenth centuries. In a work of Petrarch that Chapman used
extensively in writing *Monsieur D'Olive*, St. Augustine is made to
utter such sentiments in his own person.[26] The mood achieves a
peak of eloquent expression in Donne's *Anniversaries* and the
sermons:

> The apostle . . . says . . .
> whilst we are in the body, we are but in a pilgrimage, and we are
> absent from the Lord; he might have said dead, for this whole
> world is but an universal churchyard, but one common grave, and
> the life and motion that the greatest persons have in it, is but
> the shaking of buried bodies in the grave, by an earthquake.
> That which we call life, is but Hebdomada mortium, a week of
> deaths . . .[27]

Senecan tragedy was understandably seized on by Renaissance
writers as an eloquent vehicle for the expression of these salutary
Christian truths, for nowhere is human depravity more insistently
portrayed or the vanity of earthly hopes more eloquently
demonstrated. Seneca was considered a classical exhibitor of the
vices and the nastiness of which human beings were capable:

> I doubt whether there bee any amonge all the catalogue of
> Heathen wryters, that with more gravity of Philosophicall
> sentences, more weightynes of sappy words, or greater authority
> of sound matter beateth down sinne, loose lyfe, dissolute
> dealinge, and unbridled sensuality: or that more sensibly, pithily
> and bytingly layeth downe the guerdon of filthy lust, cloaked
> dissimulation and odious treachery: which is the dryft whereunto
> he leveleth the whole yssue of ech one of his Tragedies.[28]

The morality of *Antonio's Revenge* seems strange to a modern
audience who see comparatively little difference, morally, between
the nightmare figure of Piero, his hands covered in blood, gloating
over his killing of Andrugio and Feliche, and the avenging Antonio,

murdering Piero's innocent son and tormenting Piero by feeding the chopped-up remains of the son to the tongueless father. But the Senecan tradition demands that a distinction be made. In Giraldi Cinthio's *Orbecche* (1541), which established the pattern for the genre,[29] both the moral purpose of depicting the horrors and the right distinction to be made between avenged villain and avenging hero (or heroine in this case) is explicit and throws much light on Marston's play—and incidentally on other Elizabethan exercises in the mode, like *Titus Andronicus* and *Hamlet*. The horrors of *Orbecche* include the presentation to the heroine, Orbecche, of her husband's head and the bodies of her two young sons, by her father Sulmone. Sulmone the King of Persia has discovered the secret marriage of his daughter, whom he wished to marry to the King of Parthia. Orbecche gets her revenge by stabbing her father and then herself commits suicide. The play explicitly condones Orbecche's act in a choric judgement, invoking 'Christian' duty:

> Ma non è stato mal a uccider lui;
> ch' a Dio non s'offre vittima più grata
> d'un malvagio tiran, com'era questo.[30]

[But it was not wrong to kill him, for no more acceptable victim is offered to God than a wicked tyrant, as this man was.]

At the end of the play the Chorus summarises the lesson that has been learnt from these gory events:

This mortal happiness of ours is truly vain and fleeting . . . whoever discerns the truth ought to fly with rapid thought to that Immortal who is where God governs in Heaven and leave this frail earth to be enjoyed by fools whose eyes are blinded by the things of this world.[31]

The morality of neo-Senecan tragedy requires us to see the avenger as caught up in a web of evil which can only be destroyed by an act of violence. Our ancestors were less squeamish about this than we are—the tyrant (whether Sulmone, Tamora, Claudius, Piero) must be put down in blood as a warning to evil-doers and in an appropriate manner: Tamora and Piero must eat the offspring of their own wickedness, Claudius's soul must be sent to hell 'unhouseled'. This is not to condone the evil of killing, but in this

world we are all in the sight of God equally corrupt and evil: 'what
men must be'. The tragic hero is justified not by his superior moral
status (hence the play's rejection of stoicism as a vanity) but by his
(or her) becoming a tool of divine justice, acquiescing—as Hamlet
finally comes to realise—in the decrees of Providence.

In *Antonio's Revenge* the key moment in this acceptance both of the
Divine Will and of his role as avenger is in the soliloquy of IV.iv. as
he laments the death of Mellida:

> Ay Heaven, thou mayst; thou mayst, Omnipotence.
> What vermin bred of putrefacted slime
> Shall dare to expostulate with thy decrees?
> O heaven, thou mayst indeed; she was all thine,
> All heavenly, I did but humbly beg
> To borrow her of thee a little time . . .
> . . . I'll not blaspheme. Look here, behold!
>
> [*Antonio puts off his cap and lieth just upon his back*]
>
> I turn my prostrate breast upon thy face
> And vent a heaving sigh. O hear but this;
> I am a poor, poor orphan; a weak, weak child,
> The wrack of splitted fortune, the very ooze,
> The quicksand that devours all misery.
> Behold the valiant'st creature that doth breathe!
> For all this I dare live, and I will live,
> Only to numb some others' cursed blood
> With the dead palsy of like misery.
> Then death, like to a stifling incubus
> Lie on my bosom. Lo, sir, I am sped:
> My breast is Golgotha, grave for the dead.

Here the Calvinistic expression of God's omnipotence and man's
littleness is linked with the idea of vengeance on God's enemies
('others' cursed blood'), culminating in Antonio's allusion to
Christ's death and defeat of death in the place of skulls. Antonio's
acceptance of the role of suffering ('The quicksand that devours all
misery') that Christ's example has shown to be the way to defeat evil
does not in the least preclude his active role as avenging agent of
God's wrath. This battle could be bloody and was accepted as such
by the warring factions of sixteenth-century Christianity and it is
absurdly anachronistic for modern commentators to foist their
non-Christian pacificism on this earlier militancy. More especially

because such pacifism is explicitly mocked by Marston in his treatment of the stoic Pandulpho's inconsistencies.

Marston makes the moral position of the play quite clear at the end when Antonio and his fellow murderers are officially commended by the two senators:

> 2ND SENATOR. Blest be you all, and may your honours live
> Religiously held sacred, even for ever and ever.
> GALEATZO. Thou art another Hercules to us
> In ridding huge pollution from our state.

There is no more reason to assume this is meant ironically than for dismissing the choric comment of *Orbecche* or Marcus's approval (endorsed by popular acclaim) of Titus's revenge in *Titus Andronicus*. Senecan Tragedy commonly dealt with the much debated question of the killing of tyrants.[32] It is a common view of Marston's age that it was a religious duty to extirpate evil rulers, and clearly the play adopts that stance. Marston's theatrical techniques have not substantially changed from those of *Antonio and Mellida*, and these techniques are precisely those best calculated to convey the moral, for, as in the earlier play, they deliberately eschew the clouding sympathy that a more naturalistic treatment of character would involve. Comparison with Shakespeare's contemporaneous *Hamlet* is here useful.

The precise relationship of these two plays is obscured by scholarly uncertainty about which preceded the other. This is much less important, however, than that the two playwrights (whether by agreement, in rivalry or by coincidence) were working on closely related material. But whereas Shakespeare—characteristically at this period—chose to centre his revenge play on the tensions the demand for revenge generates in his hero, and so make the play above all a study in personality, Marston takes the opposite course. Using the dislocating techniques that had successfully shocked and entertained his audience in *Antonio and Mellida* he deliberately avoids the dangers (and rewards) of emotional involvement in the affairs of his hero, to keep the sight lines clear for the moral implications; moral implications which Shakespeare was content to muddy in the search for empathy between audience and hero. Clearly each man knew his trade, for the different approaches are appropriate to the differing circumstances of the theatre for which the plays were written. Reavely Gair has described Marston's technique as 'Quasi-operatic'[33] and while this somewhat overstates the case, the frequent punctuation of the dialogue with music (a feature of the boys' companies generally) adds an element of non-realistic artifice that assists the other devices of dislocation to a similar end. More especially because, as in *Antonio and Mellida*, the ideal harmony of the music is explicitly contrasted at one point with man's disharmony:

> ANTONIO. Wilt sing a Dirge, Boy?
> PAU. No, no song: 'twill be vile out of tune.
> ALBERTO. Indeed he's hoarse; the poor boy's voice is cracked.
> PAU. Why, coz, why should it not be hoarse and cracked,
>   When all the strings of nature's symphony
>   Are cracked and jar? Why should his voice keep tune,
>   When there's no music in the breast of man?

(IV.v.65–71)

The characteristic artifice of drawing attention to the stage conditions (the boy actors) is of course another basic device of dislocation.

The play abounds in theatrical moments that excite 'admiration' and call attention to their own staginess. As with *Antonio and Mellida*, however, the *admiratio* is closer to witty 'surprise' than the 'wonder' of such earlier Senecan imitations as *Titus Andronicus* or William Alabaster's *Roxana* whose effect on one member of its audience at Cambridge in 1592 was that she 'fell distracted and never recovered'.[34] Piero enters at the beginning of the play 'his arms bare, smeared in blood, a poniard in one hand' and his opening lines have the shock impact of a Metaphysical poem:

> Ho, Gaspar Strotzo, bind Feliche's trunk
> Unto the panting side of Mellida.

In the third scene of the play an *aubade* is proposed in which Antonio and his mother (and the audience) are led to expect Mellida to appear in the early morning to greet him:

> The heart of beauty, Mellida appears
> See, look, the curtain stirs . . .

When the curtain is drawn it reveals, strung up, the dead body of Feliche 'stabbed thrice with wounds'. Marston's deaths in this play are all brilliantly stage-managed for the maximum shock effect, as with the throttling of Strotzo or even more with Antonio's stabbing of the young Julio after the audience has been led to believe he is to be spared. Act II begins with a brief dumb show in which Antonio and his mother lay their tear-stained handkerchiefs on Andrugio's coffin. Acts III and V similarly begin in dumb show. There are, too, the same kind of language dislocations we found in *Antonio and Mellida* and abrupt changes of character, as in the scene where Pandulpho, having preached stoic patience, immediately bursts into tears over his son's body (IV.v.). Even odder is the mad transformation of Antonio into a fool blowing bubbles. A recent student production of the play in my own college in Swansea, which presented the play very convincingly as an exercise in the theatre of cruelty, none the less baulked at this scene of bubble-blowing as beyond the range of a modern audience's range of tolerance. Marston, however, in this scene is simply exercising his basic technique of keeping us free from emotional entanglement: the scene reminds us forcibly of the underlying imagery of folly that connects the two plays, as Finkelpearl brings out well in his reading of the play.[35] As in *Antonio and Mellida* comic intervention, especially through insane Balurdo, enables Marston to engineer rapid changes in tone and mood.

Marston's highly sophisticated theatrical techniques of detachment, which are used with such skill in this play and to such serious moral purpose, have not been appreciated, simply because the standard of judgement involved is so often that of Shakespeare. Harold Jenkins, for instance, complains that whereas the ghost in *Hamlet* is coherently integrated into the action of the play, Andrugio's ghost 'is heard on disconnected occasions',[36] and he dismisses the device as a bungling attempt to copy Shakespeare. But the function of Andrugio's ghost is perfectly coherent in terms of its function in the moral theme of the play, which is Marston's central concern. Unlike the Ghost of King Hamlet, Andrugio's Ghost is morally unambiguous. He has been sent to spur Antonio on to carry out the decrees of Providence (V.i.10). Before he retires to the world of the blessed (III.i.43), he announces unequivocally the theme of divine justice:

> O now triumphs my ghost,
> Exclaiming, 'Heaven's just; for I shall see
> The scourge of murder and impiety'.

(V.i.23–5)

Shakespeare's concern is to keep the Ghost's role and exact status doubtful to allow full development of the psychological tension in the hero that this uncertainty creates; and because we are required to share Hamlet's feelings we must share his dilemma. In *Hamlet* even the Ghost is humanised to draw the audience's sympathies. Marston's method is diametrically opposed; his primary aim is to dehumanise, to strip away sentiment, to exploit theatricality in the interest of a moral clarity that most modern readers (though I would guess not modern audiences accustomed to Bond or Brenton) find hard to take. For the picture it presents of humanity is not lovely: the play asks us to see man in the cold light of the realities of Vietnam and Afghanistan (not to mention things nearer home): 'what men were and are . . . what men must be'.

The chronological order of *Antonio's Revenge, Jacke Drum's Entertainment*[37] and *What You Will*[38] is uncertain. A plausible but by no means certain chronology would assume that the reference in the tragedy to 'the rawish dank of clumsy winter' is as much to a literal as to a figurative winter and that the play follows immediately after the first part of *Antonio and Mellida*, that is, that it dates from winter 1599/1600, and that *Jacke Drum's* song of 'This month of May' records the acting of the play in spring 1600 with *What You Will* (not published until 1607) following in 1601. The failure to see *What You Will* carefully through the press (unlike Marston's usual practice) and the hiatus in his output before *Malcontent* appears in 1604, with its flattering dedication to Ben Jonson (by which time Marston had joined Jonson as a playwright of the larger 'private' theatre of Blackfriars) supports Gair's conjecture[39] that Jonson's satire on Marston in *Poetaster* had stopped the rapid flow of Marston's plays.

Whatever the exact sequence and circumstances of *Jacke Drum* and *What You Will*, their relationship to Jonson is, as is usually recognised, one of the interesting things about them. The relationship between the two men is of secondary importance and in any case Marston's personality, on the evidence we have, is well nigh irrecoverable. But the dispute over their attitudes to the theatre is central to our concern with the drama of the period. *What You Will* takes up the argument with Jonson more explicitly in the Induction, which Marston uses to challenge Jonson's exalted view of the playwright as exempted 'from the gloomy multitude'.[40] In contrast the Induction argues that art is entertainment and that what pleases most is likely to be best:

> Music and poetry were first approv'd
> By common sense; and that which pleased most
> Held most allowed pass: no, rules of art
> Were shap'd to pleasure, not pleasure to your rules.
>
> (ll.59–62)

This directly challenges the poet who boasted that he 'from no needful rule . . . swerveth',[41] and it equally challenges the core of Jonson's argument in *Poetaster* (and indeed his central position as an artist) that the poet has a sacred duty to reveal the truth of which he is the custodian, not merely to entertain them (for example, *Poetaster*, IV.vi.30–78). In *Poetaster* Jonson reproves Crispinus (Marston) for debasing art's high calling and asserts through the mouth of Augustus Caesar the special place and responsibilities of the poet in a civilised community, having Maecenas compliment Augustus for his defence of the poet:

> Your Majesties high grace to poesie,
> Shall stand 'gainst all the dull detractions
> Of leaden souls.
>
> (V.i.33–5)

This is reproof indeed, but it is largely undeserved. For, as we have seen, Marston's plays up to this point had been concerned with serious issues, for all their dazzling display of theatrical virtuosity. It was Jonson who had yet to learn that there was no necessary opposition between entertainment and speaking truth, for though he aspired to the Horatian end of 'teaching sweetly' it was not until *Alchemist* that a deep-seated tendency to oppose the teaching and the sweetness was finally exorcised.

It is in *What You Will* more than in any other of his plays that Marston combines entertainment with serious moral comment, perhaps under the pressure of Jonson's hectoring. It is true that even in the Prologue of *Antonio and Mellida* he had claimed to be providing 'The worthless present of slight idleness', but it is a disclaimer not to be taken seriously. In *Jacke Drum*, however, ideas tend to be at the service of the entertainment. Serious ideas are floated in the play, Mamon, the bourgeois entrepreneur, who is satirised in morality fashion as a personification of covetousness and whose role in the first three acts as a rival to Pasquil for

Katherine's love, as well as a satirical target, is given some prominence, disappears completely (we learn later he has been sent to Bedlam) with a farewell speech that parodies morality exits:

> bondes, house and ship, ship, house and bondes, Dispaire, Damnation, Hell, I come, I come, so roome for Mamon, roome for Usury, roome for thirtie in the hundred. I come, I come, I come. (III.HW, p. 219)

We are being asked to believe Mamon is no threat, or rather, we are not being asked to think of Mamon at all, except as a theatrical device, a contrast with what Jonson was later to do with Sir Epicure Mammon or Middleton with his sardonic commentaries on filthy Lucre. There is a notable contrast, for instance, between the tragic seriousness of Audrey's song 'Let the usurer cram him in interest that excel' as she tends the dying Dampit in *A Trick to Catch the Old One* (IV.v.1–4) and the easy-going cynicism of Marston's song in *Jacke Drum* (II.i.HW, p. 197).

The flippancy with which Marston treats serious problems in this play is also apparent in his treatment of Brabant Senior, the bombastic critic who is often taken as a caricature of Ben Jonson[42] and the cause of Jonson's disaffection with Marston. Certainly Brabant Senior (like Jonson) has decided views on contemporary poetry; he strongly disapproves of Marston's plays, which are made the subject of a discussion towards the beginning of Act V (V.HW, p. 234). Here Brabant shows a preference for the humorous comedy Jonson had come to specialise in: the boys of Paul's (he complains) 'produce / Such musty fopperies of antiquitie, / And do not sute the humorous ages backs / with cloathes of fashion.' Like Lorenzo Junior, who has the playwright's general approval in *Every Man In His Humour*, Brabant Senior collects gulls to amuse himself by deriding them. Whether Brabant Senior represents Jonson or simply stands for overbearing and unreasonably critical assurance in general (as he is characterised by Ned Planet, III.HW, p. 229), his treatment at the end of the play accords more with village farce than serious satire. Brabant Senior attempts to play a joke on the pathologically lecherous French Monsieur by introducing his own wife to him as a prostitute, only to find he has been cuckolded by the Frenchman. It is true that Planet, at the end of the play, attempts to relate Brabant's punishment to his crime and the familiar solemnity of man's littleness in relation to God's greatness is sounded:

> Why Foole, the power of Creation
> Is still Omnipotent, and there's no man that breathes
> So valiant, learned, wittie, or so wise,
> But it can equall him out of the same mould
> Wherein the first was form'd.

> (V.HW, p. 240)

But the interconnection of mirth and moral seem more than a little strained.

Planet's role in the play may well be (as Finkelpearl argues[43]) to suggest stability in a turning world and his pronouncements often sound like the authorial voice:

> Why the soule of man is nought but simphonies,
> A sound of disagreeing parts, yet faire unite
> By heavens hand, divine by reasons light.

> (V.HW, p. 235)

This reminds us of Pandulpho's reference to music in *Antonio and Mellida* (IV.v.68–71), though Planet's emphasis is more optimistically on the restoration of the harmony lost at the fall of man. Perhaps Marston could assume an audience of sufficient sophistication not only to pick out this subdued note of affirmation in the barrage of farce and lampoon the play exhibits but also to see the hotch-potch itself as a symbol of the city of man. The disruptive techniques already commented on in other plays are again used and this certainly implies a high degree of sophistication in the audience. For a modern reader however (there has been no modern audience) the farce would seem to assimilate everything to itself.

In *What You Will* the process of retreat from overt moral statement is taken a step further, perhaps—as I have suggested—as a defiant retort to Jonson. The Induction argues forcibly that artistic value resides in the opinion of the audience (a familiar enough argument to the modern critic) against Jonson's basic contention that value is a transcendental quality inhering in the work of art itself. But to what extent are the views of Doricus and Philomuse in the Induction representative of their author, or are we again being entertained with the irony we meet in the Prologue of *Antonio and Mellida*? In *What You Will* the question is much harder to answer. Marston again in this play adopts the techniques of both *Antonio and Mellida* and *Jacke Drum* of interweaving an element of love intrigue with a variety of satirical scenes. The mood is again one of comic detachment, in which Marston encourages the audience to participate in the play as a theatrical event. Again there is much discussion of the nature of play-acting, there are allusions to particular problems associated with the boy actors; one scene discusses the recruitment of boy actors. We are in a self-conscious theatre that thrives on the destruction of illusion. What is less easy to see is whether this fiction is, as in the other plays discussed so far, being used as a metaphor, for not only is there no clear guidance within the play, but those characters for whom we might look for guidance are themselves undercut. We are in the Swiftian world of *Tale of a Tub* where even the guide is one whose imaginations are 'exceedingly disposed to run away with his reason'.

In *Histriomastix* Marston had employed an authorial guide in Chrisoganus, the heroic scholar whose credentials were unambiguous. In *What You Will* the author takes on the fool's habit in the person of the disillusioned scholar Lampatho Doria with whom he explicitly identifies himself in having Quadratus call him by the pseudonym Marston had used for his satire; 'Don Kinsayder' (l.531). Like Marston Lampatho has been a railing satirist, but he is eventually mocked out of this humour by the Epicurean Quadratus, rejects the life of scholarship and eventually turns lover. The scene in which he expresses his disillusionment with his former ways in a charming speech, where he confesses he knows as little as his spaniel 'Delight', expresses a scepticism that, while it does not contradict the position taken in earlier plays, would seem to be more fundamental:

> A company of old frenetici
> Did eat my youth, and when I crept abroad,
> Finding my numbness in this nimble age,
> I fell a-railing; but now soft and slow,
> I know I know naught but I naught do know.
> What shall I do, what plot, what course pursue?
>
> (ll.880–5)

Lampatho's theophily (821f.) anticipates the sweeping condemnation of mankind in Rochester's great satire. In Christian terms this is the fideistic viewpoint found in one of Marston's favourite authors, Montaigne. In *Histriomastix* the same Socratic dictum is quoted by the hedonist Mavortius and rejected by Chrisoganus, who argues dogmatically

> If wee have this wee call Scientia
> We must have truth of meere necessity . . .

(Histriomastix, I.HW, p. 250)

It looks as if Marston has shifted his philosophical ground somewhat since *Histriomastix* to a more thoroughgoing scepticism which casts doubt on the possibility of discovering truth; hence the lack of a guide in the play and the cause of much confusion in trying to understand it. This is no more an irreligious view in Marston than it is in Montaigne or Swift, indeed such fundamental scepticism concerning human knowledge became a special mark of Calvinistic thought in Marston's lifetime.

That Marston's position is still essentially Christian in *What You Will* is demonstrated by the role given to Albano in the main plot. This plot, taken from Plautus's *Amphitryo* via the Italian of Sforza d'Oddi, has the supposedly dead Albano return home to find not only that his wife is besieged by suitors, but that his brothers-in-law Randolfo and Adrian have persuaded a perfumer, Francisco Soranza, to personate him, to head off a French suitor, disapproved of by the brothers. Much is made of the ease with which people are fooled by appearance, especially by clothes, to reinforce the theme of the foolishness of man's aspiration to the truth. The rejected suitor Jacomo remarks as Francisco is dressed for his part:

> I warrant you, give him but fair rich clothes,
> He can be ta'en, reputed anything.
> Apparel's grown a god, and goes more neat;
> Makes men of rags, which straight he bears aloft,
> Like patch'd-up scarecrows to affright the rout
> Of the idolatrous vulgar, that worship images,
> Stand aw'd and bare-scalp'd at the gloss of silks
> Which like the glorious Ajax of Lincoln's Inn
> (Survey'd with wonder by me when I lay
> Factor in London) laps up naught but filth
> And excrements, that bear the shape of men . . .

(ll. 937–47)

Here I think we can detect, if fleetingly, the 'meta-voice' of the play
and it has a religious ring when, for instance, the contrast is implied
between the 'vulgar's' idolatrous worship of the God of clothes with
the wise man's ability to discover the truth beneath the appearances
(as in *The Tale of a Tub* there is an alternative to the world of fleeting
appearances). The reference to the newly invented water-closet in
Lincoln's Inn ('a jakes') which Marston must have known, and
perhaps used, in his days as a law student introduces the vocabulary
of Christian humiliation we have already seen as characteristic of
Marston in the discussion of *Antonio's Revenge*. If there is a guidance
in this world of appearances then it comes in unexpected moments,
through the mouths not of wise men—as it does in *Histriomastix*—
but in moments of revelation to the fools and knaves which make up
the people of this world. As the Neoplatonists (and Spenser) taught,
the veil of obscurity can only occasionally be lifted to reveal the
naked truth for those whose eyes are not dazzled by its
contemplation.

One such moment is from Albano when he returns to find no one
will believe he really is Albano and that he is mistaken for Francisco:

> Doth not opinion stamp the current pass
> Of each man's value, virtue, quality?
> Had I engross'd the choicest commodities
> Of Heaven's traffic, yet reputed vile
> I am a rascal. O dear unbelief,
> How wealthy dost thou make thy owner's wit!
> Thou train of knowledge, what a privilege
> Thou giv'st to the possessor; anchorst him
> From floating with the tide of vulgar faith,
> From being damn'd with multitudes; dear unbelief!

> (1247–56)

Again the religious note is unmistakable in the comment and the
'unbelief' that Albano praises is clearly the kind of Montaignean
scepticism that prevents a man being deceived by appearances. Yet
this moment of revelation does not confer any special status on
Albano as a character, who is, at the end of the play, accepted back
into the world of appearances from which he is temporarily
estranged; a very different fate from those who see the light in

Middleton's more sardonic comedies, like Whorehound of *Chaste Maid*. The ending of the play suggests a tolerance and acceptance of man's ignorance and stupidity more akin to Jonson's catholic morality than Middleton's fierce Calvinistic logic. Yet a puzzle remains, for Albano's aristocratic rejection of appearances would seem to run counter to the popularist aesthetic principles enunciated by Doricus and Philomuse in the Induction. This either suggests an element of irony in the Induction or that the 'common sense' appealed to by Doricus is common only to the privileged coterie audience of Paul's theatre—what Jonson, in his theatre, called 'understanders'. If the latter is the case, then the 'pleasure' the play would excite includes the pleasure obtained from understanding. The fact that it is Quadratus who at the end of the play recalls us to this promise of pleasure suggests some irony of intention.

It is typical of Marston's method in *What You Will* that the most authoritative figure of the play, the overbearing 'four-square' Quadratus, who is given the play's final words, should represent what is ultimately to be rejected. Quadratus is an epicure who believes that the best that can be made out of life is to enjoy what pleasures it affords. In his principal role as a commentator on the people and events of the play much that Quadratus says is true—his scornful treatment of Lampatho's habit of railing at mankind for instance, certainly suggests a saner response to the idiocies of the world he inhabits. Quadratus has often been thought to be a portrait of Ben Jonson,[44] but while he has some of the qualities for which Jonson was notorious—his aggressiveness and self-confidence, his tippling—there are even more dissimilarities, as Finkelpearl points out.[45] The overriding difference is that Jonson's satirical stance was in the service of a transcendental truth, a Christian truth, that he thought it his sacred duty to convey. Quadratus is essentially an intellectual fool playing with ideas and people as a source of entertainment. It is typical of him, for instance, that he can encourage Lampatho to turn amorist with contradictory 'anti-Platonic' and 'Platonic' arguments that women's beauty is worth sacrificing his soul for: 'for whose sake / A man could find in his heart to inhell himself' (l.1581), and that women's beauty is a revelation of heavenly beauty (l.1588) and then mock Lampatho as a fool for falling in love:

God make thee a good fool, and happy and ignorant, and
amorous, and rich and frail, and a satirist, and an essayist, and
sleepy, and proud, and indeed a fool, and then thou shalt be sure
of all these.

(ll.1598–1601)

Quadratus is never clearly repudiated in the play—for the play
allows the audience to make 'what you will' of the picture it
presents, but Iacomo's comment in Act V contrasting Cato, whose
heroism Quadratus is commending, with Quadratus himself carries
conviction (as Finkelpearl argues) '[Cato] was valiant and honest,
which an epicure ne'er was'. Quadratus is trying to persuade the
jaded Duke of Venice to hear a play he has devised on Cato's suicide
as a refined entertainment. The climax of the play, says the cynical
Quadratus, is to be the discourse on the soul's immortality, as Cato
lies dying:

To kill oneself some ay, some hold it no:
O these are points would entice away one's soul
To break's indenture of base prentisage,
And run away from's body in swift thoughts
To melt in contemplation's luscious sweets.
Now my voluptuous Duke, I'll feed thy sense . . .

(ll.1981–6)

The irony that the debate on the immortality of the soul is to be
treated as an epicurean entertainment is made clear by the
interruption of the proceedings on Albano's arrival to seek and
obtain justice of the Duke, so that the play of Cato is never in fact
performed. The 'real' world has intruded to destroy these aesthetic
games. In this Marston has given not only his judgement on
Quadratus but his underlying view of drama as more than a bid for
the audience's pleasure.

The *Malcontent* marks a new departure for Marston as his
description of his muse as 'reformed' in the Epilogue acknowledges.
He had switched his allegiance from the children of Paul's to the
Blackfriars theatre, in which company he acquired a one-sixth share
in February 1604 and in that year the play—uniquely for Marston—
was prepared for a production at the Globe; this, together with the

three editions of the text in the same year, suggests an exceptional popularity. Yet another new development is indicated by the fulsome dedication to Ben Jonson and the declaration in the Address to the Reader that he 'proposeth to himself no more ends than God and virtue do' shows a marked change of tone towards the Jonsonian stress on morality, compared to the defiant challenge to Jonson of the Induction of *What You Will*. The stagecraft of the play too suggests that Marston was trying a new tack and making a bid for a wider popularity than that of his small coterie audience of Paul's.

In technique *Malcontent* is much less original than the earlier plays. The dislocationary detachment of the earlier plays gives way to an appeal to the audience's emotions. Some of the old disruptive techniques re-appear—but now accommodated within the more orthodox framework of a well plotted play in which the characters have an easily recognisable consistency of personality and motive. A good example of this is seen in the principal character whose two dissimilar roles of Altofronto and Malevole are given the logical connection that one is the disguise of the other. Marston has abandoned the metaphor by which a stage world of disconnected fragments represents this great stage of fools, in favour of a coherent image that utters its similar philosophy rather than formally represents it. In this respect *Malcontent* is a drastic simplification of Marston's theatrical techniques and its popularity then and now is as much a consequence of its greater accessibility than of any intrinsic superiority. Indeed, in attempting to compromise with other people's ideas of a play (in particular, Jonson's) Marston has clouded his own vision.

For while Marston's underlying view of the world has not substantially changed, the image by which it is conveyed is less appropriate for encompassing it. In some ways indeed Marston's view is made more explicit and insistent here, in such an outburst, for instance, as Malevole's

> World! Tis the only region of death, the greatest shop of the devil, the cruel'st prison of men, out of which none pass without paying their dearest breath for a fee.

(IV.iv.27–9)[46]

The *vanitas* theme is as central to *Malcontent* as it is to Marston's earlier plays and Malevole must be presumed to speak for his author

in this passage and in the next scene when he consoles the deposed
Pietro for the loss of his Dukedom:

> Think this: this earth is the only grave and Golgotha wherein all
> things that live must rot; 'tis but the draught wherein the
> heavenly bodies discharge their corruption; the very muck hill on
> which the sublunary orbs cast their excrements. Man is the slime
> of this dung pit, and princes are the governors of these men; for,
> for our souls, they are as free as emperors . . .

(IV.v.107–13)

This is a return to the simpler didacticism of *Histriomastix* and, as in
that apprentice play, the interspersed satire illustrates the dross that
is to be repudiated.

The desire to amuse a wider audience by adopting more popular
techniques distorts the message. In the character of Piero in
Antonio's Revenge Marston created a Machiavel villain who not only
vividly illustrated the depths of depravity men were (and are)
capable of sinking to but stood at the centre of a world that showed
mankind as 'the slime of this dung pit'. Mendoza, the Machiavel of
Malcontent is by comparison a bungling villain, easily outwitted by a
change of clothes and an empty box, so little a threat that at the end
he can be kicked out of doors as the only punishment for the crimes
he would like to have committed. As a stage villain he is both
sufficiently type-cast to be easily recognisable for what he is and
sufficiently individual to be entertaining as a realistic character, as
for instance in his lyrical praise of women (I.v.33–50) which changes
abruptly to denunciation when he finds himself rejected by Aurelia
(I.vi.78–93). But these concessions to realism exact a price.

As tragi-comedy Marston brings his play to a happy romantic
ending in which the forces of good represented by Altofronto and
Maria triumph unambiguously against evil. In the earlier tragi-
comedy *Antonio and Mellida* Marston contrives an equally romantic
conclusion, but because the stage techniques deliberately eschew
too close an identification of the audience with the lovers, the *vanitas*
theme is uncompromised; we can see the temporary happiness of
Antonio and Mellida as one of the characteristic ups and downs of
fortune. The ending of *Malcontent* however challenges the *vanitas*
theme. This is most starkly so in the triumph of the virtuous Maria,
who within the realistic terms of the play's image clearly repudiates

the notion that all humanity is as vile as Malevole tells us it is. (The problem is avoided in *Histriomastix* by allowing allegory to predominate over realism.) Yet we cannot simply repudiate Malevole's view (even if we thought that to be Marston's intention) because he too is vindicated in the triumph of virtue at the conclusion of the play. Malevole is very much a character caught between two concepts of dramatic presentation. His double role as noble ruler and scourging satirist is a brilliant device for exposing the vices of the court society in which he operates, but it presents Marston with formidable problems in terms of character realism that he does not altogether succeed in overcoming. As Michael Scott shows in a perceptive analysis of the play,[47] Marston tends to provide us with two incompatible psychologies for his character, that of the noble Altofronto who, with *lèse-majesté*, lets Mendoza off lightly at the end of the play and the neurotic malcontent who is kept awake at night while the normal world sleeps:

> In night all creatures sleep;
> Only the malcontent, that 'gainst his fate
> Repines and quarrels—alas, he's goodman tell-clock!
> His sallow jaw-bones sink with wasting moan;
> Whilst others' beds are down, his pillow's stone.

> (III.ii.10–14)

This is essentially soliloquy, addressed to the audience, for Bilioso, who is on stage, hardly needs more evidence of Malevole's spleen.

Shakespeare, with a related problem in *Measure for Measure* keeps the Duke off centre most of the time and has an ability to create a sense of realism in his characters to which Marston was unwise to bring himself within range of comparison. It is particularly ironic that he should do so in a play dedicated to Ben Jonson. Marston has too fine a sense of the theatre not to provide in *Malcontent* an extremely skilful intrigue comedy; as theatre it works well, but it fails—as earlier plays do not—to do more than that, to use that theatrical world as a metaphor for a vision of mankind's place in the universe.

In both *The Dutch Courtesan* (1604–5) and *The Fawn* (1604) Marston set his sights lower: in both he is concerned more with specific moral problems than a general metaphysical view: *The Dutch Courtesan* announces as its theme 'The difference betwixt the love of a

courtesan and a wife'. The Prologue to *Fawn* declares 'Your modest
pleasure is our modest scope . . . mere spectacle of life and public
manners', and promises to avoid bawdy 'that most common sin of
vulgar pens' (the appeal is to the better sort of audience). In both
plays Marston is content to appeal to the specific audience of
Blackfriars in a narrower sense than his appeals to earlier audiences.
To fill the Blackfriars playhouse regularly with its capacity of about
700[48] was a very different proposition from appealing to the small
coterie audience of about 100 or so at Paul's, and Marston's
concessions in technique were no doubt bowing to simple economic
laws. Malevole advises in *Malcontent*: 'do not turn player. There's
more of them than can well live one by another already' (IV.iv.4–5).
Changes in substance too, from the earlier Calvinistic emphasis on
the depravity of the world to a rather more tolerant stance, reflects
the change from a predominantly city to a predominantly courtly
audience. Both *Fawn* and *Dutch Courtesan* continue that orthodoxy of
plotting and characterisation that marked the change in technique
between *Malcontent* and the earlier plays. *The Fawn* repeats the basic
situation of *Malcontent* in having its protagonist, Hercules, Duke of
Ferrara, appear through most of the play in disguise so that, like
Malevole, he can sustain a satiric, choric role and at the same time
participate in the action in disguise as Faunus. The subject of the
play is one close to the hearts of the Jacobean gentry: flattery. To a
ruling class that depended so much on patronage dissimulation
became a stock-in-trade and for the losers (no doubt the majority of
Marston's audience) it appeared particularly abhorrent. 'His
greatest enemies are his flatterers' says Bacon of a king,[49] a
discovery Hercules makes as he learns to flatter his way into favour
at the court of the Duke of Urbino:

> By Him by Whom we are, I think a prince
> Whose tender sufferance never felt a gust
> Of bolder breathings, but still liv'd gently fann'd
> With the soft gales of his own flatterers' lips
> Shall never know his own complexion.

> (I.ii.305–10)

Flattery is the principal subject of the play, but not the only one,
for, as in *The Dutch Courtesan*, the main theme is to be 'intermixed'
with other matters and if bawdy is to be eschewed (as it largely is by

the standards of the 'popular' theatre) sexual matters are not. Another difference between these Blackfriars plays and those he wrote for Paul's is the much greater concern with sexual matters in the later plays, again presumably because this would have a wide-ranging appeal to an audience that was young, modish and predominantly male. Much of the satire concerns the sexual irregularities of the court of Urbino and the sexual 'humours' of such as Don Zuccone, who is constantly suspecting an innocent wife, Nymphadoro, whose 'humour' is to love women in general, and the villainous Herod, who earns his living by satisfying the sexual needs of women including the wife of his brother, Sir Amoroso Debile-Dosso. As his name tells us, Debile-Dosso is impotent, in spite of the variety of aphrodisiacs he plies himself with. Such subjects as these were dealt with in the verse satires and, as there, their appeal is more that of the sex scandal exposés of the modern popular press than the discussion of a serious social problem. These 'humours' characters in the Jonsonian manner are largely incidental to the plotting of the play, though they contribute to the general theme of the corruption of court life in Urbino under the gullible, too easily flattered Duke Gonzago. But sexual matters also relate to the plot in that Hercules sets out to use his disguise to indulge a sexual appetite that has had to be curbed for the sake of political convenience, while his journey to Urbino is to observe his son Tiberio's conduct of a courtship of Gonzago's daughter that he has entrusted to him on his own behalf. In the course of doing his father's wooing Tiberio's dislike of women is cured and he falls in love with the Duke of Urbino's daughter. The play ends with romantic celebration in which both Dukes join in approval of their children's pairing after a 'trial' in which 'Cupid' punishes those who have offended in various ways against love.

As with *Malcontent*, Marston does not entirely abandon his earlier techniques of disruption in this play, but they are tempered to meet the requirements of a romantic plot where the principals, especially the lovers Tiberio and Dulcimel, and to some extent Hercules, are presented for the audience's sympathy and approval. Marston achieves an element of witty surprise, for instance, in reversing the usual sexual roles of father and son in making Hercules seek for sexual adventure while the son shuns it, but the cure of both in the reversion to type at the end suggests a normality that is repudiated in the earlier plays. Dulcimel, the romantic heroine, similarly surprises us by her outspokenness in rejecting the customary qualities of the heroine: 'Constancy and Patience are virtues in no living creatures but sentinels and anglers' (III.i.256), but like other outspoken women in Marston's plays (Crispinella in *Dutch Courtesan* is another) the unorthodoxy is verbal more than behavioural. Marston, like a Jacobean Bernard Shaw, is more concerned with theatrical shock effect than with seriously challenging moral orthodoxy. The same kind of role reversal is illustrated in the minor figures: Zuccone, for instance, arrives (in Act II, scene i) boasting that he never interferes in his wife's love affairs and assures his audience 'I lay not with her this four year', but he becomes frantic with jealousy when he thinks she is pregnant by another man. Dondolo in the same scene also illustrates the inconsistency of men when, having argued the absurdity of praying for the dead (because they cannot hear prayer), he immediately takes superstitious exception when Zoya curses the soul of the past Duke of Urbino (306–12). But these are local absurdities that may be righted—as Zoya does in punishing her husband's jealousy. Disruption is overcome and subsumed in the vision of reconciliation and order at the end. In the Jonsonian manner disruption is seen as aberration needing cure, rather than as being a fundamental condition of humanity, hence the use of a Jonsonian 'trial' scene at the end in which aberrant matters are put right.

The process of sacrificing thematic consistency for theatrical effect goes furthest of all in *The Dutch Courtesan*, which is the most Shavian of all Marston's comedies (though the sentiments are conservative and repressive rather than radical and liberal). The Prologue is defiantly un-Jonsonian in announcing 'We strive not to instruct, but to delight', but characteristically this bold announcement is considerably qualified by the aside 'Best art presents, not what it can, but should'—which seems to be claiming for the play a representation of ideals, not simply a response to things as they are. It is typical of the play that boldness should turn out to be equivocation. Certainly, as in all Marston's plays, ideas are foremost; the debate generated by the clear contrasts between Freevill's tolerant libertinism and Malheureux's orthodox Christian morality, between Crispinella's outspokenness and Beatrice's modest reticence, between the Mulligrub's getting and Cocledemoy's spending, are presented starkly; but the very clarity of the issues (as with Shaw) leads to contradiction and confusion in the attempts to resolve them. The result is often entertaining comedy, but at the expense of confusion of thought.

The abstract patterning of the play has been noted by several modern commentators. Finkelpearl remarks that 'the allegorical element is maintained . . . by means of the characters speaking to an unusual degree in the generalized language of moral sententiae, faculty psychology, and philosophy'.[51] R. K. Presson has provided a thorough-going allegorical reading of the play in which Malheureux is the Everyman figure and Franceschina is the Devil.[52] George Geckle's interpretation sees the play as a study of Temperance,[53] while Michael Scott sees the play as an unsuccessful attempt to combine Montaigne's moderate libertinism with Neoplatonic doctrine.[54] The differences between these readings are, however, less important than the need felt to examine the abstract patterning of the play. Marston has encouraged this by announcing his 'argument' at the beginning of the play. As is his wont, he seems to be demanding attention for the ideas he is discussing and yet at the same time obscuring the discussion by the way the ideas are presented.

The character of Freevill is a case in point. A clear opposition is set up early in the play between Freevill's moderate sensuality and his friend Malheureux's strict and Puritanical rejection of sexuality outside marriage. Almost all the critics agree that the play implies a rejection of Malheureux's unfortunate stance, partly because he, like Shakespeare's Angelo in *Measure for Measure*, fails to sustain it and partly because Freevill—seemingly favoured by the play's argument—is assumed to be right in his attempt to shock his friend into virtue;

> Therefore, to force you from the truer danger,
> I wrought the feigned, suffering this fair devil
> In shape of woman to make good her plot . . .
>
> (V.iii.43–5)

Yet the lesson Malheureux learns thereby is close to his initial position, a position that Freevill so clearly rejects in arguing for sexual permissiveness in the first scene. Are we to believe that Freevill has himself undergone a conversion? The play certainly does not make that clear, for Freevill advocates the usefulness of brothels after he has fallen in love with the chaste Beatrice and rejected his former mistress Franceschina. On the one hand Beatrice (who represents the type of purity to which Malheureux has aspired) assures Freevill 'your virtue won me' (III.i.201), on the

other hand Freevill himself explicitly repudiates the idea that his
behaviour towards his friend is entirely virtuous:

> But is this virtue in me? No, not pure;
> Nothing extremely best with us endures.
> No use in simple purities; the elements
> Are mix'd for use . . .

(IV.ii.39–43)

This sounds very much like Marston's accustomed view of human
sinfulness, but it is contradicted by the presence of Beatrice's
unequivocal virtue throughout the play. Scott is probably right that
Freevill's inconsistencies stem from Marston's attempt to reconcile
Montaigne's sensuality with traditional Christian teaching (or as
Scott argues, Neoplatonism) in the play. But why should he have
wanted to do this? The most likely explanation seems to me that he
wanted to startle his audience by the bold use of Montaigne's ideas
because it was too good a *coup de théâtre* to miss and even though it
obscured the central theme of Freevill's conversion. The
'conversion' was further weakened by Marston's habitual dogmatic
view that perfection is beyond human reach.

Had Beatrice remained simply a symbol of virtue there would be
no necessary inconsistency between her perfection and the thesis of
human sinfulness that is illustrated through the other characters,
but again Marston's striving for effective theatre in his new realistic
mode made an appeal to the audience's emotions irresistible when
Beatrice hears of the supposed death of her lover. This scene (IV.iv.)
is written to obtain the maximum emotional response from the
audience and confirms our need, as we watch (or read) the play to
consider *The Dutch Courtesan* in terms of real human relationships, in
spite of the debate element and the abstract patterning. It is in these
terms above all that the characters so often fail to conform to their
type requirements.

The best example of this is the 'diabolic' Franceschina, who is
repudiated in the play's moral scheme as someone whose passion
totally overrides her reason. But in human terms (as Scott notes)
Franceschina is more the victim of Freevill's brutality, cast aside, as
Scott says, like one of Cocledemoy's properties. The play simply
does not cohere at the two levels, partly of course because the moral
level itself is not entirely coherent. Freeville is not—as we see
him—a man of virtue, but an insensitive egotist who is even willing

to let Beatrice suffer torment in the process of proving a 'moral' point (as he himself admits V.ii.44f). The play constantly fails also by eliciting different moral judgements from those required by the moral patterning. Cocledemoy following—as Finkelpearl has shown—the pattern of Freevill in the main plot, also has the role of exposing hypocrisy. But his treatment of the Mulligrubs, while excellent theatre in its series of spectacular practical jokes, impresses one in human terms more with his roguery than with Mulligrub's guilt (which we hear about but scarcely see in action). In this case there must remain the suspicion that Mulligrub is primarily being pilloried for being a citizen before an audience of gentry. *The Dutch Courtesan* is a superbly theatrical play and it works brilliantly as theatre, if by that we simply mean it is exciting while it lasts. It lacks what Jacobean theatre at its best consistently provides, however, a serious and coherent response to life; by Jacobean (and Marston's) best standards, therefore, it is a failure.

Marston (effectively) ends his brief career as a professional dramatist with the heroic tragedy *Sophonisba*. Here he leaves the comic world of confused motives and sinful deeds for a simpler world of virtue triumphing over compromise. The address to the reader declares that pleasure was not his only concern in this play. The abstract theme of virtue triumphant, however, puts something of a damper on the action. The central figure, the heroine Sophonisba, is too exemplary to be interesting in spite of sharing a Shavian outspokenness with earlier Marston creations like Crispinella in *The Dutch Courtesan*. Moreover Sophonisba's heroic constancy succeeds in reducing her chief antagonist, the villain Syphax, to a state of comic ineptitude as he adds failure in war to failure in love. Marston's decision to concentrate on the 'wonder of women', as Sophonisba is described in the play's sub-title, is not only the preference of 'poetry' over 'history' he announces in the Address to the Reader, but a preference for moral abstraction over incident, and as such deprives the play of what political interest the struggle between Rome and Carthage, depicted in the action, might possess. *Sophonisba* therefore marks a final stage in that process of increasingly moral explicitness that had been set off by Jonson's mockery. Marston's theatrical effectiveness weakens progressively in a loss of a coherent satirical vision, that finally disappears altogether in *Sophonisba*. Perhaps Marston felt as much, for he retired from the professional stage, apparently leaving the play unsupervised through the press.

5
George Chapman

Of the major dramatists of the Jacobean period George Chapman is the least understood and the most underrated. He has partly himself to blame; for the cult of obscurity that he fostered in his non-dramatic poetry and that insistence on the learned nature of his poetic art, which he shares with Jonson, have led commentators either to see the drama as fitfully dark, or alternatively as a quasi-serious by-product of his major life's work, the translations of Homer. There is an element of truth in both these views: his drama is often difficult, its language opaque, its coherence difficult to rediscover and there seems little doubt too that he started work for the stage—if we can judge him fairly by what remains of his earliest work—as a hack writer earning a scanty living from Henslowe's shrewd purse, while he sought the god-wot of Elizabethan aristocratic patronage. But this is only, for the theme of this chapter, a small part of the story. For Chapman became, during the Jacobean period, one of the most popular and successful playwrights of the 'private' theatres, and is one of the great playwrights of this period.[1] The title pages of the original editions witness to Chapman's success: *May Day* was 'divers times acted at the Blacke Fryers'; *Monsieur D'Olive* 'was sundrie times acted by his majesty's children at the Blackfriars'; *The Widow's Tears* 'was often presented in the blacke and white Friars'; *The Revenge of Bussy d'Ambois* 'hath often been presented at the Private Play House in the white Fryers'; the *Revenge* also bears witness to the popularity of the earliest Bussy play to which it was a sequel. *Bussy D'Ambois*'s popularity is also attested by its appearance in second issues within a year of its publication in 1607. The importance of the *Byron* plays can be measured by the international stir that their performances occasioned, the French ambassador insisting on the censorship of passages in *The Conspiracy of Byron* that he found offensive. When in 1612 Webster, in his address to the reader before *The White Devil*, stresses the high seriousness of his art, it is to the 'full and heightened style of Master Chapman' that he first turns for emulation.

Chapman's major achievements as a playwright are entirely confined to that period of less than a decade from 1600 when the open air 'popular' theatres were challenged by the 'private' boys' companies. Like Marston and to a lesser extent Jonson, Chapman was inspired by the privileged audiences, primarily of the Blackfriars theatre, but also of Paul's. Chapman was to be stimulated, like his friend Jonson and like Marston, Middleton and Shakespeare, by the heady atmosphere of theatre rivalry in that decade, to transmute dramatic competence into excellence; all the more remarkable in Chapman's case because he was an older man than Shakespeare (himself a late developer), an older man too, incidentally, that the founding father of Jacobean drama, Kit Marlowe. Out of Chapman's long life—he was born in 1559 and died in 1634—only a little more than one decade matters for his connection with the theatre. By 1600, however, he had certainly become outstandingly competant as a dramatist in the hard school of Henslowe's rack renting. His last contribution to the repertory of Henslowe's Admiral's Men is the well-made *All Fools*, a play, incidentally, that may well have had the honour of inaugurating the new Fortune Theatre in 1600 to judge by the opening remarks of the Prologue. His last serious contribution to the stage dates from around 1612. His dramatic work falls into three phases: the first, up to about 1602, in which he prefers a theatrically brilliant comedy of intrigue based on Latin models, whose best example is *All Fools*; a middle period of mythic plays that are his outstanding contribution to Jacobean theatre; and a final period in which he tries to establish an austere neo-classical tragedy. In this he reverses Shakespeare's progress from the neo-classical *Coriolanus* to the mythic drama of the late romances.

Chapman's earliest extant plays, *The Blind Beggar of Alexandria* (1596), *An Humorous Day's Mirth* (1597), *All Fools* (1600), *Sir Giles Goosecap* (1601) and *May Day* (1602) suggest primarily an author gradually coming to terms with the demands of his medium, and with considerable success, but not finding in the theatre a congenial mode for the expression of his more serious ideas. The success of these plays—and all seem to have been popular with their audiences—is largely a technical one in the sense that they successfully provide entertainment, but fail to stimulate the mind beyond the confines of the theatre. It would be wrong to undervalue their achievement, none the less, because it was on the technical mastery of the theatre in these plays that Chapman could found his major dramatic achievement later. In *All Fools* and *May Day* in particular he shows a masterly handling of complex plots and a deftness in characterisation that at its best—as in the drunken boaster Quintiliano of *May Day*—has an almost Shakespearean panache; above all the language of these plays shows a masterly adaptation of verse toward dramatic realism. As a man learned in the classics Chapman not surprisingly took the decision to found these comedies on classical (and neo-classical) example. *All Fools* rests heavily on the Terentian models of *The Self Tormentor* (*Heauton Timorumenos*) and *The Eunuch* (*Eunuchus*), while *May Day* has Alessandro Piccolomini's neo-classical comedy *Allessandro* as its source. He was not the first Elizabethan to use latin models for his comedy, but in contrast—say—to Shakespeare's use of Plautus in *Comedy of Errors*, Chapman is far more concerned to convey the tone of secular realism of the original and so initiates that move away from surrealistic romance (that writers of his own generation like Greene and of course Shakespeare favoured) towards that drama of contemporary city life that was to triumph in the hands of younger men like Marston, Jonson and, above all, Middleton.

A brief comparison of Chapman's *All Fools* with Middleton's early comedies is instructive both in showing how much Chapman anticipated the fashion for satirical city comedies and also—even more importantly—in showing the essential differences between the humanistic, basically optimistic attitudes of the older playwright and the gloomy view of man of the younger playwright's Calvinism. The difference is partly to be explained too by the difference between the Terentian and the Plautine models in comedy. *All Fools* shares with a number of Middleton's comedies the basic situation in which the natural exuberance of the younger generation finds itself thwarted and blocked by its more rigid elders. Both the fathers in Chapman's play, Gostanzo and Marc Antonio, pride themselves on a wisdom that proves itself folly. The fathers oppose their son's marriages only to find themselves outwitted. Both Rinaldo and Valerio share the cynical attitude of the Middletonian hero: Rinaldo declares 'My future is to win renown by gulling' (V.i.11) while Valerio sees gulling as the world's principal activity, singing a song that has a remarkably Middletonian ring:

> Nay, never shun it [the Court] to be called a gull,
> For I see all the world is but a gull,
> One man gull to another in all kinds.

A merchant to a courtier is a gull,
A client to a lawyer is a gull,
A married man to a bachelor, a gull,
A bachelor to a cuckold is a gull
All to a poet, or a poet to himself.

(II.i.359–66)[2]

This is a characteristic of the Middletonian world where men are 'like fishes, one devours another' (*Puritan Widow*, I.ii.71) or where 'A lord maintains [a courtesan], she maintains a knight, he maintains a whore, she maintains a captain' (*Your Five Gallants*, III.ii.103–4) where 'Cozenage in the father wheels about to folly in the son' (*Michaelmas Term*, IV.i.88). Even the association of commercial and sexual vice reminds us inevitably of Middleton's comic world. But the differences are even more striking. Valerio's words have none of the bite, the bitter cynicism of Middleton's language, where men devour one another, women drink men down in their hellish lusts. Valerio in fact is not a Middletonian cynic essentially, but a romantic hero who has married the girl of his heart before the play begins and merely tricks his father into accepting his choice—which at the end he does with a good grace. Men are shown here, not as essentially evil, but as made in God's image, all fools perhaps, but not all rogues. So the play ends in the kind of general benevolence that even Middleton's later romantic comedies fail to achieve.

It is characteristic of Chapman's idiosyncratic career as an artist that, having done more than anyone to prepare the way for the new realism, he abandoned it just as it was coming into its own, in order to move to new (and more interesting) ground in *The Gentleman Usher*, *Monsieur D'Olive* and *Widows' Tears*—his last three comedies. His earlier comedy innovates also in its tendency towards the kind of social satire that—again—it was the younger generation's achievement to exploit to the full. Satiric drama was not unknown to earlier playwrights—indeed, the morality play tradition fostered a satirical attitude to all things worldly—but the new satire has less of this fundamentalist approach and in the hands of Jonson, at least at first, is as much concerned with folly as vice, with bad manners as bad morals. Here Chapman's *An Humorous Day's Mirth* and *Sir Giles Goosecap* are as innovating as the neo-classical intrigue comedy. The satire of manners which Chapman introduces in *An Humorous Day's*

Mirth shares with neo-classical comedy the mood of secular realism and it is not coincidental that these two kinds of comedy develop alongside each other, but the play differs in placing much less emphasis on plot and much more on the behaviour of the characters. It differs from earlier satire in having little moral implication, thus one of the scenes (Scene vii) is devoted to exposing the tendency to cliché in fashionable speech. In this scene Lemot (an observer figure with a concern for 'the word') demonstrates to a fellow courtier, Catalian, how he can anticipate the responses of his inter-locutionaries. The scene has the cleverness of a review sketch and much of the ephemerality of its kind. It anticipates, before the new satire had made its mark, attempts at social satire in Marston and such a play as Jonson's *Every Man Out of His Humour*.

Chapman's early stage successes were, it seems, principally in comedy, though we have it on the authority of the over-sanguine Francis Meres, writing in 1598, that Chapman (like Shakespeare) excelled in both comedy and tragedy.[3] On the existing evidence it would seem that Chapman's preference for comedy at this period stems from a certain artistic detachment from the theatre rather than a compulsive urge to comedy. Even in these lighter pieces of entertainment, however, he allows some of his more serious preoccupations as an artist to intrude. His introduction, for instance, of the figure of the melancholy artist Dowsecer in *An Humorous Day's Mirth* or Clarence in *Giles Goosecap* is a private joke of the kind Alfred Hitchcock indulged in, in his brief film appearances. Dowsecer has little function in such plot as there is in *An Humorous Day's Mirth* and only appears in two of the play's fourteen scenes. In one of these (Scene 7) he gives an emblematic 'reading' of a picture, a sword, a codpiece and hose placed for him by the king and his courtiers so that his comments can be overheard. It is highly appropriate that Chapman's representative in this play should be skilled in the interpretation of emblem, for the emblematic is Chapman's most characteristic mode of expression. Dowsecer duly allegorises these objects in terms of the vanity of the world to the concealed approval of the king who finds Dowsecer's comments 'perfect judgement'. This brief intrusion of a much more serious level of comment reveals for the audience a level of truth that Chapman is mostly content to leave hidden in these earlier comedies, though it becomes central to the later plays. The habitual world of Chapman's earlier comedy is (as with Jonson) the muddled, foolish world of man where glimpses of the truth are fitful and obscure. Only the exceptional man like the 'rarely learned' Dowsecer who 'hateth company and worldly trash' (as the king tells us) can penetrate the world of comic appearances to the divine truths which it conceals. Something of the nature of these 'divine truths' is hinted at in Dowsecer's entrance, quoting Cicero's *Tusculanae Disputiones*:

> What can seem strange to him on earthly things,
> To whom the whole course of eternity,
> And the round compass of the world is known?
> A speech divine, but yet I marvel much
> How it should spring from thee, Mark Cicero,
> That sold for glory the sweet peace of life,
> And made a torment of rich nature's work,
> Wearing thyself by watching candle-light,
> When all the smiths and weavers were at rest,
> And yet was gallant, ere the day bird sung,
> To have a troop of clients at thy gates,
> Armed with religious supplications,
> Such as would make stern Minos laugh to read.

(Scene vii, 67–79)[4]

This is a somewhat cryptic statement of a standpoint that becomes more overtly stated in the later drama and most directly stated in the *Revenge of Bussy*: the need for men (like the smiths and weavers here) to atune themselves to the rhythms of God's will in the world ('rich nature's work'), and the absurdity that men (Cicero in this case) can see and understand the good but fail to obey its demands—'For the good that I would, I do not' as St. Paul writes in the *Epistle to the Romans* (7:19).

These earlier comedies express, as it were, the flip-side of Chapman's philosophy. It is only when he has an audience that he can trust 'will accept acceptable matter in plays . . .' free from 'any vain estimation of the vulgar' as he puts it (characteristically) in the dedication of *The Widows' Tears*, that his comedies become the vehicles for the exposition of his most deeply held beliefs and that he, at the same time, turns again to the more exalted genre of

tragedy. This audience he finds in the 'private' theatres of
Blackfriars and Paul's. The last comedies (if we exclude for the
moment the lost *Old Joiner of Aldgate* written for Paul's in 1603) were
written for Blackfriars.

The Gentleman Usher, the first of these more serious comedies, was
written just before the closing of the theatres in early 1603 in a
particularly virulent outbreak of the plague, which lasted to March
1604. In this play we leave the neat, enclosed world of the well-made
neo-classical comedy and move towards the allegorical world of
divine revelation that is at the heart of Chapman's art. These late
comedies have been compared—and rightly—with Shakespeare's
late romances (which they anticipate). Both Chapman and
Shakespeare share in these plays that optimistic vision, more
characteristic of the older generation than of their successors, of a
benevolent God intervening to save man from the consequences of
his own sinfulness and take upon themselves the mysteries of
things by which God is shown to transmute evil into good. Whereas
Shakespeare's vision is sustained with a lyrical grace that 'commits a
rape upon the soul' (as was said of Donne), Chapman, more
philosophically, asks us to learn an emblematic language the
mastery of which will reveal the truths hidden to the unskilled.

The first two acts of *The Gentleman Usher* centre on separate
emblematic presentations. These are acts of initiation for the
audience into the magical revelations later in the play. The play
starts in the familiar world of intrigue comedy: Alphonso, Duke of
an unspecified Italian city (Chapman's equivalent to the 'coast of
Bohemia') is incongruously enamoured of the young Margaret,
daughter of the Earl Lasso, and is in rivalry with his own son Prince
Vincentio. Margaret, of course, prefers the younger man. Alphonso
is the bad ruler, without adequate knowledge of himself or others,
who favours the villainous Medice (whose real name is revealed to
be Mendice, a compound, J. H. Smith suggests, of '*mendace*' and
'*mendico*', liar and beggar).[5] Medice's influence over his master has
to be overcome so that the Duke can recognise his own failings and
come, as he eventually does, to recognise the propriety of his son's
claim to Margaret's affections. The victory of good over evil is not,
however, achieved by human agency alone but by the help of
miracle and revelation.

In the first act of the play the Duke decides that he wants to see a
play he had devised 'wherewith we will present our beauteous love'

(I.i.171), rather than attend his usual boar hunt. When the pedant Sarpego presents some lines for approval these are rejected as fustian even though Sarpego demonstrates his knowledge of stage matters by acting a few lines from Plautus's play *Curculio*. The Duke decides to supply his own speech and has Medice learn it in readiness for the performance that is to take place at the Earl Lasso's house in front of the Earl's daughter Margaret, under the direction of the earl's steward, Bassiolo, the gentleman usher of the title. The show turns out to be an allegory of the Duke's passion for Margaret, in which the Duke finds himself struck down by Margaret in the figure of the goddess Diana as he is about to slay a wild boar that attacks him. His wound enables some 'carnal spirits' to appear and bind him. An Enchanter then explains the allegory by which the boar represents Margaret's cruelty and her role as Diana represents her beauty. The Duke has entered with his hands bound and at the end of the scene pleads with Margaret to untie him, which she does reluctantly. Medice, who was to present the allegory, fluffs his lines and has to be helped out by Vincentio's kindly adviser, the courtier Strozza, which he does ably in spite of constant barracking by his friend Vincentio, who finds the performance better than the speech.

The purpose of this playlet within the play has puzzled commentators, but it has two functions, one of which is to introduce the mode by which the play is to be interpreted. The rejection of Sarpego's Plautine offering shows Chapman repudiating his own classical affiliations in this play in favour of the allegorical interpretation of romance. But it also parodies the new mode. The Duke's allegorical method is a product of ignorance—hence the appropriateness in Vincentio's eyes of having Medice, 'one unlearn'd' as he says and one too who appears for the masque dressed as the savage wood god, Sylvanus, speak the lines. Moreover the Duke's interpretation of his allegory forces the emblematic figures out of their customary use for his own purposes. The figure of Diana, for instance, usurps the traditional role of Venus; indeed the boar hunt and the Duke's captivity is intended to recall to an Elizabethan audience the myth of Venus and Adonis, for Chapman adds such detail as the myrtle grove, sacred to Venus. In the most usual Renaissance reading of the Adonis myth, the goddess of love overcomes the forces of death. The interpretation of poetic meaning was not, as Chapman explains elsewhere, an arbitrary matter, it demands learning and supernatural aid:

rich Minerals are dig'd out of the bowels of the earth, not found in
the superficies and dust of it; charms made of unlerned characters
are not consecrated by the Muses, which are divine artists, but by
Euippes daughters, that challeng'd them with meere nature . . .
(Dedication of *Ovid's Banquet of Sense*)[6]

It is true that in a later account of the interpretation of the 'allegorical
fictions of Poesie' he allows the poet 'the use and application of
these fictions' but the fictions themselves get their potency from
their antiquity: 'These have in that kinde, beene of speciall
reputation; as taking place of the rest, both for priority of time, and
precedence of use; being borne in the ould world . . .'.[7] The Duke
and his henchman Medice show neither the learning needful for
serious understanding nor respect for the ancient myths. Indeed,
the Duke's manipulation of myth for his own selfish purposes is
exactly that fault condemned in Chapman's disquisition on allegory
where he rebukes those who give up 'their understandings to their
affections'.[8]

The parodic masque of Act I, Scene ii is therefore the anti-masque
(the comic introduction) to the serious application of the allegorical
method in the later half of the play. It also, as an anti-masque
should, foreshadows the action of the main action. Alphonso's
fictitious wounding, for instance, anticipates the actual wounding
of Strozza in a boar hunt in Act IV, as the fictitious hunt itself
anticipates the actual hunt during Act III, the fictitious binding of
Alphonso's arms anticipates the imprisonment of Margaret in Act
V, Scene i. From the play-acting of Act I we move into the world of
transcendent reality in the later half of the play.

But before we are allowed to enter into this real world we are
required to witness a further entertainment. In Act II the Duke
Alphonso's fantasies are further indulged by a masque prepared by
the pedant Sarpego, in which Margaret—addressed as if she were
already the Duchess—is required to watch an entertainment whose
theme, as explained by Sarpego, is 'The fault of virgin nicety' and if
the moral is not sufficiently clear it is spelt out in a language of
befitting crudity:

> This, lady and duchess, we conclude:
> Fair virgins must not be too rude;

> For though the rural wild and antic
> Abus'd their loves as they were frantic,
> Yet take you in your ivory clutches
> This noble duke and be his duchess.

(II.i.291–6)

The manifest incoherence of the masque in which Margaret is both assumed to be and exhorted to become Alphonso's duchess, in which virgin modesty rather than 'rural wildness' is seen as 'rudeness', in which beauty and opportunism are absurdly linked, are a further comic statement of the absurdity of allowing 'affection' to distort truth. The absurdity of a world dominated by selfish passion is now fully exposed: we are prepared to move forward from comic disruption towards a world of harmony and reconciliation.

Both the entertainments of Acts I and II are under the general supervision of Bassiolo, who throughout the play acts as the catalyst of the action. He is a fool, vain and absurd, but then, as Vincentio remarks when Strozza's simpleton nephew Pogio confesses himself a fool: 'Therein thou art worth us all, for thou knowest thyself' (III.ii.222). Bassiolo is the artist's surrogate, he brings to light the state of things as he finds them. In the first two acts he has presented the prevailing absurdity for inspection. Vincentio punningly remarks, in congratulating him on his efficiency:

> . . . even as in a turnspit call'd a jack
> One vice assists another, the great wheels
> Turning but softly make the less to whir
> About their business, every different part
> Concurring to one commendable end,
> So and in such conformance, with rare grace,
> Were all things order'd in your good lord's house.

(III.ii.12–18)

In Act III, as the play moves from the absurd world of Alphonso's wilfulness, towards a God-centred harmony, Bassiolo becomes (again largely unwittingly) a catalyst for good, helping Margaret and

Vincentio (not always quite in the way he intends) to confirm their love for one another.

The road to harmony and reconciliation, however, is not an easy one. It involves suffering and pain before the divine will becomes manifest. Strozza and his wife Cynanche and the young lovers Margaret and Vincentio are the principal agents of the new order. The evil that prevails in Alphonso's court and that is represented above all in Medice's villainy shows its true nature in Medice's plot to assassinate Strozza during a boar hunt. The assassination nearly succeeds. At the beginning of Act IV Strozza is carried on stage with an arrow lodged in his side. Strozza's physician, Benevenius, advises that any cure will be hazardous, 'One last hope rests in Nature's secret aid'. Strozza's response is to rail at 'The torturing delays of slavish Nature' and he threatens to commit suicide as the most rational course of action. Will is opposed to Nature: we are still in a world where man is at cross purposes with divine will.

Strozza must learn to curb his own will in accordance with Nature. His wife Cynanche, whose name signifies 'collar' and who represents the disciplined spiritual life,[9] urges patience in explicitly Christian terms:

> Pains are like women's clamours, which, the less
> They find men's patience stirred, the more they cease.
> Of this 'tis said, afflictions bring to God
> Because they make us like him, drinking up
> Joys that deform us with the lusts of sense,
> And turn our general being into soul . . .

(IV.i.60–5)

Strozza hesitates but is soon raving against his fate again as his wife urges him to 'salve with Christian patience pagan sin'. This scene is interrupted by a comic love dialogue between Margaret and Vincentio (maladroitly assisted by Bassiolo) which, skilfully breaking into the melodramatic tone of the previous scene, continues to further Chapman's central theme of the triumph of God's love over the world's resisting material forms. Margaret and Vincentio are brought together by a love that transcends both the social impediments to it and the formal processes deputed by man to control it. Margaret refuses to allow the course of 'God and Nature' (the terms are virtually synonymous) to be circumscribed by man's wayward inhibitions:

Are not the laws of God and Nature more
Than formal laws of men? Are outward rites
More virtuous than the very substance is
Of holy nuptials solemniz'd within?
Or shall laws made to curb the common world,
That would not be contain'd in form without them,
Hurt them that are a law unto themselves?
My princely love, 'tis not a priest shall let us,
But since th'eternal acts of our pure souls
Knot us with God, the soul of all the world,
He shall be priest to us, and with such rites
As we can here devise we will express
And strongly ratify our heart's true vows
Which no external violence can dissolve.

(IV.ii.133–46)

This apparent arrogance is in fact spiritual humility, for Margaret wishes to submerge her own will in that 'law of God and Nature' which sets apart the spiritual from the sensual man. The lovers, however, have also to learn, like Strozza, that the process of purification involves suffering, and we must follow them, like Strozza, through privation and near-despair before at the end of the play they too arrive at harmony with God's laws.

The next scene is contrived to illustrate how the process of spiritual purification requires God's direct intervention and tests the faith in the miraculous world of God's intentions that is the basis of all Christian belief. For now that Strozza reappears we find he has undergone a conversion of faith: he no longer seeks to assert his own will in committing suicide but resigns himself to the will of God ('My free submission to the hand of heaven', IV.iii.43). The resignation brought about by his wife's 'divine advice' (IV.iii.3) opens a world of revelation to him ('humility hath rais'd me to the stars / in which I sit and see things hid from human sight'). Here too we find the paradoxical notion, already encountered in Margaret's speech, that humility involves exaltation. The revelation that the arrow in his side will miraculously fall from him in seven days is a prophecy that is duly fulfilled. The scene is a bold attempt by Chapman to introduce the central tenets of his faith into secular comedy. The tone of tender marital harmony that is recaptured in the scene serves to assert (as does the main plot) the agency of human love in the process of God's universal love.

This perhaps is as far as secular drama can go in the assertion of Christian faith. Chapman's art has often been mistakenly thought too influenced by classical example to be thoroughgoingly Christian. But to Chapman (as to most Renaissance learned men) there was no essential clash: classical learning rightly interpreted through a reading of its 'hieroglyphics', would lead to Christian truth.[10] Chapman's contemporaries were right to add to the words on his tombstone, after the epitaph 'poeta Homericus, Philosophus verus', the words 'etsi Christianus poeta' ('and more especially a Christian poet'). All Chapman's writing is underpinned by his Christian faith, his most explicit statement of which comes in the powerful 'Hymne to our Saviour on the Crosse' that he published with *Petrarch's Seven Penitentiall Psalms* in 1612. Here he reveals his faith as humanist and Anglican, rejecting the Calvinistic gloom that tends to dominate the thought of his younger contemporaries, for an assertion of man's likeness to God's image:

> Wherein stand we for
> Thy heavenly image, Hels great Conqueror?
> Didst thou not offer, to restore our fall
> Thy sacrifice, full, once, and one for all?[11]

The Gentleman Usher is built on a masque-like pattern and once more shows Chapman exploring new ways that are to be picked up subsequently by other poets, notably by Ben Jonson in his later Court Masques. The play's masque-like qualities would be even more apparent in production, for it exploits the song and dance characteristic of the boys' theatres. The first two acts are both 'antic' (comic) and 'anti-'masque, showing the false values from which the counter-movement of Acts III to V is to liberate the audience. It is an experiment in using the secular stage to reveal religious truth and skilfully exploits the techniques of realistic comedy, mastered in the earlier plays, to reach out towards divine allegory. In the two remaining comedies, *Monsieur D'Olive* and *Widows' Tears*, Chapman yet more skilfully succeeds in achieving a secular statement of religious ideas, avoiding even that limited display of the miraculous found in *The Gentleman Usher*. His two last plays are truly great comedies brilliantly combining theatrical effectiveness with coherent moral statement. (It is a measure of the extreme conservatism and timidity of the modern theatre, incidently, that neither play has been performed on the professional stage.)

Like *The Gentleman Usher*, *Monsieur D'Olive* is a play about resurrection. More obviously and more powerfully than in the earlier play we are plunged in the beginning into an atmosphere of frustration and sterility. Swinburne, in his excellent essay on Chapman, rightly calls the opening of the play 'one of the most admirable in any play'.[12] But where in *Gentleman Usher* the sterility is represented in terms of absurdity, here the pervading mood is one of gloom, of life blocked off and perversely thwarted. Both the Countess Marcellina's withdrawal from the world of daylight in pique at her husband's unjust jealousy of her (suitably platonic) relationship with her admirer, Vandome, and Count St Anne's morbid vigil over his deal wife's body are perverse acts that would deny life and love—the theme is central too to *The Widows' Tears*. The best commentary on his morbidity is perhaps to be found in that 'Hymne to our Saviour' already referred to, where Chapman berates those (highly fashionable) puritans who wallow in sin 'and like Moules / Grovel in earth still, being advanc't to heaven' (l.186). In the poem Chapman rejects the pessimistic Calvinistic stress on man as inevitably perverted by sin (so common in the works of his contemporaries):

> O blasphemie
> In hypocriticall humilitie!
> As we are men, we death and hell controule,
> Since thou createdst man a living soule.
> .   .   .   .
> When casting off a good life's godlike grace,
> We fall from God; and then make good our place
> When we returne to Him: and so are said
> To live: when life like His true forme we leade
> And die (as much as can immortall creature:)
> Not that we utterly can ceasse to be,
> But that we fall from life's best quality.

> (198–201, 206–12)[13]

A marginal gloss on the lines I have omitted here reads: 'We do not like men when we Sin, (for as we are true and worthie men, we are

God's images)'. The modern reader needs to be familiar with the prevailing Jacobean mood of gloom and doom to appreciate fully the pugnacious optimism of these lines. It is in their spirit that both *Monsieur D'Olive* and *Widows' Tears* are written. Both plays are a spirited rejection of that terrifyingly ugly view of man depicted in much of Marston, Middleton and Webster.

Monsieur D'Olive takes us through the process of recovery to a life led in God's 'true forme'. The principal agent of the recovery is Vandome, Marcellina's platonic lover and the brother of Count St Anne both that his sister's body must have Christian burial, 'that it Marcellina's husband, describes it, IV.i.98)[14] of bringing both Marcellina and St Anne back to life. Like Hercules (who frequently in Renaissance mythology represents Christ himself)[15] Vandome brings them both from death-in-life to a life of love, pleading with St Anne both that his sister's body must have a Christian burial, 'that it may reassume a form incorruptible' (II.i.44) and then encouraging his interest in Marcellina's sister Eurione who has fallen in love with him: 'To make you happy in a life renew'd' (IV.i.65) as he afterwards explains to the Count.

Vandome's role as a rescuer from the dead can be more easily understood in reference to Petrarch's *Secretum*, which Chapman uses (in places verbatim)[16] as a source for several of the speeches where Vandome is persuading St Anne to cure himself of his grief by taking on a new love (quoting Ovid's *De Remediis Amoris*—III.i.23). This would seem to be profane enough advice. But the speech derives closely from a speech Petrarch puts in the mouth of St. Augustine in the third book of the *Secretum*[17] where the saint explains to Petrarch that his love for Laura, however chaste, is sinful and that it must be cured before his soul is ready to take flight to the love of God: 'Nothing so much leads a man to forget or despise God as the love of things temporal, and most of all this passion that we call love'.[18] St. Augustine quotes the same line from Ovid in arguing that it is preferable even to 'go from one passion to another' (that is, change one love for another) than to remain attached to a mere creature of God.[19]

In the opening speech of the same scene St Anne confesses that his deep grief over the loss of his wife has driven him to thoughts of despair and suicide. This derives closely from a passage in the second book of the *Secretum* where Petrarch confesses to an insuperable melancholy that St. Augustine diagnoses as the deadly sin of 'accidia'.[20] The whole purpose of the *Secretum* is to demonstrate the need for the soul to free itself from temporal concerns by accepting God's will, and this may include (as St. Augustine argues) having the humility to accept the natural limitations of the flesh. This is precisely Vandome's lesson for St Anne and later Marcellina. It is a vanity of pride to fail to adapt to the natural processes God has decreed for mankind—at one point of the *Secretum* Petrarch refuses at first to contemplate the possibility of Laura's death and is sharply reproved by St. Augustine for his worldliness.[21] Just as Petrarch must be cured of the spiritual vanity of his love for Laura, which is an impediment to his spiritual freedom, so St Anne must leave the idolatry to his grief and accept God's will that everything in this life is ephemeral. In urging this Vandome quotes in Latin the very line that St. Augustine adapts from Virgil: 'Heu fuge dilectas terras, fuge litus amatum' (III.i.46).[22] Literally this would seem rather inappropriate to St Anne—it only becomes appropriate if we understand St Anne's grief as self-indulgence. Vandome's task with Marcellina is considerably more difficult, for Marcellina's love affair with a metaphorical death is not an outcome of natural grief inordinately indulged, but a wilful act of denial. Her shutting out of sunlight, her perverse turning of day into night is a violation of nature. Marcellina's page describes the two women, Marcellina and Eurione 'condemn'd to darkness' in their 'jail' and, indulging in un-Chapmanesque bawdy, explains that he is their giant 'set to guard them/My name is Dildo' (V.i.33), Marcellina suffers from spiritual onanism. To break this false virginity Vandome must engage her feelings for someone else, 'drive passion out with passion' and so 'restore her/To her most sociable self again'. Vaumont, her husband, also sees this in sexual terms, praying to the goddess of childbirth, Lucina, to assist with a healthy rebirth (V.i.14). Vandome achieves his task by making Marcellina jealous of her husband, who she thinks is being unfaithful to her. This is the 'divine wit' that brings Marcellina 'out of her cell' (VI.i.96–7). Having achieved it Vandome has completed his Herculean task 'the solemn votary is revived . . . th' Herculean labour's past' (V.i.254, 257). The darkness of the cell gives way to the light of love between the couples, Vaumont can reappear to his wife as 'a sun will clear your beauties' (V.ii.26). Vandome has achieved his Hermetical role as the divine messenger of love.

To this main action the comedy of Monsieur D'Olive acts as a comic commentary. D'Olive's role is similar to Bassiolo's in *Gentleman Usher*. He is the comic negative of the play's positive serious concerns, brought out from (in his case) well-deserved obscurity—the Duke describes it as 'entombment' (II.ii.59)—to be his country's ambassador; like Vandome he is a messenger, though his journey turns out to be unnecessary. In contrast to Vandome's embassy of light, D'Olive foolishly concerns himself with the opaque matters of court foppery and court estime, being preoccupied (as MacLure rightly notes)[23] with money. Swinburne complains that this comic counter-theme to the play disturbs the play's seriousness, but it really functions in a more subtle, more theatrically effective way, as did the opening two acts of *Gentleman Usher*, to define the false world which Vandome's divine comedy of love's harmony is escaping. MacLure is right, I think, to connect the zany D'Olive with Chapman himself,[24] not so much because of the mock-melancholy D'Olive affects, but because in rejecting D'Olive's comic world Chapman is making a gesture of repudiation of the role he has had to assume, of theatrical comedian. D'Olive is Chapman's wry comment on the compromises forced on the artist by his medium.

Altogether it is difficult to praise *Monsieur D'Olive* too highly. It presents a solemn theme in a manner that is both highly entertaining and totally compelling. As in all Chapman's plays (unlike Shakespeare's) the interest is not primarily in the characters, who function principally as emblems of those ideas whose dynamic the plot represents. But this is a drama that transcends the mere drawing of individual character (as indeed does Shakespeare's) by showing us a world of archetypal forms, where the essential engagement with the audience is at levels of feeling's mysteries. Yet the profundity is worn with amazing grace and lightness; the entertainment is as much in the sense of sustaining as of amusing its audience.

The Widows' Tears is equally impressive and if still largely unperformed, has at least earned the praise of those academics who have taken the trouble to study it. Yet it is also a very puzzling play, for its tone of tolerant cynicism seems quite unlike that of the religious seriousness of the previous two comedies. Chapman was a restless artist and rarely attempted the same thing twice. The boisterous worldly tone of the play seems to relate it more to *May Day* and *All Fools* than its immediate predecessors, and indeed the moral suggested by the title of *All Fools* is apt enough for *Widows' Tears*. There are, however, obvious thematic connections with the later comedies: the theme of resurrection—now, however, brilliantly represented through grotesque farce—is shared with both *Gentleman Usher* and *Monsieur D'Olive*. Modern commentators on the play have found it expounds 'a bitter theory of human nature':[25] MacClure calls it an 'amorality' play,[26] and Swinburne had characterised it as 'brutal exuberant fun', speculating that Chapman might have been taking his revenge in the play on all womankind for some personal slight.[27] Exuberant the play certainly is, but not brutal or amoral, which would be uncharacteristic of the man—'poeta Christianus'. For all its farcical air *Widows' Tears* is a serious and moral play. If *Monsieur D'Olive* is Chapman's *Cocktail Party* (where Harcourt-Reilly's Herculean role is remarkably like that of Vandome's), *Widows' Tears* is more like (though less like) his *Confidential Clerk*.

The crucial difficulty in interpreting *Widows' Tears* is in understanding the role of the swashbuckling hero, Tharsalio. Modern interpretation sees him usually as a successor to Rinaldo in *All Fools*, a cynical rake whose declared aim is 'to win renown by gulling'.[28] One of the play's recent editors quotes H. M. Weidner's description of Tharsalio as a 'Machiavellian malcontent' and points to what she regards as Machiavellian echoes in the play.[29] Certainly much of Tharsalio's behaviour encourages us towards such a view. He is of a noble family that has come down in the world and he is determined to regain his place in society through the exercise of self assertion—Machiavellian *virtù*. There is obviously material here for a Webster or Middleton. But nowhere does Tharsalio show the malevolence of a Machiavel; on the contrary he is unfailingly good-humoured and tolerant even when he suffers humiliation from the widow Eudora, whose hand he sues for. He seems to regard the seduction of Eudora as something of a joke, and yet there are all the signs that he makes a perfectly responsible and kindly husband to her after their marriage. It is thoroughly characteristic of him that his primary concern, when he discovers the chaste Cynthia is really no better than she should be, is to fly into exstacies of self-congratulation that his cynicism had been justified, his only disappointment being that he wavered in his cynical expectations briefly (V.i.52–7). But that he is not merely the cynical rake is equally demonstrated by that moment of doubt at the beginning of the scene when he confesses to his companion Lycus that he feels 'fear and shame' that he risked Cynthia's death through starvation in putting her faithfulness to her husband to the test (V.i.14).

Even the self-confessed Machiavellianism turns out to be strongly qualified in ways that come to have special significance to the theme of the play as a whole. When Cynthia accuses him of having 'drunk too much of that Italian air' (I.i.13), his reply at first would seem to justify her accusation:

> No, sister, it [Italy] hath refined my senses, and made me see with clear eyes, and to judge of objects as they truly are, not as they seem, and through their mask to discern the true face of things. It tells me how short-lived widows' tears are . . . all which I believe as a Delphian oracle, and am resolved to burn in that faith.
>
> (I.i.138–45)

Smeak points to Chapter 15 of Machiavelli's *Il Principe* as the authority for this speech where Machiavelli declares his intention of writing the truth as it is rather than as people imagine it to be.[30] The extreme secularism of Machiavelli's stance here, however, combines very oddly with Tharsalio's admittedly somewhat ambiguous reference to the Delphic oracle. The voice of the Delphic oracle was the voice of Apollo, the sun god, and, as Shakespeare uses it in *Winter's Tale*, in Renaissance thought the voice of the Christian God.[31] Chapman is careful with his classical references and is intentionally suggesting a transformation of the Machiavellian sense of reality by asking us to see how people are in the light of God's truth.

For Tharsalio, like Vandome in *Monsieur D'Olive*, is an agent of the divine truth. Like Vandome he has the Herculean task (he himself compares his bid for Eudora with Hercules's wooing of Omphale— II.iv.183–92) of bringing life out of death. Modern commentators are too ready to see characters as personalities rather than as functions—an attitude engendered (often appropriately enough) by the peculiarities of Shakespearean dramatic techniques. As I have already argued, Chapman is rarely interested in characters as people: they are more frequently, like Jonson's, functions of an argument. Tharsalio's role is primarily as a moral agent to expose the emptiness of Eudora's and Cynthia's heroic aspirations to virtue, not because they are women—for the play is not in the least a satire on women—but as they are 'in the likeness of sinful flesh'. Tharsalio's 'boldness' (his name is based on the Greek word θαρσαλεος, confidence) is not that of the Machiavel, but like Strozza's, that of the visionary who has seen the true nature of things; hence he acknowledges that the goddess Confidence is a 'blind deity' (I.i.172), her truths are inward. But Tharsalio's vision is of the flux of fortune that controls all earthly things and the Augustinian sense of the presumptuousness of those that would, like Eudora, Cynthia and Lysander, rise above it. Only an acceptance of it can transcend it, so while Tharsalio acknowledges 'Confidence' in preference to 'fortune' as his deity (I.i.1–14) the confidence of his vision tells him (as it does St. Augustine) that in this world fortune rules, hence his apparently inconsistent assertion of the power of fortune in his own life (I.i.31).

The last of Chapman's comedies exemplifies in its two central characters, the widows of the title, that critique of heroic virtue, that is also the central concern of Chapman's major tragedies, the first of which, *Bussy D'Ambois*, had preceded *Widows' Tears*. Like Bussy, Eudora and Cynthia set themselves up as models of heroic virtue and the purpose of the comedy, as of the tragedy, is to demonstrate the hollowness of that pride in virtue that is generated by self-will, for both Eudora and Cynthia are merely indulging their vanity in their grief. Their vow of faithfulness to their dead, or supposedly dead, husbands is not a virtue born of inner truth but a hypocritical respect for 'opinion', a vanity that presumes it can escape the promptings of nature to which we are all heirs:

> Certain moral disguises of coyness, which the ignorant call modesty, ye borrow of art to cover your busk points; which a blunt and resolute encounter, taken under a fortunate aspect, easily disarms you of; and then, alas, what are you? Poor naked sinners, God wot . . .
>
> (III.i.93–8)

At this stage Tharsalio's language has the acerbity of the satirist, but as with *The Gentleman Usher*, the play moves away from either comic or tragic disruption towards the harmony imposed by love. This harmony is duly celebrated in the hymneal masque in Act III celebrating Tharsalio's marriage to Eudora. Hymen, the god of marriage, is played by Tharsalio's nephew, Hylus, whose beauty captivates Laodice, Eudora's daughter. Laodice's prayer to Venus to aid her love is duly answered in the final movement of the play. Music begins the masque as Tharsalio (his satirical mood now abandoned) prays to heaven to serve, 'As I my heavenly mistress' (III.ii.80). Hymen proclaims the marriage the work of Destiny 'Ordain'd past custom and all vulgar object'—echoing Margaret's words to her lover in *The Gentleman Usher* (IV.ii.131–46). The harmony of the occasion is finally expressed through a dance in which the 'Bride and the rest' join Hymen and his troop of six Sylvans in joyful celebration. The presence of the wood demons reminds us that this is the divine harmony expressed through the medium of the natural world. So Act III ends with the earlier jarring notes resolved, discord has resolved in concord: 'All things by strife engender' (I.ii.190).

But the instability of the natural world demands that the process has to be endlessly repeated, and in Acts IV and V we watch the movement re-enacted in the relationship of Tharsalio's brother and his wife Cynthia. Immediately before the marriage masque Cynthia has sworn eternal faithfulness to her husband and casts a shadow on Eudora's 'sunshine' by her lament for his absence. The absence however, is contrived by Tharsalio, who here again plays the Herculean role of bringing life from the dead, for Cynthia's rigid adherence to her vows is presented as death in life, enacted suitably enough in her husband's tomb. Whereas Eudora's inhibition, like St Anne's in *Monsieur D'Olive*, is a result of natural grief for the dead, Cynthia's moral state is more akin to Marcellina's, though a more subtle and insidious example. Cynthia is wedded to an idea of faithfulness, and is willing to thwart her own nature to assert her ideal, much as Marcellina chooses to deny her natural relationship with her husband because she considers he has impugned her chastity. Lysander is convinced of his wife's heroic virtuousness:

> O Cynthia, heir of her bright purity,
> Whose name thou dost inherit, thou disdain'st
> (Severed from all concretion) to feed
> Upon the base food of gross elements.
> Thou art all soul; all immortality.
> Thou fast'st for nectar and ambrosia,
> Which till thou find'st and eat'st above the stars,
> To all food here thou bidd'st celestial wars.

> (IV.ii.181–8)

As in the tragedies, the heroic pretensions are to be measured against Christian humility to make their absurdity apparent. Cynthia in the words of her maid, Ero, will have to 'learn to live as other mortals do'.

Lysander's confidence in his wife is undermined by his brother's hints that she may not be all she seems. He agrees therefore to put her to the test by pretending to go away on a journey and then being reported dead. On hearing of his 'death' she retires with her maid into her tomb with the intention of starving herself to death. Lysander returns in disguise as a soldier to make love to her and test the sincerity of her earlier protestations and is encouraged when he finds Ero prevailing on her mistress to eat and drink. The disguised husband appeals to her to choose life rather than the living death of her abstractions:

> I would have you live, and she [Ero] would have you live freely, without which life is but death. To live freely is to feast our appetites freely, without which humans are stones . . .
>
> (IV.iii.63–6)

Against this Cynthia can only plead that her reputation is at stake—a confession of pride that Lysander treats with scorn.

The process of Cynthia's resurrection becomes literally an escape from a living tomb, but not before Chapman has achieved a complicated and dramatic set of manoeuvres involving the animation of dead bodies—actual and supposed. In Act V Chapman turns theatrical property into symbol. Lysander has got access to Cynthia's tomb by having himself appointed as one of the guards of the crucified bodies, whose security is entrusted to him on pain of his own death. Tharsalio, coming to the tomb, sees Cynthia making love to a common soldier and decides a suitable punishment would be to steal one of the crucified bodies (unaware that the soldier is his brother). Tharsalio 'climbs the cross' (V.i.72) to obtain the crucified body as a means of harrowing sin. As Tharsalio takes the dead body from the cross he observes the truth of human nature that the widows wished away: 'He that believes in error, never errs'(V.i.80). Cynthia's response to her lover's predicament, when he discovers he has a lost a corpse, is to offer to supply her husband's corpse in its place. Through the theatrical brilliance of farce Chapman shows Cynthia now willing to sacrifice the dead for the living (the Christian parallel is precise) where formerly she was offering the living as sacrifice for the dead. When the tomb is opened there is, of course, no body in it, so that Cynthia's earlier heroic gestures have been shown to be based on nothing.

That human judgement is bound to err in this 'topsy turvey

world' as one of the soldiers describes it (V.iv.33) is given one further farcical illustration in an episode in which the corrupt governor of Cyprus tries Tharsalio's companion Lycus for the murder of Lysander. In the course of the trial the Governor outlines the reforms he intends, parodying the ideas of the perfectability of man we have been shown to be so mistaken, to an accompaniment of Tharsalio's cynical asides. But the cynicism is not the final note of the play. Lysander is brought forth, the trial is stopped and Tharsalio brings in the two young lovers, Hylus and Laodice, whose nuptials are about to be celebrated. Human nature is to triumph over abstraction. Tharsalio's last words are to remind us of the compromises and ambiguities which flesh is heir to as he calls his brother once more to take his wife:

> So brother, compound the strife,
> And think you have the only constant wife.

The Widows' Tears was the last of Chapman's unaided comedies and it is perhaps—if not the most profound—the most skilful. Chapman was still to write, however, a share in the lively city comedy of *Eastward Ho* with his friend Ben Jonson and the tolerated Marston. Chapman had already led the way in city comedy with the lost play *The Old Joiner of Aldgate* (some knowledge of the plot of which survives), and in *Eastward Ho* we have an example of the sheer professionalism of these three men of the theatre. The play neither attempts the mystical profundity of Chapman's major comedies nor has the visionary satire of Jonson's great plays, but as an example of the entertainment devised for the sophisticated audiences of Blackfriars it would be hard to beat. There was one more attempt at comedy, *The Ball*, which we only have in a version revamped by James Shirley for a later generation of playgoers.

Before he had finished with his major comedies Chapman's mind had turned again towards tragedy. We cannot be sure when *Bussy D'Ambois* was written, but the consensus of modern scholarship regards 1604 as the likely date of its first performance. The 1607 Quarto title page affirms it 'hath been often presented at Pauls' and it seems to have remained a popular play, for an edition of 1641 reasserts 'it hath often been acted with great applause'. Its presentation at Paul's theatre confirms the research of modern scholarship that it was conceived as a serious play for a select audience—caviare to the general. Yet its succeeding popularity is a measure of Chapman's ability to combine erudite doctrine with theatrical aplomb at the height of his career as a dramatist. The erudition however has proved a stumbling block for the modern critic, for at this distance in time it is not easy to pick one's way through the welter of iconographical and mythical readings which Chapman habitually calls for. The difficulties are compounded by the substantial differences between the earlier and the later editions and the uncertain date and authority of the changes. If, as seems likely, in at least some cases the alterations are Chapman's, however, we can be sure that the 1607 version represents Chapman's earlier intentions, and as I want to discuss the play in the context of the comedies he was writing contemporaneously, I shall use N. S. Brooke's edition of the play, which is based substantially on the 1607 quarto.[32]

Seen in the context of our discussion of the late comedies, which he must have been writing around the same time as he was working on *Bussy*, the tragedy is as coherent as it is dramatically impressive. The central problem for the critic is in estimating the degree of admiration to be accorded to the hero. Bussy is not only an outstanding heroic figure, endowed with the Renaissance quality of self-confidence, *'virtù'*, but more interestingly, he is a man dedicated to a notion of virtue, 'I am for honest actions, not for great' he says (I.i.127)—and the play sets out to examine the viability of that notion. In the opening scene Chapman establishes Bussy as a man of natural virtue who has set himself against the worldly temptations of power-seeking, preferring a 'green retreat', a world of 'obscure abodes' where he can meditate on the vanity of things. Yet this other-worldliness is hardly the product of the resigned will, it is a 'cloistered virtue', even if we hesitate to accept Monsieur's cynical estimate that Bussy is simply 'discontented with his neglected worth' (I.i.47). Bussy's opening words justify our suspicions that his other-worldliness is that of the malcontent:

> Fortune, not Reason, rules the state of things,
> Reward goes backwards, honour on his head . . .

Accordingly the comparative ease with which Monsieur tempts him from his retreat into the great world hardly surprises us.

The situation in this opening scene inevitably recalls the theme of *Monsieur D'Olive*. Like Marcellina, Bussy prefers the darkness of his own self-righteousness to the daylight wickedness from which they are both in retreat; like Marcellina's, Bussy's virtuousness is a form of pride. But in this case also, as with the comic D'Olive, the call from virtuous obscurity to compromising light turns out to be fraught with dangers that expose the venture to failure. In accordance with Renaissance Aristotelian poetic the comic D'Olive is inferior to the ordinary man and his downfall is ridiculous, Bussy is a great man and his failure is accordingly tragic. Bussy's tragic progress is a Christian commentary on the heroic ideal, but it is also a Christian commentary on man's frailty in a corrupt world.

The ideal that Bussy exposes is the ideal of natural self-sufficiency, a further manifestation of the pride that has activated his initial contempt for the world. His motives are tainted from the beginning. The ambiguity of Bussy's moral stance is illustrated in Chapman's characteristic emblematic manner in the first encounter with the courtly after his decision to move into the great world. Monsieur sends his steward Maffé with 1000 crowns to Bussy, but Maffé only offers him 100. Bussy detects the cheat and cuffs Maffé. His dominance and freedom are asserted even at the moment when he is compromising his freedom by accepting the bribe. We are rapidly shown the consequences of his pride in the two great heroic 'matters' of love and war. As soon as Bussy arrives at court he becomes the subject of envious gossip and this leads to a duel in which his three enemies and two of his friends are killed. Bussy is the only survivor. As a heroic act the event is impressive, but a different light is placed on it when the king describes the deaths as 'wilful murders' which are 'ever past our pardon' (II.i.149–50). The king has been established on his first appearance (in I.ii.) as a man of virtue in his praise of the English Queen (Elizabeth) and disapproval of the confusion of the French court; his judgement of Bussy's role in the duel is therefore a reminder of those alternative standards to Bussy's and Monsieur's heroism, that are ultimately to be vindicated. Bussy refuses to accept the king's pardon of 'such foul pollution' on the grounds that he is above the law:

> Who to himself is law, no law doth need,
> Offends no king, and is a king indeed.

> (II.i.203–4)

Nicholas Brooke asks us to compare this with Strozza's claim in *Gentleman Usher* that 'A virtuous man is subject to no prince',[33] but the situation is quite different: Strozza is asserting the demands of virtue over those of obedience to a tyrant. Bussy is claiming the right of self-interest. Nor is the king's criticism of Bussy affected by his later judgement that Bussy is a good man whose 'native noblesse' would make law and therefore kings unnecessary were all men the same (III.ii.91ff.). These words are indeed reminiscent of Strozza's in *Gentleman Usher*. Bussy has just been entertaining the king with satirical denunciations of vice in this scene and the king knows nothing of the adulterous affair that Bussy is at this time conducting with Tamyra. In the context of the action the king's comments are unconsciously ironic, but in any case his remarks are couched in conditional terms: if everyone were like Bussy (as the king conceives him) the pre-lapsarian world could indeed be restored. We know that neither Bussy, nor anyone in the Court, nor indeed any man in this post-lapsarian world is 'in his native noblesse'. Bussy's tragedy is that the nobility he strives for is beyond human reach in this fallen world.

The affair with Tamyra, the heroic love affair that eventually brings about Bussy's death, is equally subjected to the judgement of Christian virtue—and it too is found wanting. Indeed here Bussy is his own judge, for as he is dying he forgives his killer and pleads with the deceived husband, Montsurry, to forgive his wife. His renunciation of his heroic *virtù* for Christian virtue is emblemised as he hands the sword that has been literally sustaining him, to his enemy (V.iii.161). Bussy has finally arrived at the state where his understanding of God's will makes clear man's (and his own) true insignificance:

> O frail condition of strength, valour, virtue,
> In me like warning fire upon the top
> Of some steep beacon, on a steeper hill . . .

> (V.iii.188–90)

His very eminence highlights man's vulnerability. Bussy is a great man: his heroic *virtù* is not in itself evil: in a perfect world Bussy's natural virtues of courage and honesty could have been exercised without sin. But in a fallen world these very virtues are flawed. Bussy's fatal flaw is that he is too late aware of his own human frailty.

Chapman highlights the inevitable corruption that attends all our

actions in this world in the role of Friar Comolet, who aids Bussy's
love for Tamyra and eventually suffers death and purgatory for his
helpfulness. The Friar illustrates clearly the corruption of good in a
fallen world, for his aid of Bussy is apparently disinterested. That
the Friar's deeds require punishment is suggested by his death and
tormented reappearance as a ghost. But before his death the Friar is
forced to meddle with the powers of darkness in seeking to find out
whether Bussy's relationship with Tamyra has been discovered.
The summoning of Behometh in IV.ii., and then again by Bussy in
V.ii., illustrates how far from virtue Bussy's *virtù* has forced him to
stray. But although the Friar is to suffer penance in the afterlife
(V.ii.266) he can also speak truth from beyond the grave, that was
denied him when living. His choric judgement on the need for
submission to God's will (which we have seen as a theme of the later
comedies) directs us to the moral interpretation of the play's tragic
conclusion. To Tamyra's words that man's life is one of grief the
Friar's ghost replies:

> 'Tis the just curse of our abus'd creation,
> Which we must suffer here, and 'scape hereafter:
> He hath the great mind that submits to all
> He sees inevitable; he the small
> That carps at earth, and her foundation-shaker,
> And rather than himself, will mend his maker.

> (V.iii.69–74)

But this is not the Friar's final judgement of the wilful Bussy, for
Bussy's virtuous death is an acceptance (at last) of God's will which
completes the *post mortem* perfection not achievable in the post-
lapsarian world. Hence the Friar's last words recognise Bussy's
death as finally transforming Bussy's *virtù* into virtue:

> Farewell brave relics of a complete man:
> Look up and see thy spirit made a star,
> Join flames with Hercules: and when thou set'st
> Thy radiant forehead in the firmament,
> Make the vast continent, crack'd with thy receipt,
> Spread to a world of fire: and th'aged sky,
> Cheer with new sparks of old humanity.

> (V.iii.268–74)

Bussy's spirit purified through suffering and death ascends, like Hercules-Christ, to oneness with the Father. The allegory is Christian: Bussy's 'natural noblesse' is inevitably tainted by the act of living in the world, but Bussy is saved by striving to achieve the virtue that eludes him. It is his death, the death of the strenuous Christian, that makes him a complete man.

Between the writing of *Widows' Tears* and the appearance of Chapman's next plays the two-part *Conspiracy* and *Tragedy of Byron* there is a gap of about three years or so, which may at least partly be explained by Chapman's imprisonment for his part in the comedy of *Eastward Ho* with Marston and Jonson in 1605. The *Conspiracy of Byron*, however, marks something of a new departure in Chapman's tragic method. The change noticeable in all Chapman's later tragedies, marks a substantial paring down of action and a greater unity of tone compared to *Bussy D'Ambois*. It cannot be a coincidence that this same change away from Senecan sensationalism towards a manner more closely reminiscent of Greek tragedy occurs in the work of Chapman's two great rivals in tragedy around this time. For in both Shakespeare and Jonson there is an attempt to re-create the classical unity of tone in tragedies about the time Chapman was writing the Byron plays. Shakespeare's *Coriolanus* of around 1608 looks like a similar attempt to create an austerer form of tragedy and the contrast between Shakespeare's 'Senecan' exuberance in *Hamlet* and *Macbeth* and the neo-classical *Coriolanus* is not unlike Chapman's change from the 'Senecan' gothic of *Bussy D'Ambois* to the more unified dignity of the Byron plays. The cause of this shift of classical emphasis can only be conjectured—in Shakespeare's case it was temporary, an experiment in an alien manner, however splendid the result. For Chapman on the other hand, it was a more permanent shift to a more congenial, less popular manner, and it may be that the original impulse derived from Chapman's enveloping devotion to his Greek studies. If Chapman were setting the pace in the theatre, it would not be for the first time.

The two-part, ten-act drama of the *Conspiracy* and *Tragedy of Byron*, for all its difference of method from the earlier plays, has some thematic connection with *Bussy D'Ambois*. Like the earlier tragedy its subject is the frailty of private virtue in the public world, but the emphasis is quite different. The interest in *Bussy D'Ambois* is on the inward man, the tainting of the good man in a corrupt world and his purification in death. The interest of the Byron plays is in the world of politics and the choices it offers between good and evil.

Again the similarity to the shift between the psychological dramas of *Hamlet* and *Macbeth* and the political concerns in *Coriolanus* is notable. Like Coriolanus, Byron is presented from the outside as it were, a public man making conscious political choices. The difference in mode can be well illustrated from Chapman's use of emblem in the Byron plays. In the late comedies and in *Bussy D'Ambois* emblem is used symbolically as a device for revealing new levels of meaning. The world of truth to which Strozza and Bussy aspire or to which Vandome and Tharsalio lead the neophytes is a hidden world which needs to be unravelled through the interpretation of hieroglyphic, the plays are journeys through the labyrinths of myth. In the Byron plays there is no mystery, the theme is declared openly in the opening prologue:

> . . . see in his revolt how honour's flood
> Ebbs into air, when men are great, not good.[34]

The Byron plays are, like all Chapman's later tragedies, 'exempla' to give 'material instruction, elegant and sententious excitation to virtue and defection from her contrary'.[35] The emphasis in the *Conspiracy and Tragedy* is on defection from vice. Here emblem is not used so much as magical symbol, but as illustration. So when the conspiratorial Duke of Savoy, just after we have heard Byron meditating treachery, points to Byron confidently sitting astride his horse as a 'witty hieroglyphic / Of a blest kingdom' (*Conspiracy*, II.ii.78–9), emblem becomes an ironic mode for distinguishing falsehood. The king, the play's touchstone of truth, appropriately remarks:

> Your wit is of the true Pierian spring
> That can make anything of anything.

Similarly when Byron, enraged at what he takes to be the king's belittlement of his mighty deeds, describes a monument he wishes to see erected to emblemise his greatness (III.ii.141–77) he demonstrates a perverse misuse of art that was associated in Act I of *The Gentleman Usher* with the state of darkness from which Strozza shows the path to virtue. It is significantly in the scene from England (Act IV), a land, in contrast to France, where order prevails, that a true perspective can be obtained through the reading of symbols. So when the 'great and eminent' Councillor (Robert Cecil?) warns

Byron of the insecurity of greatness founded on vice, he points to the 'hieroglyphic' of the stars where it is the fixed stars that appear to wander and the wandering stars that are steadfast:

> A perfect hieroglyphic to express
> The idleness of such security

> (IV.i.207–8)

Chapman has learned to trust his elite audiences of Blackfriars to look on truth unveiled, as the uncharacteristic perspicuousness of the language throughout also witnesses. The interest in the Byron plays is not, then, in learning to interpret a mysterious language of truth, but in watching the consequences in Byron of ignoring truths that are manifest. Byron is the great man who fails to found his greatness on virtue and arrives at his tragic end by a perversion of will. The strength of the plays is in their demonstration of the inescapable logic of perverse choice as Byron's follies of grandeur lead him to oppose over and over again the rightful authority of his king. The inexorable nature of Byron's fall has something of the fatefulness of Greek tragedy, though in Byron's case the tragedy stems from wrongful choice not the vicissitudes of circumstance. The premises of Chapman's tragedy are always essentially Christian. The success of the plays in spite of their mangled state (a victim of the Jacobean censorship) derives from Chapman's ability to give genuine tragic status to the hero in spite of his wrongfulness. Byron is no 'Senecan'-type monster, but a man of outstanding ability, fretted by the limitations of subordination. However inexcusable, his restlessness is fully comprehensible and we find no difficulty in having some sympathy for him. The feeling of inexorableness is enhanced by the two-part presentation, for the second part realises the tragic potential explored in the *Conspiracy*, a play which is an example of the tragedy of happy ending. The massive impressiveness of Byron's character, in spite of his wilfulness, gives the tragedy a monolithic dignity not often obtained in Jacobean tragedy.

The *Revenge of Bussy D'Ambois* is, like the *Tragedy of Byron*, a sequel, but it is more in the nature of an afterthought. Here Chapman is more concerned with excitation to virtue than with 'deflection from her contrary' so the tragic tension created in the

Byron plays by the conflict between greatness and virtue is missing. The *Revenge*, written some six or seven years after the writing of *Bussy D'Ambois*, follows the mode of the Byron plays in its concern to illustrate a moral and in its tone of moral gravity. Chapman's habitual use of character emblematically, in this case to embody moral values, results in the characters bearing little relation to their appearance in the earlier Bussy play. The wise and just king of *Bussy D'Ambois* becomes the treacherous and unstable monarch of the *Revenge*, the Guise, who had plotted Bussy's assassination in the earlier play, becomes the avenger's friend and aide. It seems unlikely then that the *Revenge* was intended as a sequel to the revival of Bussy as has been suggested.[36] Its chief theme is the central preoccupation of Chapman's last three tragedies, for it shares with *Caesar and Pompey* (c.1613?)[37] and the *Tragedy of Chabot* (c.1613?) the concern to define the virtuous man. Clermont, the avenger of the *Revenge of Bussy*, shares with Cato in *Caesar and Pompey* the stoical virtue that leads to their suicides in protest at the corrupt world in which they have been forced to play a part. In all three of these plays the hero chooses private virtue in preference to public success and acclaim. Chapman is not interested, in these plays, in discovering the path of virtue, but merely in illustrating it. All three heroes are born (as it were) virtuous men and the plays exist to display their qualities. In the *Revenge* and in *Caesar and Pompey* the display of virtue involves ethical dilemmas and the drama of the *Revenge* in particular is generated from Clermont's uncertainty about the ethics of revenge. This indeed is one of the few Jacobean plays that take seriously the moral issues involved for the Christian in private revenge. Chapman's play raises and clarifies those issues which *Hamlet* so confusingly refuses to address itself to. Clermont possesses that trust in God and the need for obedience to His will that Chapman made the touchstone of virtue in the late comedies (we saw it as a central theme of *Monsieur D'Olive*):

> He that strives t'invert
> The Universal's course with his poor way,
> Not only dust-like shivers with the sway,
> But, crossing God in his great work, all earth
> Bears not so cursed and so damn'd a birth

> (III.iv.71–5)

Later Clermont is given the most detailed and most unequivocal expression of this doctrine in all of Chapman's work:

> And know you all (though far from all your aims
> Yet worth them all, and all men's endless studies)
> That in this one thing, all the discipline
> Of manners and manhood is contain'd:
> A man to join himself with th'Universe
> In his main sway, and make (in all things fit)
> One with that All, and go on round as it;
> Not plucking from the whole his wretched part,
> And into straits or into nought revert,
> Wishing the complete Universe might be
> Subject to such a rag of it as he . . .

(IV.i.135–45)

In these late plays Chapman's sententiousness is constantly liable to over-rule his sense of the dramatic.

Clermont's difficulty, then, is not in the disposition to do God's will, but in the difficulty of recognising it (a difficulty both Chabot and Cato so completely overcome that what dramatic conflict remains comes from the external opposition to the hero's virtue). At one point in the play Clermont is inclined to interpret God's will in quietistic terms, suggesting that private revenge is always wrong:

> I repent that ever
> (By any instigation in th' appearance
> My brother's spirit made, as I imagin'd)
> That e'er I yielded to revenge his murther.
> All worthy men should ever bring their blood
> To bear all ill, not to be wreak'd with good:
> Do ill for no ill; never private cause
> Should take on it the part of public laws.

(III.ii.109–16)

Clermont's conversion from this passivism is not, however, the result of internal debate, for that would be to suggest an uncertainty in recognising good from evil that is contrary to his sense that 'Good and bad hold never / Anything in common' (III.iv.54–5). His change

comes by direct intervention from outside in the person of Bussy's
Ghost, who argues that God's will rises above all personal feeling,
so that the virtuous man becomes God's instrument of justice:

> When (by true doctrine) you are taught to live
> Rather without the body than within,
> And rather to your God still than yourself;
> To live to Him, is to do all things fitting
> His image, in which, like Himself we live;
> To be His image is to do those things
> That make us deathless, which by death is only
> Doing those deeds that fit eternity;
> And those deeds are the perfecting that justice
> That make the world last, which proportion is
> Of punishment and wreak for every wrong,
> As well as for right a reward as strong.
> Away, then! Use the means thou has to right
> The wrong I suffer'd. What corrupted law
> Leaves unperform'd in kings, do thou supply,
> And be above them all in dignity.

(V.i.84–99)

This revelation from the next world precipitates Clermont to his act
of revenge and the killing of Montsurry, Bussy's murderer, is
consummated by the ghost of Bussy, the Guise, Monsieur, Cardinal
Guise and Chatillon who 'dance about the dead body'. Clermont's
earthly duties are done. He cannot exact revenge for the Guise's
death since: 'There's no disputing with the acts of kings' (V.v.151).
The king's treachery has brought about the Guise's death.

   The last three of Chapman's tragedies, while they lack the
dramatic excitement and complexity of *Bussy* on the one hand and
the noble, epic expansiveness of the Byron plays on the other, share
with the Byron plays that tone of august dignity that renders them
the most successful attempt in English to emulate the grandeur of
classical Greek tragedy. *Caesar and Pompey* is perhaps the most
successful of the three, for the inevitably static quality of Cato's
virtue is dramatically counterpoised by the more human fallibility of
the chief opponents, Caesar and Pompey. In this play Chapman
returns to the opaque and difficult language of *Bussy* and the late
comedies and there is some return too to the earlier methods in the

brief intrusion of comedy (II.i.) but essentially the play is illustrative of Chapman's last phase of dramatic writing where the purpose is above all 'the excitation to virtue'. One interesting thematic element is Cato's defence of suicide, where the Roman stoic asserts his faith in the resurrection of the body and soul (IV.v.126–36) and in which Homer is quoted in defence of Christian doctrine. However pagan the matter, the doctrine remains that of a Christian poet.

The weakest of these three plays is undoubtedly *The Tragedy of Chabot*, but this is almost certainly to do with Shirley's participation. Although it was composed (apparently) around the same time as *Caesar and Pompey*, like the latter play it seems it was not performed during Chapman's lifetime. By 1613 or so Chapman may have lost interest in the stage in his pursuit of Homer and his austerity may have been losing favour with Jacobean audiences. Shirley's revision for performance in any case shows a completely different appeal to the audience from Chapman's; Chabot's goodness is primarily presented for our sympathy and for the pathos of his fall from the king's favour. It is characteristic of the play that Chabot's death, in stark contrast to the heroic suicides of Clermont and Cato, should be of a broken heart and that the last scene of the play should present the tottering and sick admiral as re-instated too late for his life to be saved. It is Chapman's usual premise that in Bussy's words, only the 'illiterate vulgars' concern themselves with 'flesh's bonds' (*Revenge*, V.i.81–2). The pathos of Chabot's end assumes the opposite: that it is tragic to lose life's prizes. Such an ending requires a presentation of character that can interest us by asking us to share its feelings. Chabot is too Chapmanesque for that, he is a hero too far outside the range of our own experience, too exemplary to appeal to us in this way. Chapman's mythic and exemplary method clashes fundamentally with Shirley's affectiveness and the play's failure helps accordingly to highlight the measure of Chapman's success as a tragic writer in those plays that are substantially his own. To the end of his productive and successful relationship with the professional stage he ploughs his own furrow, uniquely producing both the finest example of mythic drama of the period in the late comedies and the nearest the Jacobean stage got to the purity of the classical drama in his tragedies. His Jacobean plays deserve a better fate than merely to be read by the scholar.

6
Thomas Middleton

Middleton is the one major Jacobean playwright whose stature went unrecognised by his contemporaries. That he was a highly successful playwright is clear from his long career in the professional theatre from 1601, when we hear of him as 'remaining in London accompanying the players',[1] to his spectacular success with A Game at Chess in 1624 (he was buried on 4 July 1627), and by his employment in the City of London in the arranging of pageants and his appointment from 1620 as City Chronologer (that is, as historian to the City). In terms of status and financial prosperity Middleton's would seem to have been one of the more successful careers among Jacobean playwrights. Yet his artistic stature went largely unrecognised until our own times; he is seldom mentioned as a serious artist by his contemporaries; Webster gives him no mention in the otherwise comprehensive roll-call of major dramatists prefacing The White Devil (a title incidently culled from Middleton's Revenger's Tragedy) while Jonson's brief comment in the conversations with William Drummond places Middleton along with Day and Markham as 'not of the number of the faithful, i.e. poets, and but a base fellow'.[2]

Jonson's remark is useful in placing Middleton in a contemporary perspective. Unlike Jonson himself, Middleton did not see his role as a dedicated artist, but as a theatrical entertainer. Middleton's attitude to his writing is illustrated in the witty and unpretentious preface to The Roaring Girl, a joint venture with Dekker, where he offers the play as an alternative to 'an afternoon from dice at home in your chambers' and where the address promises merely 'venery and laughter'. A consequence of this casual view of his trade is that there is no attempt to collect and preserve his work in folios like those of Jonson, Shakespeare and 'Beaumont and Fletcher' and no attempt to see the plays carefully through the press, as with Webster and Chapman. What plays of Middleton were published during his lifetime were published in inelegant and often slapdash quarto; a considerable amount of his work was published either without the author's name (as with Michaelmas Term, the first version of the title page of *A Trick to Catch the Old One* and *The Revenger's Tragedy*) or simply by initials (for example, *A Mad World My Masters*, or the second title page of *Trick*). This, of course, has led to problems in identifying the canon in modern times, so that even now, after much labour spent on attribution, plays like *Revenger's Tragedy*, *The Puritan Widow* and *The Yorkshire Tragedy* are in hot dispute.

Jonson's dislike was no doubt sharpened by the fact that whereas he saw himself as a Court poet of conservative, Anglican tendencies, Middleton's connections (as Margot Heinemann has comprehensively shown) were Puritan and with the City of London. I have already (in Chapter 1) expressed my view that Paul's Theatre catered primarily for a City audience and it was in the tiny Paul's Theatre that Middleton (after the almost inevitable few years of Henslowe's treadmill) first made his name. If Middleton was a theatrical entertainer, therefore, he was for much of his career an entertainer of a sophisticated, elite audience. He seems to have taken over as chief playwright of Paul's boys around the time that Marston was switching his allegiance to Blackfriars (1602/3) and his satiric realism owes much to Marston's example. Like Marston he uses contemporary reference as the groundwork for religious allegory, but with Middleton the surface realism is more insistent and the allegorical implications both less obvious and more consistent. So convincing, indeed, and so self-consistent is his picture of the actual world of London life that critical comment has constantly overlooked or dismissed the religious intention. It is characteristic of Middleton to use real-life incidents and people as the source material of his plays, as he does with the story of 'one Howe, a broker' in *Michaelmas Term*,[3] with Mary Frith in the *Roaring Girl* and, most conspicuously of all, with the contemporary political situation in *A Game at Chess* (1624).

Middleton's work for the professional theatre falls roughly into three stages: a period from his earliest extant plays *The Family of Love* (1602?) and *The Phoenix* to *A Chaste Maid in Cheapside* (1613) characterised by a series of brilliant comedies of London life; a second period from around 1613 to around 1620 when he seems to be searching, not wholly successfully, for new modes of dramatic expression, to some extent in response to the fashion for romantic comedies established by Shakespeare at the end of his career and by Beaumont and Fletcher; and finally a short but triumphant period in which he wrote his finest two tragedies *The Changeling* (with

Rowley) and *Women Beware Women*. It is the early period that marks
Middleton's most distinctive contribution to Jacobean theatre.
Middleton's most characteristic mode is irony, an irony generated
by an implied contrast between things as they are and things as they
should be. The main reason for the success of such early comedies as
Michaelmas Term, *A Mad World, My Master*, and *A Trick to Catch the
Old One* (all published in 1607/8) and *Chaste Maid* is in their brilliant
juxtaposition of vividly realised actuality with an implied reality at
another (religious) level. The contrast is the Augustinian one
between the corrupt and temporary city of man and the eternal city
of God[4] which is hidden for most of mankind, 'solde under sinne' as
man is. As in St. Paul 'flesh' and 'spirit' are seen in Middleton as
irreconcilably opposed: 'flesh lusteth against the Spirit and the Spirit
against the flesh and these are contrary one to the other'.[5] In the
plays of the middle period the sharp contrast between the two
worlds weakens because a romantic element both diminishes the
sense of actuality and allows the intrusion of the world of the spirit
in less convincing ways.

Middleton's finest comedies exploit the absurdity of a mankind
busying itself with its own destruction—the image of the world as a
madhouse recurs throughout Middleton's work from the aptly
named *A Mad World* to Andrugio's answer to the Duchess in *More
Dissemblers Besides Women* (1615) when she asks 'How long have you
been mad?' 'Mad? A great time lady; since I first knew I should not
sin, yet sinned' (V.i.85–7)—the allusion is to St. Paul, *Romans*, 7:
14–15. In *The Changeling*, where the metaphor of the world as a
madhouse is made into a structural principle by the contrast
between the two plots, Isabella complains that in the lunatic asylum
'here's none but fools and madmen', to which the attendant Lollio
replies 'and where will you find any other if you should go abroad?'
(III.iii.15–16).[6] Vindice in *The Revenger's Tragedy* meditating on the
vanity of the world underscores its madness:

> Surely we're all mad people, and they
> Whom we think are, are not; we mistake those;
> 'tis we are mad in sense, they but in clothes.

> (III.v.80–2)[7]

The roots of Middleton's thoughts here lie in Calvin, who refers in
the *Institutes* to man's innate 'imbecility' (Bk I, ch. 18, 3). Behind

Middleton's vision of a mad world is the Christian paradox of the foolish wise and the wise foolish, the tradition exploited by Erasmus in his *Praise of Folly*. The vision is essentially comic because it ironically juxtaposes two opposed concepts of man, as of the flesh and of the spirit. In an early collaboration with Dekker, the first part of *The Honest Whore*, the two playwrights had concluded their play with a madhouse scene in which the Duke of Milan visits the madhouse for his entertainment—for the Jacobeans Bedlam was a place of wry laughter.

In the City comedies the madhouse of this world is presented with an apparent fidelity to the actual that makes the joke both telling and frightening. The City of London is referred to in *A Chaste Maid in Cheapside*, for instance, in minute detail so that we can plot the movements of the characters from the Yellowhammer's shop in the West Cheap in 'the heart of the City of London' (I.i.94) to Trig Stairs and Puddle-wharf from which Tim Yellowhammer suspects his sister may have eloped by boat (IV.ii.5, 7),[8] (modern editors wisely supply a plan of Jacobean London to help readers find their way around the play). As Parker has shown in the Introduction to his edition, the play abounds too in references to contemporary events (pp. xxx–xxxv). In all this Middleton is wanting to identify (in time-honoured fashion) the world about him in London with the Babylon of Christian homily. Accordingly the picture presented is one of getting and spending (as much in their sexual meanings as in their economic). London is dominated by the lusts of the flesh whether it is the commercial greed of the senior Yellowhammers, and Allwit (who lives by his wife's prostitution) or the sexual obsessiveness of the aptly named Touchwoods and Sir Walter Whorehound or such mere idiosyncratic obsessions as Tim Yellowhammer's aspirations to scholarship and poetry that make him more concerned to beat his tutor to a funerary poem than with the actual fact of his sister's sickness (V.ii.18–21). Middleton's attitude to the vanity of scholarship—as foolish a vanity as any other in this homiletic tradition—incidentally helps to explain Middleton's lowly view of his own calling (a Puritan response in contrast with the high Anglican and Catholic respect for art and the artist). But in Middleton's 'London' we are not so much concerned with particular sin as sinfulness itself, the state incident to being human. In man's fallen state sinfulness is endemic and any particular sin simply a manifestation of the general state, so that fornication is seen as much in terms of buying and selling as commercial greed is seen in

terms of lust, neatly summed up in such punning as: 'No mar'l I
heard a citizen complain once / That his wife's belly only broke his
back' (III.ii.65–6), where the struggle for food and fornication is
promiscuously intermingled. Each individual is compelled by his
own species of greed to pursue a narrow self-interest that isolates
him from his fellow, so when Moll Yellowhammer sings the
touching song in her sickness on the loss of her love, her mother can
only comment 'O I could die with music—well sung girl'. The
incongruities in the response of one character to another show us a
world that does not add up, a comic world of irreconcilable
contradictions, the resolution of which can only be achieved by
escape to another plane of reality.

Whenever this transcendental reality intrudes, however, it too
inevitably results in incongruity, for the two levels of experience
are totally discontinuous—as St. Paul and Calvin teach. One of the
finest moments of Middleton's irony in the play is when the
wounded Whorehound announces to the Allwits his rejection of his
sinful past, only to be met by the husband's belief he is raving (the
Christian madness of the wise) and the wife's comment 'He is lost
for ever' (V.i.51). In the upside-down city of man, to be saved is to be
lost for ever. The intrusion of the other world is, as Calvinistic
thought would have it, sudden and unaccountable, for there is
absolute discontinuity between the two planes of being.
Whorehound's conversion is as sudden as it is unexpected and, as
he says 'by chance':

> . . . if I had not
> Wak'd by chance, even by a stranger's pity,
> I had everlastingly slept out all hope
> Of grace and mercy.

(V.i.28–31)

The bustle of Cheapside with all its frenetic activity is in reality
nothing but the sleep of death.

Middleton reminds his audience of the Christian truths with
which the way of the world is contrasted in a variety of ways
throughout the play. Three of the scenes in the play involve the
celebration of Christian ritual: Lent, baptism and the burial of the
dead. In each of these the solemn events get manipulated and
distorted by the perversity of human nature. The scene in which

Whorehound's seventh bastard (by Mrs Allwit) is baptised is perhaps the funniest in the play, as we measure the greed and backbiting of the gossips against the solemn nature of the Christian feast. As the guests (including two male Puritans) mouth their polite congratulations, Allwit stands aside and comments on the greed with which they help themselves to the food:

> Now out comes all the tassell'd hardkerchers,
> They are spread almost between their knees already;
> Now in goes the long fingers that are wash'd
> Some thrice a day in urine; my wife uses it.
> Now we shall have such pocketing: see how
> They lurch at the lower end!

> (III.ii.50–4)

Allwit of course congratulates himself that it is Whorehound, not himself, who has to pay for it all. This liking for multiple level action in which opposed planes of experience (the gossips/the Allwits'/Whorehound's/the Christian) are juxtaposed, relates to Middleton's allegorical method, for just as there is absolute discontinuity between levels of vision, so within earthly society the self-preoccupation of the individual leads to discontinuity of viewpoint between one person and another. Life is, literally, knock-about. In man's sinful state all men are islands.

The presence of Puritans as subjects of Middleton's attack in the play might be thought curious in a playwright of Puritan sympathies, but the subject of attack is hypocrisy, the failure to live up to Puritan professions. As with his class satire, which ranges widely from Welsh country girl to the courtly Lady Kix, Middleton is spreading his net to encompass the great variety of reprobates in the City of Man. Moroever the various plots are schematically arranged to illustrate the multifarious and perverse nature of man's degeneracy. Thus Touchwood Senior's super-fecundity is balanced by Sir Oliver Kix's sterility, Mrs Allwit's super-abundance of illegitimate children with Lady Kix's longing for an heir, Whorehound's absurd jealousy with Allwit's absurd complacency. In these City comedies the City of God is present largely by implication, though clearly the comedy could not work if the audience were not constantly able and willing to supply the Christian standards that make such ironies as the Allwit's disgust at Whorehound's conversion viable. In *A Mad World, My Masters*, the true nature of the genial world of Sir Bounteous Progress and his trickster grandson Follywit is more explicitly revealed in a scene in which the devil appears in the guise of one of the characters. Like Whorehound in *Chaste Maid*, Penitent Brothel (whose name similarly juxtaposes spirit and flesh in comic oxymoron) undergoes a crisis of conscience in the course of the play and renounces his lecherous ways. The devil's appearance in the guise of Penitent's former mistress, Mrs Harebrain, focuses the audience's attention briefly on the allegorical nature of the surface realism in a play that might otherwise be seen (as it often has been) as light-hearted depiction of contemporary society.

In *A Trick to Catch the Old One*,[9] perhaps the finest of the comedies and Middleton's most notable comic achievement, the awareness of other-worldly standards is allowed to remain inferential. The audience is asked to share the uncertainty and deceptiveness of appearances with the characters. The London world depicted, though with much less circumstantial detail than in *Chaste Maid*, is every bit as sordid. Character vies with character to cheat and outwit each other, the hero Witgood merely being one of the most astute of the tricksters—as his allegorical name suggests. Here too we have the world of getting and spending in which commerce and sex are entwined and ultimately inseparable. Here however there are no diabolic manifestations to point to the allegorical dimensions of the play, nor even the sudden Pauline conversion that reminds us of the distinction between the saved and the damned in *Mad World* and *Chaste Maid*. It is true that at the end of the play Witgood, having cheated back the deeds of his mortgaged patrimony from his uncle and having palmed-off his whore on the unspeakable miser Walkadine Hoard and married the lady of his choice, goes through a form of repentance (in company with the cast-off whore), but this is clearly so perfunctory and the irregular octosyllabic form so ambiguous in tone that the scene becomes a parody of the conventional moral ending.

In this mad world of ribaldry and mockery the voice of sanity has to be sought by indirection and by inference—as it does in the larger world outside the theatre—for this is not a world that God and the devil have totally abandoned. The presence of the devil is as strong in this play as in *Mad World* and Middleton images it through a subplot that at first sight seems to have little to do with the main action of the play. Three scenes are devoted to the decline into dipsomania of the usurer Dampit, whose name is explicitly likened to his role as one of the damned (his first name is Harry—old Harry to Witgood, I.iv.37) 'There's pits enow to damn him, before he comes to hell' sings his mistress Audrey at the beginning of the last scene (IV.v.). Dampit as a damned soul is constantly linked with hell and the Devil 'Did not I tell you he lay like the devil in chains when he was bound for a thousand years' says the mocking Lamprey (quoting the Book of Revelation, 20:2), who has come to enjoy the spectacle of Dampit's sordid decline: 'a slave in this world and a devil in the next' (IV.v.59). The moral of Dampit's end is rehearsed by both Lamprey and Dampit's fellow-usurer Gulf (the name again pointing to the affinity) who with supreme irony comments: 'O Dampit, here's a just judgement shown upon usury, extortion and trampling villainy' (IV.v.150–1). Gulf is one of those typical Middletonian characters who, in the words of St. Paul, 'allow not that which I do' (*Romans*, 7:15).

The Dampit plot, which in terms of action is completely independent of the main actions of the play, is thematically linked with the theme of damnation, through a network of verbal echoes that connect Dampit above all with the apparently successful hero Witgood. Ironically it is Witgood's own description of Dampit as 'the most notorious, usuring, blasphemous, atheistical, brothel-vomiting rascal' (I.iv.12–13) that gets echoed throughout the play in descriptions of Witgood himself as a 'rioter wastethrift and brothelmaster' (I.iii.26); 'a spendthrift, dissolute follow . . . A very rascal . . . A midnight surfeiter . . . The spume of a brothel house' (II.ii.30–4); 'a brotheller a wastethrift, a common surfeiter' (II.i.3–4); 'proclaimed rioter, penurious makeshift, despised brothel-master' (II.i.196–7); 'a prodigal, a daily rioter, and a nightly vomiter' (IV.iii.19–20). Dampit's usury, too, not only connects him to such usurious figures as the Hoards and Lucre but to the hero again, who is even willing to 'foresweare brothel at noone day' to get back the deeds of his mortgaged land and who, in an ecstasy of joy when the deeds are recovered, addresses them as 'the soul of my estate' (IV.ii.87). Witgood is as sordidly materialistic as the professed usurers of the play. There is also a network of references to hell binding the characters together in a society of the damned: Witgood, taken to prison for his debts cries out 'I am in hell here, and the devils will not let me come to thee' (IV.iii.61–2). The damned in Middleton often speak better than they know. Equally damned are the usurers Hoard and Lucre. In Act I, Scene iii we find them fighting bitterly with one another:

HOARD. O that I had as much power as usury has over thee!
LUCRE. Then thou wouldst have as much power as the devil has
over thee.

These characters are living already locked in the hell of God's
election, like Dante's souls in *Inferno* 'whom anger overcame' (*Inf.*,
VII, 116). It was a distinction of Calvinistic thinking to convert
heaven and hell into earthly phenomena. Like Dante's damned,
Middleton's characters are in constant strife one with the other.
Hoard and Lucre are no sooner forcibly separated in this scene, than
we move to another short scene of anger in which Moneylove, a
suitor for the hand of Joyce Hoard, strikes his rival Freedom and
challenges him to a duel. Middleton shares his vision of mankind
with the Calvin of the *Institutes* where man is seen as wholly corrupt,
'nothing else but concupiscence' (*Institutes*, Bk II, ch. 1, 8) and
where salvation is for those few whom God elects to save. In
Middleton's mad world it is mostly for the weak and the outcast, like
the prostitute Audrey, lovingly tending the dying Dampit, who has
the signs of salvation about her. The power of Middleton's vision
stems from his finding in contemporary London a convincing and
precise vehicle for his allegory.

This grim view of the world in the earlier comedies diminishes
considerably in the middle-period plays, as the sharp contrast
between good and evil weakens. Middleton's first response to the
new fashion for romantic plots is the rather ambiguous comedy *No
Wit, No Help Like a Woman's* (c.1611).[10] Retaining some of the
features of the City comedy such as the London setting, the theme of
trickster son against 'blocking' father, the satire on riches and
worldliness, the action of the play none the less takes us into a world
of romantic love, of unexpected revelations and strange
coincidence. For instance, the young hero, Phillip Twilight, is no
longer the witty trickster (though his part includes spending the
money given to him to ransom his mother and sister and marrying
his heart's desire) but a melancholic who three times threatens
suicide in the course of the play. The girl he marries secretly in
France turns out to be the daughter of his father's friend Sunset,
while the girl Sunset believed to be his daughter turns out to be the
daughter of Sir Oliver Twilight. There are equally complicated and
improbable plots involving disguise and revelation, like that in
which Mistress Low-Water (the woman of the title) wins back the
fortune from the widow of the man who cheated her family out of it,

Goldenfleece. Mistress Low-Water disguised as a man pays court to Widow Goldenfleece and wins her hand; when the true situation is revealed Widow Goldenfleece is quite content to marry Mistress Low-Water's brother, Beveril, instead. The nomenclature suggests that Middleton had not abandoned his customary liking for allegory here and the fact that so many of the names point to moments of time in nature (Twilight, Sunset, Weatherwise, Low-Water) indicates the central opposition in the play between time and the timeless. Weatherwise, one of the fools of the play, is mocked because as an astrologer he claims to have an insight into the mysterious workings of nature. However, Mistress Low-Water, the play's heroine, understands that God's mysteries are a matter of faith, not science:

> There is no happiness but has her season,
> Wherein the brightness of her virtue shines:
> The husk falls off in time that long shut up
> The fruit in a dark prison; so sweeps by
> The cloud of miseries from wretches' eyes,
> That yet, though fal'n, at length they see to rise;
> The secret powers work wondrously and duly.

(I.ii.142–8)

The play's unlikely events are to illustrate the wondrous workings of these secret powers. The theme contrasts the foolish who trust in earthly things with those who submit themselves to God's will: the heroine guides us once more:

> I feel a hand of mercy lift me up
> Out of a world of waters, and now sets me
> Upon a mountain, where the sun plays most,
> To cheer my heart even as it dries my limbs.
> What deeps I see beneath me, in whose falls
> Many a nimble mortal toils,
> And scarce can feed himself! the streams of fortune,
> 'gainst which he tugs in vain, still beat him down,
> And will not suffer him—past hand to mouth—
> To lift his arm to posterity's blessing . . .

(II.iii.252–61)

The imagery here (echoed in Mrs. Low-Water's name) has unmistakable Biblical echoes: the shining mountain, for instance, suggests the description of Jerusalem in the Book of Revelation (21: 10–11) which the Geneva Bible glosses: 'by this description is declared the incomprehensible exellencie which the heavenlie companie do enjoye'. The romantic ending in which each Jack has his Jill assures us that the secret powers are essentially benevolent, as the last lines of the play make explicit:

> Heaven still relieves what misery would destroy;
> Never was night yet of more general joy.

By comparison with earlier City comedies, *No Wit* falls uncomfortably between the stools of satire and romance. There is too much in it of the old vision of secular depravity to ignore and it tends to set the tone for the play.[11] Yet the stress on the miraculous nature of God's bounty and the improbable events which are its vehicle requires a suspension of disbelief not easily compatible with satiric deflation. Perhaps Middleton himself sensed that the right balance had not been achieved here, for in his next comedy, *Chaste Maid*, he returned to the general satire on mankind that had provided the initial impulse for his best early comedies.

Chaste Maid in any case provided him with the last opportunity to write for boy players,[12] and this may have sent him back to the satiric comedy he had perfected for the Paul's audience. After *Chaste Maid* he wrote for adult players, as he had done intermittently throughout his earlier career. Increasingly he was in demand for masques for special City occasions such as the masque of the *Inner Temple* (1619) which interestingly takes up a theme related to that of *No Wit* in a more obviously allegorical manner by contrasting the unruly days of festival presided over by Almanac with the timelessness of heavenly virtues who 'By making Time their King / See, they're beyond time rear'd'.[13] Middleton's work for the popular stage at this time, however, goes through a period of not entirely successful experimentation: with such romantic comedies as *More Dissemblers Besides Women* (c.1615); and with *The Widow* (1616) and with 'problem' plays in which he focuses more narrowly on particular problems such as duelling in *A Fair Quarrel* (with Rowley) and euthanasia—especially its effects on the young—in *The Old Law*. Both plays are skilful, professional comedies and a recent revival of *A Fair Quarrel* has shown it to be still very stageworthy, but it lacks that seering vision of man's sinfulness that charges the early comedies with their ironic energy.

It is in the late tragedies that this animating conviction again becomes the central issue, but now—as befits tragedy—seeing the problem from the inside (as it were) outwards, centring on the sinner rather than the sinfulness, sharing with the audience the feeling of what damnation means. Middleton's first excursions into tragedy go back to his earliest work for Henslowe and the lost tragedy *The Viper and Her Brood* mentioned by Middleton in a law suit of 1608. But any discussion of Middleton must take into account the possibility (probability would seem more appropriate in the first two cases) that he was the author of the anonymous *Revenger's Tragedy* (1608),[14] the so-called *Second Maiden's Tragedy* (1611) and the one-act *Yorkshire Tragedy* (c.1606). *The Yorkshire Tragedy* is a remarkable playlet about wife- and baby-battering. Advertised in the 1608 Quarto as 'lamentable but true', its realism of psychology and manner is thoroughly Middletonian, as is its suggestion that the husband is diabolically possessed. The lack of individual names (also a Middleton trait) asks us to see this story of an immature spendthrift releasing the frustration of his poverty in violence against his family as a general commentary on man 'sold under sin' while (again characteristically) the woman pays the price. The play acts as an interesting comment on the sentimentality of Dekker's similar attempt to depict violence in the immature male in the character of Matheo in *II Honest Whore*—a character that Middleton had helped to create in the first part of *The Honest Whore*. That *The Yorkshire Tragedy* impressed its contemporaries is suggested by its being the only one of the 'four plays in one' of which it was a part to achieve publication.

The Revenger's Tragedy is a very moralistic version of the horror play that Marston had so successfully exploited theatrically in *Antonio's Revenge*. The theatrical effects in Middleton's play—startling as are such scenes as the death of the nameless Duke, poisoned by kissing the skull of the woman whose death he caused—are always subordinated to the moral that the wages of sin is death. This the avenger (Vindice) too discovers as he somewhat unexpectedly and arbitrarily betrays his role and that of his brother as murderer of the Duke at the end of the play. *The Revenger's Tragedy* in many ways points forward to the two late tragedies: like *The Changeling* the action is focused through the eyes of the central character, whose damnation for participation in sin is the subject of the play, so that, unlike the comedies, the audience is asked to participate in the hero's feelings—an appropriate enough technique for adult players. As in *Women Beware Women*, however, Middleton finds it difficult to sustain interest in his central figure as a personality in his overriding concern to illustrate what his hero stands for at a more abstract level. The result is a final act (as in the later play) where the audience is further and further distanced affectively from the action. This is partly a result of the speed with which the events are presented, partly of the arbitrariness with which the events are related (in order to make the perfectly valid moral point of the essential inconsequentiality of evil). Theatrically this 'alienation' effect succeeds in exploring the logic of absurdity and the only time I have seen the play acted (by students) I was not surprised to find the last act disconcertingly funny, especially in the final scene where Vindice, Hippolito and two noblemen appear as Masquers in honour of the new Duke's enthronement and begin a new round of killings that reminds the audience rather of those lines of dominoes set up in order to be suddenly cast down. Middleton attempts a similar use of the Masque—with equally unsettling results—in the last act of *Women Beware Women*. *The Revenger's Tragedy* in fact reveals why Middleton is essentially a comic writer, for essentially he has little interest in individuality, as his nomenclature throughout the play illustrates. More like Jonson's theory than his practice, Middleton illustrates human aberration as a sure indication of sinfulness and individuality as a sign of depravity.

The absurdly named *Second Maiden's Tragedy* (a name given by the Jacobean censor) written for Shakespeare's company in 1611 is a more deliberate attempt to come to terms with the tragic genre, and perhaps initiates Middleton's attempts to break out of the ironic mode in which he had so conspicuously excelled. On first impression, indeed, the play scarcely resembles Middleton's work at all. In place of the characteristic focus on sinfulness the tragedy places two innocent victims at the centre of the drama, the deposed King Govianus and his betrothed (called 'Lady' throughout) the daughter of the time-serving nobleman Helvetius. The focus is on innocent suffering as both Govianus and the Lady are subject to the attentions of the usurping Tyrant. Rather in the manner of the usurping King of *Philaster* (which play Middleton may have been influenced by) the Tyrant is morally unable to destroy the man he has deposed, but tortures him by allowing him to marry the Lady and then keeping them apart. His attempts to seduce the Lady end in her heroically committing suicide—a theme Middleton had dealt with, if somewhat differently and more doctrinally, in the poem *The Ghost of Lucrece*. Like Philaster, Govianus plays a somewhat passive role, even to the extent of being unable to wield the sword at his Lady's bequest, but whereas Philaster's passivity stems from political consideration, Middleton characteristically emphasises the religious when for instance Govianus expresses his contempt for this world's glories:

> The loss of her [the Lady] sits closer to my heart
> Than that of kingdom or the whorish pomp
> Of this world's titles that with flattery swells us
> And makes us die like beasts fat for destruction.

> (I.i.59–62)[15]

The *contemptus mundi* theme, here so overtly stated, consistently underlines the assumptions of Middleton's work from the very early paraphrase of the *Wisdom of Solomon* onwards. Equally characteristic is Govianus's continuing in a satirical vein as he reflects on the fickleness of women (63–7). For once the satire is unjustified, the Lady symbolising Virtue as she does and excusing at the allegorical level Govianus's infatuation for her.

As we would expect, Middleton is at least as concerned to depict the evil that threatens as the innocence that suffers and the perverted Tyrant out-Senecas the Senecan in his enormities—he is the only stage necrophiliac of the Jacobean Theatre as far as I am aware. Again characteristic is Middleton's allusive use of a sub-plot (in the manner of *Trick* and *The Changeling*) as a moral commentary on the main action; in this case the sub-plot offers us a contrasting picture of a reprobate woman sexually betraying her husband (the contrast inverts the relationship of the *Changeling* plots), the sub-plot presenting us with a picture of sin rampant that is usually Middleton's central concern. The effectiveness of this tragedy, however, is in Middleton's success in interesting us in the affections of virtue, and especially in the portrait of the Lady, whose heroic suicide is powerfully and convincingly achieved in spite of the overt moralising: 'there is no heaven but after death' (III.i.243). The contrast between the 'heavenly' victims and the hellish sinners ('I cannot call this life that flames within me/But everlasting torment' agonises the Tyrant—IV.ii.32–3) shows us we are in the customary Middletonian world of discontinuity between planes of reality. Like all Middleton's sinners, the Tyrant is doomed by the sins of the flesh over which he has no control: 'In vain my spirit wrestles with my blood / Affection will be mistress here on earth' (V.ii.1–2).

The somewhat ramshackle *Hengist King of Kent* (c.1616)—more frequently referred to by the sub-plot title of *The Mayor of Queenborough*[16]—would seem to be another Middleton experiment to break out of habitual limitations, in this case by resurrecting the kind of 'mixed' chronicle play popular in the days of Robert Greene and continued in the popular theatres. The theme of the play (as usual with Middleton, the organising principle) is the familiar use of a contrast between the worldly and the other-worldly, presented unusually as a contrast between the brief reign of the holy Constantius, a monk whom we find reluctant to succeed his father to the throne of Britain at the beginning of the play, and the ruffians who succeed him:

> Think with how much willingness and anguish
> A glorified soul parted from the body
> Would to that loathsome jail again return:
> With such great pain a well-subdu'd affection
> Re-enters worldly business.
>
> (I.i.50–4)

Once chosen as King he frets at the worldly pomp required of his office:

> Wonder of madness! can you stand idle,
> And know that you must die.
>
> (I.ii.51–2)

The contrast is the familiar Pauline one between the mad world of conspicuous consumption and the world of the spirit. Constantius refuses to marry the proferred Castiza (a name Middleton uses incidentally, in *Phoenix* and *Revenger's Tragedy*) because as a monk he has been dedicated to chastity. The distance between ourselves and Jacobean habits of mind is nowhere clearer than in the play's assumption that Constantius's irresponsible political attitudes are not only praiseworthy but exemplary—and commentators on *King Lear* might usefully take note. Constantius is duly killed by the usurping Vortiger (the episode depicted in dumb show) and we are plunged into a period of political chaos as the unpopular and unscrupulous Vortiger takes over power supported by the German mercenaries Hengist and Horsus. Middleton here skilfully uses the loose form of the chronicle play to give the sense of flux and disorder rife in this kingdom of sin, including the introduction of the comic 'Mayor of Queenborough' scenes that give the play its alternative title (it is perhaps appropriate to the disorderly world of the play that even the title should be in doubt). The world of Vortiger, Hengist and Horsus is a world of selfish expediency, the mad world of getting and spending, in which sexual incontinence is as conspicuous as the greed for power and property. It is, moreover, a world doomed to destroy itself by its internal contradictions as we are explicitly reminded by the triumphant legitimists at the end of the play: 'See, sin needs / No other destruction than it breeds / In its own bosom' (V.ii.76–8).

Two great tragedies end Middleton's career as a stage dramatist (apart from the brilliant, but occasional, *Game at Chess*, too bound up in the politics of the day to be resurrected for a modern audience, the anti-Spanish theme is again reflected in the Spanish setting of *The Changeling*). It is not clear when Middleton wrote *Women Beware Women*, but the late date of around 1621/2 is now widely accepted as likely.[17] In both tragedies Middleton returns to the great theme of the early comedies, the corruptions of the flesh that lead to the damnation of the soul, but now this theme is looked at tragically to arouse terror and pity, rather than dispassionately, to arouse laughter. Both tragedies concern themselves with apparent innocence that conceals corruption and appropriately this is symbolised in the character of a young woman, fair on the outside, corrupt within. The names of both heroines point ironically to their apparant virtue: Beatrice-Joanna ('she who blesses, the gift of the Lord'), Bianca 'the white lady'—both (resuming the dialogue with Webster) are 'white devils'.

From the very opening of the play it is clear that Beatrice-Joanna of *The Changeling*[18] is 'sold under sin'. In the opening scene Middleton lays stress on her wilfulness as she determines to reject the suitor insisted on by her father: 'I'll want my will else' says Vermandero, to which Beatrice replies: 'I shall want mine if you do it' (I.i.214–16).

Vermandero's serving man Deflores, himself infatuated with
Beatrice, shrewdly sees this quality as uppermost in Beatrice 'She
knows no cause . . . but a peevish will' (I.i.103). In this battle of
wilfulness he pits his will against hers, as he proclaims to the
audience at the end of the scene:

> . . . If but to vex her, I'll haunt her still:
> Though I get nothing else, I'll have my will.

(I.i.232–3)

All these assertions, it should be noted, are asides. Middleton sets
up an immediate ironic contrast between the outwardly polite,
courtly world of Vermandero's castle and the turmoil beneath it in
the souls of the principals which isolates them from one another.
Wilfulness is the classic condition of those who inhabit the city of
man as Augustine defines it.[19]

Beatrice, on the surface, has everything going for her: she is rich,
beautiful, desired. But the play brilliantly unfolds the inner
corruption which dooms her. To achieve her 'will' she has Deflores
kill Alonzo de Piracquo, her father's choice for her, to free herself
for the man she loves, Alsemero. Deflores, seeing this as an
infallible way of getting power over her, kills Piracquo and in one of
the greatest scenes in Jacobean drama comes to her for the wages of
his sin—bringing with him the ringed finger of the murdered man to
remind Beatrice of what she has had him do. In the most subtly
modulated dialogue it gradually dawns on Beatrice that she is not
only an accomplice of the murderer, but has put herself entirely in
his power. Her disgust as she realises he is demanding that she
sleeps with him is brilliantly punctured by Deflores:

> BEATRICE. Thy language is so bold and vicious
>   I cannot see which way I can forgive it
>   With any modesty.
> DEFLORES.   Push, you forget yourself;
>   A woman dipp'd in blood, and talk of modesty!

(III.iv.124–7)

Deflores is outstandingly ugly and Beatrice is physically repelled by
him, but increasingly as the relationship develops she finds herself

identifying with him until she admits 'I'm forc'd to love thee now, / 'Cause thou provid'st so carefully for my honour' (V.i.47–8). The ironies dazzle. She has come to understand that their surface difference hides a spiritual sameness.

It is important to notice in Middleton's handling of the relationship of Beatrice and Deflores that Beatrice's character does not 'develop' in the Shakespearean sense, that is, *change* in character (as Macbeth does). Middleton is not in the least interested in individuality as such but in revealing the nature of sinfulness. Beatrice simply comes to recognise what has been true of her from the beginning, that she is 'sold under sin'. Like all Middleton characters she is an emblem of the quality to be illustrated, and to attempt to impose modern ideas of individuality on his drama (ideas that partly stem from Shakespearean practice) is totally to distort his purpose. Beatrice is one doomed to die eternally, one whom God has pre-ordained to damnation, as both she and Deflores come to recognise:

> O come not near me sir; I shall defile you.
> I am that of your blood was taken from you
> For your better health, look no more upon't
> But cast it to the ground regardlessly,
> Let the common sewer take it from distinction.
> Beneath the stars, upon yon meteor
> Ever hung my fate, 'mongst things corruptible . . .

> (V.iii.150–6)

Here the metaphorical meteor (Deflores) reminds us of the actual meteor that signals the fate of the reprobates in the last scene of *Revenger's Tragedy*. Beatrice here recognises that she has been doomed inexorably by her affections (her 'blood') and that her affinities with Deflores were there from the beginning. Deflores himself realises they are both damned eternally: 'now we are left in hell' (l.164). The symbolic function of the action is reinforced by a contrasting sub-plot (the work of the more genial William Rowley) in which Isabella, wife of the mad-house keeper, keeps her virtue among the overtly mad.

An understanding of Middleton's attitude to character obviates much of the critical discussion concerning Bianca in *Women Beware Women*.[20] The apparent change from innocent (and attractive) wife

to vicious courtesan is of little interest to Middleton, who is
concerned once again to illustrate the corruption of the flesh in a
worldly society 'sold under sin'. Like Beatrice, Bianca is doomed
from the beginning by an ineluctable fate—as is made clear in the
brilliant metaphor of the chess game played out between her
mother-in-law and the panderess Livia during Bianca's seduction by
the Duke of Florence (II.ii.). Bianca is a pawn in a game in which all,
however powerful, have their fate dictated from above. The choric
figure of the Cardinal (the Duke's brother) returns to the image of
the chess-board in the last lines of the play to distinguish absolutely
between the black and white kings of the damned and the elect:

> Sin, what thou art, these ruins show too piteously.
> Two Kings on one throne can not sit together,
> But one must needs down, for his title's wrong;
> So where lust reigns, that prince can not reign long.

> (V.ii.222–5)

Mulryne has pointed to the importance of the search for peace of
mind by the characters of the play, especially Bianca,[21] but the irony
of the action is that she is looking in the sinful world for a peace
'which the world cannot give'. In *Women Beware Women* Middleton
reinforces his picture of the fallen world by having the sub-plot
parallel, rather than contrast with, the main action. The Isabella of
Women Beware Women helps to illustrate the total depravity of a
carnal world. It can be no accident that Middleton gets another
playwright to create the virtuous Isabella of *The Changeling*.

So insistent is Middleton on this picture of general depravity that
he is willing to risk the kind of audience alienation more appropriate
to comedy in a series of contrived deaths at the end of the play like
those at the end of *The Revenger's Tragedy*. The wedding masque at
the end of the play described appropriately by Mulryne as 'at once
farcical and horrible'[22] has an impeccable symbolic logic to it—as
Mulryne shows, but it is difficult to reconcile it with the affective
treatment of character of the earlier part of the play. For all their clear
emblematic function Bianca, her husband Leantio, the bawd Livia
especially, are brilliantly realised; realistic characters with whom we
can sympathise. We must not look for psychological depth in these
characters but we can be satisfied with their psychological
semblance. It is only when at the end the puppet-like implications of

their behaviour become apparent through the mechanisms of their disintegration that the audience viewpoint is changed radically and disconcertingly. Middleton's propensity for the absurd finally gets the better of him. Not so in *Changeling* where the focus is more consistently on the two damned souls, Beatrice and Deflores. To the end we can pity them; indeed, part of the power of this extraordinary play is that we cannot ourselves be sure at the end that we are not like them.

7

John Webster

The White Devil's address to the reader asks that the play be judged in terms of the author's fellow dramatists and he lists, presumably in order of preference, the characteristic qualities of their works; Chapman first for his 'full and height'ned style', 'the labor'd and understanding works of Maister Johnson', the 'no less worthy composures' of Beaumont and Fletcher and then together the 'happy and copious industry' of Shakespeare, Dekker and Heywood. The grouping is significant. The address makes a plea for the play as 'labor'd and understanding' and echoes Jonson's themes of the seriousness of the dramatist's calling and the need for an audience who are 'understanders' not mere readers,[1] while the full and heightened style of the play equally proclaims its allegiance (though its effects are very different from Chapman's). Jonson and Chapman, the two learned men of the professional stage, are the model; the professional entertainers, from Beaumont to Heywood, are acknowledged secondarily as successful men of the theatre.

Yet Webster holds a strange position in Jacobean theatre. In all probability he was not a professional playwright, at least in the sense that his collaborators Dekker and Heywood were, for after the first few years as a Henslowe hack he seems to have returned to the family business of coach-building; nor can he seriously be compared with the two great dedicated literary men whose leadership he acknowledges. Certainly he is not a playwright with the vision of heroic greatness that burned in Chapman, nor with the moral crusade which provides the dynamism of Jonson's greatest plays. Webster accepts the moral commonplaces of his age, much as Shakespeare does, as the basis of a drama that is above all theatrical. Yet, again, he is not like Beaumont and Fletcher where the theatricality is the end rather than the means. Commonplace the viewpoint may be, but it is realised at its best with a power, truthfulness and compassion which give Webster's best work a distinctive voice in a theatre of supreme distinction.

Compassion might seem an odd word for a dramatist whose most famous scenes involve pathological cruelty calculated for the maximum theatrical effect, yet the sense of what people suffer, doomed or saved alike, is what gives distinction to Webster's Grand Guignol world of exotic cruelty and surprising turns. There is something contradictory in Webster's combination of mannerist oddity with his feeling of pity for the human lot, but it is a contradiction that smacks of truth. That we are doomed to die and that some of us are doomed to die eternally is the commonplace of the great tragedies, the distinction is in Webster's ability to remind us what this commonplace feels like.

Under the tutelage of Dekker in the early years it is not surprising that Dekker's somewhat sentimental *bonhomie* should colour their collaborations. Webster started in the professional theatre, like so many other aspirants to dramatic greatness, as a journeyman for Philip Henslowe. Only one of these collaborations survive, and that in truncated version, the *Famous History of Sir Thomas Wyatt* of 1602/3. By 1604 Webster (with Dekker again) had moved up-market to the little theatre of the Paul's Boys in a London City comedy called *Westward Ho*. Here already we find the Websterian combination of corrupt intrigue and human sympathy. The play has a Machiavellian Italian, Justiniano, out to demonstrate the frailty of women by spying on his wife, and in a series of counterplots we are involved in the seedy world of the bawd Birdlime whose customers include an earl (seeking the favours of Mrs Justiniano) and the respectable London merchant citizens Honeysuckle, Tenterhook and Wafer. In a complicated series of manoeuvres of which Webster (whose address to the reader prefacing *Devil's Law Case* boasts that the 'grace' of his play lies in the tortuous action) must have felt proud, the citizens' wives take on courtier lovers to disturb their husbands, without any thought of actual depravity. As Mrs Tenterhook explains in a Websterian passage:[2]

> They shall know that Citizens wives have wit enough to strip twenty such gulls: tho we are merry, lets not be mad: be as wanton as new married wives, as fantasticke and light headed to the eye, as fether-makers, but as pure about the heart as if we dwelt amongst em in Black Fryers.   (V.i.159–63)[3]

The irony at the expense of the Puritans in the reference to the feather-traders of Blackfriars (and no doubt also at the expense of the courtier customers at the rival theatre) does not carry over into irony at the expense of the citizens' wives because they do remain pure in heart in a world where corruption is always threatening, but never triumphs. The grotesque and the heartfelt are in characteristic juxtaposition here. Webster shares with his fellow citizen Middleton a sympathy with the humbler and weaker, and the message of the play resides in the triumph of the powerless over the powerful: of citizen over courtier, of women over men. The triumph of Mrs Justiniano over both the libidinous Earl and her suspicious husband, who shares his misogyny[4] with more distinguished Webster reprobates, is not unrelated (though on a different plane of theatrical effectiveness) to the Duchess's hard-won purity of heart in the grotesque world of Amalfi.

A second 'Ho' play, *Northward Ho*, similarly addressed to the Paul's audience, seems both to witness to the success of the first and to be an attempt to cap the rival Blackfriars' *Eastward Ho* produced in 1604/5 by the combined talents of Marston, Jonson and Chapman. Like the earlier *Westward Ho*, but in contrast with the Blackfriars play, which is more than a little equivocal about citizen virtues, *Northward Ho* again demonstrates the superiority of the London citizen over the gallant and the wife over the husband. Mrs Maybery both rejects the advances of the gallants Greenshield and Featherstone and shames her husband's suspicions. The play is more neatly plotted than the earlier collaborative venture, but the certainty of virtue's bourgeois triumph throughout makes the play somewhat anodyne by comparison. A Middletonian sub-plot in which son cheats father unsuccessfully also lacks bite and is interesting mainly because the offended father—the playwright Bellamont—would seem to be a stage portrait of George Chapman.[5] It is a sympathetic portrait, which suggests that the rival companies were cashing-in on each other's successes rather than engaging in academic criticism (as academics have sometimes thought) and implies we should take at face value the compliments to the rival company's plays in the Prologue to *Eastward Ho*. Interesting though it is to have a picture of the great man on the contemporary stage Bellamont is not a particularly interesting comic character, his invariable rectitude adding to the general inoffensiveness of this competent, but routine play. Dekker's spirit is in the ascendant.

Northward Ho, written in 1604/5, would seem to have been the last of Webster's professional plays, for there is now a long gap in his writing for the theatre during which he must have returned to the commercial world to help his father and his brother run the successful coach-building firm in West Smithfield.[6] For we cannot suppose that, however long it took him to write *The White Devil*, he was doing nothing else prior to its production in 1611/12. The laborious nature of the enterprise attested in the address to the reader is amply confirmed by the evidence of painstaking labour in the work itself. A variety of modern scholars, culminating in J. W. Dent's *John Webster's Borrowing* (1970), have shown that Webster's method in his major plays is to borrow heavily from a variety of literary and historical works. Yet it would be a mistake to think of *The White Devil* as of solely literary inspiration. In his ability to make his historical figures come alive Webster more resembles Shakespeare than either Jonson or Chapman. And just as Shakespeare imbues his wholesale borrowings with the conviction of actuality so Webster convinces that his macabre world has a local habitation and a name.

Clearly the seven or so years between *Northward Ho* and *The White Devil* mark a considerable change in Webster's methods and moods, but the difference is not so marked as has been thought. The fact that the tragedy is the first of Webster's unaided plays might well account for the more sombre mood, for even with Dekker's easy benignity the 'Ho' plays are not gay comedies. Both suggest a tawdry, seedy London where swindling and sexual squalor are commonplace—where, for instance, the lubricious Greenshield is delayed from finding his wife in bed with his friend in 'dirty Ware' because 'taking bitter pills, he should prove a loose fellow if he went and so durst not go' (*Northward Ho*, IV.i.244–5). The scatology is Dekker's, but it is not out of place. Webster differs from both Jonson and Middleton—whose depiction of the squalid is every bit as acute—in providing us with unexpected exotic blooms from the dunghill. It is mostly the women who achieve this transformation, Mrs Mayberry sticking firmly to the path of virtue under attack from the fashionable and supicion from her husband in *Northward Ho*, the citizen wives in *Westward Ho*. In *White Devil* the case is more complicated—and interesting—but it is not essentially altered.

The ground base of *The White Devil* is that Jacobean belief in the vanity of the world and of the impending collapse brought on by the weight of man's sinfulness. The metaphysical implications of this, however, that are central to Middleton, are to Webster simply the conditions which govern each individual soul and it is the struggle of the individual within this system that principally concerns him as a dramatist. It has been observed that Webster frequently refers to domestic details in the tragedies. Inga-Stina Ewbank, for instance, points out the prevalence of domestic imagery in *The Duchess of Malfi*,[7] and in *The White Devil* Flamineo in particular is constantly illustrating his cynical philosophy with the minutiae of Jacobean life. This tendency, apparent also in the early comedies, to centre interest in the actual world and treat it for what it is rather than for what it should or might be, however coloured by Webster's metaphysical assumptions, anchors the interest in the people of the plays, not in what they illustrate. Webster's tennis shirts, caged birds in a summer garden, the buttery-hatch thronged at opening time, the shoes that stink of blacking, the mention of kindling flax that perhaps records an actual fire in Webster's London neighbourhood[8] and countless other examples, tell us of a real world of men and women. This world may be merely shadow in the light of eternity, but it seems solid enough while we are here—nor is Webster willing to labour the point that this is so much the worse for us.

Modern criticism of both *The White Devil* and *The Duchess of Malfi* has tended to swing away from the earlier emphasis on the pathos of the plays, with its assumption that Webster's central interest is in character, towards a concern for the metaphysical implications. It is the pathos of the Duchess's death that the first modern critic of Webster, Charles Lamb, emphasises[9] and, more acutely than most subsequent critics, he notes that Vittoria Corrombona almost persuades her judges (and us) that her manifest guilt is innocence.[10] To Leonora Brodwin this appeal of passion to our compassion is so strong that it overrides the guilt: 'despair in all other worldly values produces an amoral devotion to their love which places them beyond good and evil'.[11] Brodwin, like many earlier critics, sees the lovers desperately clinging to a love that temporarily keeps a hostile and meaningless universe at bay. The pathetic reading of the two tragedies fosters its own existential metaphysic, which J. R. Mulryne describes as 'anguished agnosticism'.[12] But more recently critics have seen both plays as examples of the theological pessimism so characteristic of the Jacobeans. M. C. Bradbrook reminds us of this mood, fostered by the contemplation of man's wickedness, in her chapter on *The White Devil* in *John Webster Citizen and Dramatist* (1980).[13] In this light the plays are to be seen not as agnostic complaints but as sermons on God's justice. *The White Devil* is truly diabolic and we are to take seriously the frequent reiterations of diabolic influence that run through both plays. Read in this light—as Joyce Peterson does in *Curs'd Example: the Duchess of Malfi and Commonweal Tragedy* (1978)—the Duchess is not the heroic innocent of earlier readings, but a chip off the same rotting block as her twin brother. Her primary sin is her political irresponsibility in marrying, in defiance of her rank, to gratify her own lusts.

Although the metaphysical assumptions of the two readings are opposed and cannot be reconciled, the response to the plays that they show are complementary. Evidence of the reaction of Webster's contemporaries shows both kinds of response. To Webster's fellow-playwright and Londoner, Thomas Middleton, *The Duchess of Malfi* is most memorable for the pathos of the heroine's dying:

> . . . thy note
> Be ever Plainness, it is the Richest Coat:
> Thy Epitaph only the Title bee,
> Write *Dutchesse*, that will fetch a teare for thee,
> For who e'er saw this *Dutchesse* live, and dye,
> That could get off under a Bleeding Eye?[14]

For Middleton, as shrewd a critic as dramatist, there is no doubting where the impact of the play lies: this is a drama of affectiveness (unlike his own) in which the audience identify with the heroine and weep for her suffering and fall. But Middleton sees no difficulty in combining that response with an orthodox moralistic reading of the tragedy, for he adds (in Latin) a comment on tragedy in general:

> As light at the Thunderer's stroke from darkness springs,
> To the wicked, doom, to the poet, life she brings.[15]

A later contemporary, Abraham Wright, complains of Webster 'in his language he uses a little too much of scripture'.[16] But Middleton and Wright interestingly single out for comment Webster's 'plainness', while another of the writers of commendatory verses to *The Duchess*, John Ford, praises Webster's 'clear pen'. This is hardly in accord with modern estimates of Webster's language, but perhaps rather refers to the plainness of the Christian teaching that they saw in the play.

Certainly for anyone at all acquainted with Jacobean habits of mind it seems particularly unlikely that the respectable London 'Cartwright-playwright', as Henry Fitzjeffery calls him,[17] should publicly espouse agnostic causes and moreover without adverse comment from his contemporaries. There was only one Marlowe

and he died young and in unfortunate circumstances. Fitzjeffery is a
hostile commentator who impugns Webster's style and his
laboriousness, but has nothing to say about unorthodoxy—the fact
that he complains about the crabbed, obscure style, however, gives
more credence to my understanding of Middleton's praise of
Webster's 'plainness'. Webster himself provides interesting
evidence in *The White Devil* to support the orthodox view of tragedy
as a duty to expose vice. Cardinal Monticelso assumes it to be the
duty of the dramatist, as of the preacher, to hold up the sin of such as
Vittoria to castigation on the stage:

> —My Lord *Brachiano*,—
> Alas I make but repetition,
> Of what is ordinary and Ryalto Talke,
> And ballated, and would be plaid a'th stage,
> But that vice many times findes such loud freinds
> That Preachers are charm'd silent.

(III.ii.255–60)

There is no reason to think that Webster's view of the stage's
function would be substantially different from Monticelso's: it had
the same responsibility as the pulpit, to expose vice for what it was
known to be—all the more necessary when vice went gorgeous.

The moral 'voice' of both plays is indeed plain and clear. Vittoria is
a whited sepulchre whose adulterous relationship with Brachiano
leads to the most appalling crimes of murder and cruelty. The
introduction of the lovers in the second scene of the play directs our
judgement unmistakably towards condemnation. Brachiano's
'Quite lost, Flamineo' (I.ii.3) soon comes to be seen as a more
appropriate comment on his eternal soul than on his love-
relationship with Vittoria. That Vittoria is to be no reluctant sinner,
that she too is lost, is established immediately in the comic pruriency
of Flamineo's conversation with Camillo in which Vittoria's refusal
to honour her marital vows are the principal subject. When the
lovers come together they do so in a darkness whose symbolic
overtones are emblemised by the attendance of the bawding black
servant Zanche; in Flamineo's words they are 'let loose at midnight'
(I.ii.189–90). The world of the lovers makes light of dark, darkness
light:

> Loose me not Madam, for if you forego me
> I am lost eternallie . . .

Vittoria is the jewel of great price in a different sense from either of Brachiano's intentions as he plays bawdily with analogies between jewel and genitalia, for the price Brachiano will pay we see in the ugly torments of his death, with its mock liturgy and his vision of the devil 'with a great cod-piece . . . stuck full of pins / With pearls o' th' head of them' (V.iii.99–101). The grotesque comedy of centring happiness on the penis defines the nature and quality of the love relationship. But Webster does not leave the moral significance to symbolic inference in this early scene: in the morality tradition he provides us with angelic comment—both good and bad—as the lovers bury themselves in each other's arms. Both Cornelia, Vittoria's mother, and Flamineo, Vittoria's demonic brother, act as chorus for the scene, Cornelia giving vice its proper name:

> Earth-quakes leave behind
> Where they have tyrannised, iron or lead, or stone,
> But woe to ruine, violent lust leaves none.

> (I.ii.208–10)

Flamineo equally speaks God's truth—for, as Bosola tell us, 'Sometimes the Divell doth preach'[18]—in praising his sister as an 'Excellent Divell'. The very artificiality of this scene with mother and brother intruding into the lovers' intimacy highlights Webster's concern that we should see beyond the affective immediacy to its metaphysical interpretation. Webster is characteristic of his age precisely because the echoes reverberate beyond the theatre. But it is characteristic of Webster that his artifice is given theatrical plausibility as he allows the choric figures to participate in the action of the scene: Cornelia, unable to restrain her feelings of revulsion, steps into the action by openly accusing both Vittoria and the 'adulterous Duke Brachiano' and forcing Flamineo to intervene on the side of the fallen angels. Cornelia's citing of Scripture 'Bee thy act *Judas-like*, betray in kissing' sets the seal on the playwright's directions.

Yet another device within the action points to the interpretative level demanded of the audience in the dream Vittoria recounts to her lover. The dream, in Flamineo's interpretation, suggests to Brachiano the need to eliminate his wife and her husband

I'll seate you above law and above scandal

But the terms of the dream, with ambiguous images of cross-sticks and yew tree,[19] suggest ominously different interpretations in which Camillo and Brachiano's duchess, with pickaxe and rusty spade, insist on exposing the bones of the graveyard to prepare Vittoria for an eternal night, the sight of which terrifies Vittoria and prevents her from praying (I.ii.239–40). Flamineo's comment dwells on the portentous nature of the dream: 'the divell was in your dream'. The precise interpretation of the dream is difficult (as modern scholars have found) but this is Webster's main dramatic point, the ambiguities allow both Brachiano's favourable reading while at the same time ominously suggesting the presence of diabolic forces and predicting the disastrous outcome of the lovers' playing the devil's game.

The conflict between the forces of death and of life already shown in the contrast between the opening scene in which the villainous Ludovico is expelled from Rome for his crimes (described as 'this gentle penance', I.i.36) and the scene we have just explained in which the adulterous lovers turn their thoughts to murder, is contained in the opening of Act II. The contrast has persisted through the wooing scene in the interventions of Cornelia, but in the beginning of Act II the forces of life—already even in the first scene seen to be ominously weak in 'these bad times' (I.i.37)—rally briefly in the interview between Isabella and her brothers with her husband Brachiano. This splendid scene between the proud Brachiano and the wronged wife is not only a superb dramatic clash of opposing powers, it is a classic Christian confrontation between pride and humility—an issue that is to be central to Webster's other great tragedy. Isabella's willingness to forgive her husband ('all my wrongs / Are freely pardoned', II.i.12–13) demonstrates a sacrificial humility in sharp contrast to the proud anger that simmers constantly in Brachiano as he confronts Francisco and the Cardinal. The theme of Brachiano's damnation is again introduced as Francisco replies to Brachiano's flippant (and so blasphemous) reference to his wife's virtue.

FRANCISCO.   would I had given
  Both her white hands to death, bound and lockt fast
  In her last winding sheet, when I gave thee
  But one.
BRACHIANO. Thou hadst given a soule to God then.
FRANCISCO.   True,
  Thy ghostly father with al's absolution,
  Shall ne're do so by thee.

                                  (II.i.66–72)

Francisco is hardly a model of perfection, but as we have seen, this
does not preclude his speaking truth. The encounter between
Isabella's brother and husband is presented as a battle of wills
between two proud men—at one point Francisco claims to
command the thunder, Brachiano likens himself to the lion (l.86).
Again Webster produces a sudden contrast in tone by introducing
the young prince Giovanni, whose military language gives a view of
true heroism in contrast to the display of personal pride we have just
witnessed, and this again leads to a further contrasting passage
between Isabella and Brachiano. Here again the scene is presented
both in moving terms as an encounter between husband and wife,
but also as typological allegory. Isabella's explanation of her arrival
in Rome is expressed as 'Devotion' and Brachiano immediately
suggests a level of meaning that points the audience to its two
contexts:

BRACHIANO.   Devotion?
  Is your soule charg'd with grievous sinne?
ISABELLA. 'Tis burdened with too many; and I thinke
  The oftner that we cast our reckonings up,
  Our sleeps will be the sounder.

                                  (II.i.150–4)

Isabella's humble piety cuts through Brachiano's equivocation and
presents us starkly with the contrast between good and evil that
runs through the dialogue. As Brachiano repudiates his marriage
vows, Isabella asserts her love for her husband in sacramental
terms: 'the sweet union / Of all things blessed' (ll.201–2). The
implications are ominous for the adulterers. Isabella constantly
reiterates her willingness to forgive; her thoughts are in his salvation
(ll.212–16) and in feigning jealousy she is even willing to take on

the burden of his sin to save him the public humiliation of having to give the real reason for the breakdown of the marriage. Isabella's saintly conduct repudiates the view that Webster's view of human nature is unduly harsh. In contrast to the Calvinistic severities of Middleton's tragedies Webster not only shows the force of virtue but demonstrates its eventual triumph.

It would be tedious, however, to plot the details of this abstract patterning—and indeed it would hardly be necessary, such is Webster's 'plainness', had these plays not been so frequently misunderstood by modern readers. The progress of evil in *White Devil* is both predictable and unequivocal. Vittoria's proud defence of her hideous crime in having her husband murdered, which modern commentators have so often praised in terms of courage, in the play's terms is a matching display of proud wilfulness to that already displayed by the fallen Brachiano. The depravity that is a consequence of their fall is nowhere in Jacobean drama more clearly illustrated than in the scene where Vittoria and the black Zanche shoot Flamineo and 'run to him and tred upon him'.[20] Flamineo's death, like the appalling suffering of Brachiano, is a measure of their guilt and depravity, 'so bad a death argues a monstrous life' (*2 Henry VI.* III.iii.30). The art of holy dying was well understood by Webster's audience and the lessons of a tormented deathbed would not have gone unremarked. Let Jeremy Taylor speak for his age:

> He that hath lived a wicked life, if his conscience be alarmed, and that he does not die like a wolf or a tiger, without sense or remorse of all his wildness and his injury, his beastly nature and desert and untilled manners—if he have but sense of what he is going to suffer, or what he may expect to be his portion—then we may imagine the terror of their abused fancies, how they see af-frighting shapes, and, because they fear them, they feel the gripes of devils urging the unwilling souls from the kinder and fast embraces of the body, calling to the grave and hastening to judgement, exhibiting great bills of uncancelled crimes, awaking and amazing the conscience, breaking all their hope in pieces, and making faith useless and terrible, because the malice was great, and the charity was none at all. Then they look for some to have pity on them, but there is no man (St. Chrysostomus). No man dares be their pledge: no man can redeem their soul, which now feels what it never feared. Then the tremblings and the sorrow, the memory of the past sin and the fear of future pains, and the

sense of an angry God, and the presence of some devils, consign him to the eternal company of all the damned and accursed spirits. (Ephraim Syrus).[21]

Dent rightly remarks that in the death scene of Brachiano there is 'no apparent endeavour by the dramatist to excite pity'.[22] Brachiano's mad ravings, centring on money (with its Middletonian sexual overtones[23]) shows a man unable to free himself from dross. We might compare this death with the equally sordid death of Dampit in *Trick to Catch the Old One*, IV.v. There is no appeal to our pity, but to terror and fear; the terrible lesson is spelt out by the murderer as they mock him (just as the Creditors taunt the dying Dampit):

LODOVICO. Devill *Brachiano*,
   Thou art damn'd.
GASPARO. Perpetually.
LODOVICO. A slave condemn'd, and given up to the gallowes
   Is thy great Lord and Master.
GASPARO. True: for thou
   Art given up to the devil.

(V.iii.150–4)

As Dent points out, the scene echoes closely the death scene of the Duke (the 'white devil') in Middleton's *Revenger's Tragedy* from which Webster obtained his title. Like the Duke in *Revenger's Tragedy*, Brachiano is damned.[24] The reference to the 'slave condemn'd' as the devil is odd, but throughout Brachiano's death throes the murderers, dressed as monks, are holding a crucifix before him and it would be characteristic of Webster's use of ambiguity to have the hanging Christ (referred to ironically by Lodovico) become the hanged Judas of Gasparo. In the previous scene (V.ii.12–13) we have been told how Flamineo, the Duke's pimp, as a baby desecrated the crucifix. Dent's observation that the devil is treated mockingly throughout entirely accords with the mocked devil of the morality tradition, whose patterns Webster follows.

The pattern, however, is not Webster's carpet. Webster is concerned primarily with the figures as people. It is the affectiveness of the great scenes: the interview between Isabella and Brachiano, the great trial scene, the deaths of Brachiano and Flamineo, where the dramatic power of the play resides. We are not being asked to sympathise with Vittoria and Brachiano but we are being asked to marvel at them; the *admiratio* (surprise, astonishment) of the Senecan tradition is central to Webster's affectiveness. The drama centres on the strength of the feelings that the characters arouse in us, rather than what they stand for in the scheme of things. In this sense Webster's drama is popular rather than elite and it is not surprising if he wrote the two tragedies for public playhouses (the Rose and the new Globe respectively). It is out of the tension between our response to these characters as people, the horror and pity of their plight, and the exposition of God's justice, that the tragedy is made. It is a tension peculiar to tragedy and helps to explain why Webster is so much more successful in tragedy than comedy. The two sides that Webster's critics tend to have taken in interpreting his tragedies are in fact the two essential angles of his tragic perspective.

The much discussed element of discontinuity in Webster's plays, the inconsequencies of speech and action that are a feature of his work, have led to comparisons with Marston.[25] But unlike Marston's discontinuities Webster's do not function primarily as illustrations of a fallen and incoherent world (though they may have been conceived in these terms) but turn out to be functions of the character realism. The sudden changes of mood and feeling in the tragedies, the sudden transitions of mood in the characters, the plots that go nowhere, like Camillo's appointment as sea commander, the quick comings and goings of characters, the abrupt breaks in thought and image, far from stretching credulity, are remarkably lifelike. Brachiano's oscillations between attempts to collaborate with his brothers-in-law and outbursts of defiance against them (II.i.) brilliantly highlight the confusions in the man's own mind. Characteristically Isabella's sudden change to a pretended jealousy of Vittoria in the same scene is psychologically motivated, these are not arbitrary dislocations—as in Marston—to symbolise a dislocated world. The 'calculated randomness' that A. J. Smith finds most remarkable in the encounter between Lodovico and Flamineo (III.iii.)[26] is certainly not imposed on the character from outside; Lodovico's sudden change of mood from friendliness to hostility when, having been pardoned, he no longer needs to identify with the malcontent outsider, is just what we would expect of the unprincipled Lodovico. Vittoria can denounce her lover's lust (III.ii.209–10) without our feeling she is the less infatuated with him. Again, Monticelso's sudden disenchantment with revenge after he has become Pope (IV.iii.120) is understandably at variance with his earlier demand for revenge on Brachiano and Vittoria (IV.i.14–23). Such inconsistencies are surely the natural expressions of the unprincipled and the erring. The evil deprive themselves of kinship by their evil: Webster is of course asserting a moral commonplace, but he depicts the theological dogma as a personal truth—hence the moving and terrifying end of Flamineo whose inability to trust anyone or anything except death ironically leads him to trust Vittoria to kill herself: 'Wee cease to greive, cease to be fortunes slaves / Nay cease to dye by dying' (V.6.252–3). The mist in which Flamineo dies is the confusion of a soul who has failed to find direction: his sister's image of the ship 'driven I know not whither' applies equally to her brother: they are, alike, lost souls. But it is not the inevitable condition of mankind: Isabella dies reverencing her husband, kneeling 'as to prayers', and her willingness to sacrifice herself for Brachiano has already been remarked. Marcello's death similarly is sacrificial:

> There are some sinnes which heaven doth duly punish
> In a whole family

> (V.ii.22–3)

Marcello, unlike his brother, has kept to the path of virtue, though as poor and disadvantaged as Flamineo. Constancy is not beyond human nature, even if it is not as common as inconstancy in the fallen world. Inconstancy is not (as in Marston's early plays) a condition of being human. Nor is inconstancy neccessarily evil, as, for instance, when the distracted Cornelia drops the knife she is about to use on Flamineo, to say: 'The God of heaven forgive thee' (V.ii.52). It has been remarked that the innocent suffer as much as the guilty in Webster's world and that the unsavoury Medici are left triumphant—but it is hardly consistent with the religion of the crucified Christ to suggest that reward and punishment in this world are measures of virtue and sin. Jacobean playwrights were too familiar with the orthodoxies of Christian belief to be tempted easily by Pelagianism.

Webster uses his inconsistencies consistently to depict characters that are convincing—both good and evil—likenesses of ourselves. It is for this reason we can admire the courage of Vittoria without for a moment questioning the justice of her end. The infatuation of the lovers is understandable, astonishing in its intensity, without our being inclined to condone it.

The Duchess of Malfi follows, in many ways, the pattern of the earlier tragedy. The tragic tension arises from our feeling of compassion and pity for souls who are out of harmony with the divine intention. There is, however, one very important difference. In The White Devil Webster has arranged his characters emblematically between the good and the bad with a Calvinistic suggestion of predestination.[27] The result is a tendency for his humane interest in his characters as people to run counter to the implications of his metaphysical patterning. In The Duchess of Malfi he finds a more dynamic formula in which the central character, the Duchess herself, progresses from darkness to light. Once again the focus is on the individual soul in relation to the divine will, but now we follow the progress of a soul's salvation.

There seems at first sight more reason why the Duchess should capture our sympathies than the criminal Vittoria Corombona. Until recently—again taking its cue from Lamb—criticism has seen the Duchess as an innocent victim of her villainous brothers and the constantly quoted 'I am the Duchess of Malfi still' has repeatedly been seen as an existential triumph of the spirit over cruelty and suffering:[28] 'an affirmation of reason and an assertion of the stoic kingship of the mind, undismayed by tyranny'.[29] More recently the play has been placed in the context of Jacobean religious discussion, notably by D. C. Gunby and Dominic Baker-Smith.[30] Gunby sees the play as an expression of Anglican pessimism while Baker-Smith assumes a Calvinistic reading; both see the Duchess as a virtuous victim of her brothers' wickedness, though Gunby remarks on her 'pride and wilfulness'. To Joyce Peterson, however, The Duchess of Malfi is about political irresponsibility: the Duchess's marriage to Antonio shows a wilful neglect of her political duties as head of state, the Duchess is truly a twin of her brother in exhibiting a similar obsessive wilfulness: 'the play bears out the dangers of unchecked individualism'.[31] The aristocratic status of the Duchess is clearly important to the play—she is referred to only by her title throughout—yet the play does not centre on political events but on the Duchess herself and her relationship to her brothers. There can be no doubt, I think, that Peterson is right to stress the wilfulness of the Duchess, but the emphasis of the play is on the personal, not the public consequences of her dereliction. Webster's protestantism, whatever its colouring, is more interested in the saving, or otherwise, of souls than in the welfare of commonwealths.

M. C. Bradbrook sees the essential fault of the Duchess as her defiance of propriety in her marriage to her servant Antonio.[32] Webster had himself discoursed and eloquently on the difference between virtuous and delinquent widowhood in the two character portraits on widows. The good widow considers 'to change her name . . . to commit a sin', she is a model of chastity whose mind is set upon things not of this world. In contrast the 'ordinary' widow is anxious to remarry, is worldly and unchaste.[33] We can see from the scene in which the Duchess woos Antonio to which type she belongs. Ironically, Antonio has been praising the Duchess's chastity to Delio immediately before:

> but in that looke,
> There speaketh so divine a continence
> As cuts off all lascivious, and vain hope.
>
> (I.i.202–4)

Not only does the hope prove justified but we are soon to see the Duchess indulging in the most pointed bawdy with her steward. The Duchess herself confesses that she has been forced to the indecorum of taking the initiative by her 'violent passions':

> And as a Tyrant so doubles with his words,
> And fearfully equivocates: so we
> Are forc'd to express our violent passions
> In ridles and in dreams, and leave the path
> Of simple vertue, which was never made
> To seeme the thing it is not . . .
>
> (I.i.509–14)

These lines are an apt commentary on the Duchess's own position: her clandestine marriage with Antonio forces them from the 'path of simple virtue'—we have already seen the Duchess lying to her brothers in assuring them, 'I'll never marry' (1.334) and she confesses to her maid-in-waiting that her life and reputation (l. 329) are in her hands, because Cariola knows her secret. The point of this

scene is not only to show that the Duchess is starting out on a sinful
path but that she does so knowingly and willingly:

> wish me good speed
> For I am going into a wildernesse,
> Where I shall find nor path nor friendly clewe
> To be my guide.

(I.i.403–6)

The biblical echoes of this imagery mark this perhaps as one of those
biblical passages disapproved of by Abraham Wright. The Duchess
knowingly embraces a lie which leads to such deceptions as her
pretending to accuse Antonio of fraud to ward off suspicion
(III.ii.211–48). When Cariola expresses her doubts that the
Duchess's profane use of the shrine at Loretto is 'jesting with
religion' we are no longer surprised that the Duchess passes it off by
retorting 'thou art a superstitious fool' (III.ii.367). Antonio is equally
well aware that for him this too is a moment of choice. His is the
traditional role of the reluctant Adam to the tempting Eve:

> There is a saucy and ambitious divell
> Is dancing in this circle.

(ll.471–2)

The sexual connotations of the imagery here make it clear that
Antonio recognises the temptation to be of lust as well as ambition,
though it is the 'great man's madness' of ambition that he recognises
as the more dangerous temptation. The scene abounds in ironic
anticipations of the Duchess's death, for Webster wrote both his
tragedies as much to be read and savoured as to be acted—they are
as bookish as they are theatrical. The lovers' ambitions to find
worldly happiness end, in the 'wild voyce of pratling visitants/
Which make it [ambition] lunatique', literally, in the lunatic ravings
that precede the Duchess's death. The kiss with which the Duchess
seals her clandestine contract with her servant-husband, she
describes aptly· as his 'Quietus' (l.532), whose traditional
associations with death (as in *Hamlet*) had been exploited in
Webster's recent poem on the death of Prince Henry.[34] Most

important of these anticipations is the moment when the Duchess orders Antonio to rise from his knees:

> This goodly roof of yours, is too low built,
> I cannot stand upright in't, nor discourse
> Without I raise it higher . . .
>
> (I.i.479–81)

Perhaps an 'understanding auditory' as well as the understanding reader could be expected to remember this moment when in the Duchess's death scene she finally arrives, on her knees, at the lowly door of humility:

> Yet stay, heaven gates are not so highly arch'd
> As Princes pallaces—they that enter there
> Must go upon their knees.
>
> (IV.ii.239–41)

Antonio succumbs to temptation, which leads him into the pathless wilderness of prevarication where he must 'double with his words and fearfully equivocate'; he must 'seeke shamefull waies, to avoid shame' (II.iii.69). The reward for his weakness is that he becomes a lord of misrule (III.ii.9), the absurd figure (to the Jacobeans) of a husband without authority and so without dignity. Bosola (like the devil) speaks true in commentating on Antonio's refusal to face Ferdinand and the Cardinal:

> This proclaimes your breeding.
> Every small thing drawes a base mind to feare . . .
>
> (III.v.64–5)

Antonio is indeed a grimly comic figure and the grotesqueness of the comedy is highlighted in the rapid succession of children that the hole-in-the-corner relationship produces, children that the Duchess describes as 'born accurs'd' (III.v.137).

　　If we were in any doubt about how we were to view this defiance of Jacobean sexual and social proprieties, Webster provides an element of disinterested comment on the Duchess's behaviour which should surely have guarded modern sentimentality from misunderstanding the play. Antonio himself reports that to the world at large: 'She is a strumpet' (III.i.30), a view of course not just of the 'rabble rout', as Antonio would have it, but of the Duchess's brothers as well. More telling is the comment Webster gives the pilgrims who watch the dumb-show of the Duchess's banishment at the shrine of Loretto (III.iv):

1ST PILGRIM. . . . who would have thought
So great a Lady, would have match'd her selfe
Unto so meane a person? Yet the Cardinall
Beares himself much too cruel . . .
2ND PILGRIM. . . . her brother shew'd
How that the Pope fore-hearing of her loosenesse,
Hath seaz'd into th' protection of the Church
The Dukedome which she held as dowager.

The political implication of the play's action is kept in the background mostly, and the purpose of these comments is largely to place the Duchess's conduct in a wider perspective of moral judgement. The claustrophobic world of the court quickly disorientates and right and wrong become almost inextricably commingled. It is important therefore that here the voice of the people unequivocally reminds us that the Duchess's 'looseness' has demeaned her and the balancing judgement on the Cardinal's cruelty reassures us that in a lunatic world the voice of sanity is speaking.

The picture of court life given in *The Duchess of Malfi* is in some ways even less attractive than that of *The White Devil*, for in the later play there is no Isabella or Cornelia to reassure us of the possibility of human virtue. Antonio's praise of the French court in the first scene of the play may suggest, in Chapman's manner, a contrast between that and the corrupt Italian court, but Antonio's idealism is so quickly swamped by the sinful reality that we may think of his praise as more that of a lost innocence than of an account of a particular society. Similarly the Italian world into which we are plunged seems, even without the generalising comments of Bosola, to be as much a picture of fallen man as of a precise time and place. Bosola's homily on the corruption of the flesh—IV.ii.122f. (like Vindice's meditation on his fiancée's skull in *Revenger's Tragedy*) is only the most obvious intrusion of Christian commonplace in a text where Webster's constant resort to *sententiae*, marked out typographically, also makes of the particular events general *exempla*. The Duchess's 'I account this world a tedious theatre' (IV.i.99), or Antonio's 'Heaven fashion'd us of nothing: and we strive, / To bring our selves to nothing' (III.v.97–8), with its reminiscence of Donne's *Anatomy of the World*,[35] are two striking examples of a tendency to Christian sententiousness that permeates the play.

In this world of exemplary evil the Duchess must find her path to salvation through suffering. She is herself aware of this:

> naught made me ere
> Go right, but Heavens scourge-sticke.

> (III.v.94–5)

To be aware of one's sinfulness, however, is not to avoid sin: 'For I do not the good thing, which I woulde, but the evil, which I wolde not that do I.'[36] The Duchess's growing awareness of her sinfulness, particularly marked in the scene where she says farewell for the last time to Antonio, still has to be translated into a genuine desire to repent. Calvin asserts in the *Institutes* that 'the foundation of our philosophy is humility' (Bk ɪɪ, ch. 2, 11) and it is this humility that the proud and wilful Duchess must learn to acquire. Certainly she has not achieved it in the first scene of her captivity when she curses the stars for her fate (IV.i.115), or when the sin of despair leads her to contemplate suicide with the sacrilegious remark 'The Church enjoynes fasting: / I'll starve myself to death' (IV.i.89–90). Here her defiance and her desire to control her own destiny shows all the old pride and wilfulness that brought her into this wilderness. Even in the last scene her defiance is uppermost until the very end; her response to Bosola's lesson on the vanity of man 'I am the Duchess of Malfi still' shows a failure to accept her fate with humility. It is only when she realises her death is imminent that the significant change occurs:

> I have so much obedience in my blood,
> I wish it in their veines, to do them good . . .

> (IV.ii.168–9)

This is a new note of resignation and acceptance which shows a genuine preparation of her soul for death—in her last moments she finds both the charity and humility without which salvation is impossible. The earlier doubts about the afterlife (IV.ii.20–1) now give way to confident belief:

BOSOLA. Doth not death fright you?
DUCHESS. Who would be afraid on't?
   Knowing to meet such excellent company
   In th' other world.

                                   (ll.215–18)

And to show that this confidence is not misplaced, she enters heaven on her knees and her last thoughts are for the contentment of the brothers who have murdered her. The Duchess's good death is contrasted with the unprepared death of Cariola. In the Duchess's final triumph Webster has again asserted the triumph of the powerless.

But while the religious implications of the play are clear, as with *The White Devil*, the Christian theme is not the centre of dramatic interest. The fact that generations of critics have failed to see the metaphysical patterning clearly is explained by Webster's concern with the theatrical impact of the suffering rather than with the journey's end. Webster's method is to engage his audience fully in the play's experience: we are asked to respond with our emotions before our intellect. Not surprisingly, therefore, the process of the Duchess's suffering rather than its significance has caught the critics' attention. This is most obviously true of the Duchess, whose sufferings Webster is most concerned to depict. Such scenes as that in which she says farewell to her husband and children (III.v.) are principally concerned with engaging our emotions:

DUCHESS. Me thought I wore my Coronet of State,
   And on a sudaine all the Diamonds
   Were chang'd to Pearles.
ANTONIO. My interpretation
   Is, you'll weepe shortly, for to me, the pearles
   Doe signifie your teares.

While we are encouraged to contrast the Duchess's grandeur with her current fall, Antonio, who might have been expected to be reassuring his wife at this point, is given the affective task of capitalising on our emotional involvement. The sadness gives way equally dramatically to fear as Ferdinand's equivocal letter is quoted, summoning Antonio: 'I want his head in a business'.

Webster's preference for immediacy of dramatic impact, for which he employs these rapid changes of mood and action, is even more striking in the depiction of the evil Ferdinand. That the play is equally about the damnation of Ferdinand and the Cardinal as of the salvation of the Duchess accounts for the last act, in which we witness the terrible sufferings of Ferdinand in his madness. For a modern audience Ferdinand, with his obsessive concern for his sister's sexual purity, is almost a sympathetic figure because his self-torment and final madness suggest he is as much a victim as an inflicter of suffering. One of the most interesting things about Ferdinand, and about Webster's play, is that once we appreciate the Duchess's behaviour for what it is, he is right to be suspicious. Ferdinand, like the avenger-villain of *Revenger's Tragedy*, Vindice, has right on his side in his concern with the family honour and responsibilities:

> CARDINAL. You may flatter your selfe,
>   And take your owne choice: privately be married
>   Under the Eaves of night . . .
> FERDINAND. Think't the best voyage
>   That ere you made; like the irregular crab,
>   Which though't goes backward, thinkes that it goes right,
>   Because it goes its owne way: but observe;
>   Such weddings, may more properly be said
>   To be executed, than celibrated.

> (I.i.351–9)

The brothers are right to warn the Duchess of the consequences of her wilfulness, but the rectitude, especially in Ferdinand's case, is undercut by the macabre nature of the imagery of the crab scuttling and the complex associations of 'executed' which suggests both a dehumanisation and a fatal outcome. Ferdinand follows this with a speech even more macabre, in which he produces his father's dagger to threaten her: 'I'll'd be loth to see't looke rusty, 'cause 'twas his': both the imagery of blood as rust, the perverse reason for sparing the dagger and the following picture of vizors and masks as 'whispering rooms' again suggest dehumanisation. Ferdinand's sudden switch too to sexual innuendo in which the penis is likened to a lamprey gives the whole speech a suggestion of perverted inhumanity that inverts the moral standing of the correspondents. At this stage of the play we do not know what right the brothers have to be suspicious, but it soon becomes clear that their accusations are not totally unfounded. *The Duchess of Malfi* abounds in examples of the Devil preaching—both Ferdinand and the Cardinal are right to be concerned about their sister's wayward behaviour, but for the wrong reasons. Both are obsessed with the nobility of their blood, as wilful a vanity (for Webster's London citizenry) as their sister's pursuit of private happiness. But what most appears in the portrait of Ferdinand (unlike his brother) is a picture of a soul in torment unable to free himself from the weight of sin or prevent his own damnation:

> Oh most imperfect light of humaine reason,
> That mak'st us so unhappy, to foresee
> What we can least prevent.

(III.ii.90–2)

We can afford to pass over Webster's three later plays, *The Devil's Law-Case*, *Appius and Virginia* and *A Cure for a Cuckold* more cursorily, remarking in passing a lost tragedy on the Chapmanesque subject of *Guise* mentioned after *The Duchess of Malfi* in the dedication of *The Devil's Law Case*. Perhaps the play on a subject that Chapman had covered in the Bussy plays was in the later Chapman manner, for we find the austere neo-classical style of Chapman's later tragedies employed for Webster's last tragic effort, *Appius and Virginia*. The austerity of the writing cuts off Webster from his chief source of interest, the power to convey intense and complex feeling through action and metaphor. The passionate eloquence of the two great tragedies, here becomes dead rhetoric. In the central scene of the play, for instance, a trial scene in which Appius tries to get possession of the virtuous Virginia as a bondswoman to gratify his lust, Virginia pleads with her father to kill her rather than deliver her up to Appius (a request to which her father eventually accedes):

O my dear Lord and father, once you gave me
A noble freedom, do not see it lost
Without a forfeit; take the life you gave me
And sacrifice it rather to the gods
Than to a villains lust. Happy the Wretch
Who born in bondage lives and dies a slave,
And sees no lustful projects bent upon her,
And neither knowes the life nor death of honour.

(IV.i.31–8)

There is no special interest in Virginia as a character here, the language has been washed bare of the psychological quirkiness of the great tragedies and she has no special individuality, she remains a type of virtuous integrity (of a Roman kind) confronted by stereotypes of villainy. Nor has Webster the intellectual fire of a Chapman to give mythic status to the opposed forces. He has forsaken his best affective talents for a drama of typological posturing. Muriel Bradbrook suggests possible political overtones in the telling of the story,[38] but if that is so, it was the politics that gave what life the play had; the play fails to rouse interest in the politics.

Of the two remaining plays, *The Devil's Law Case* is the more interesting. It is partly a return to the intrigue comedy of the early years, but charged with a seriousness that relates it both to the 'problem' comedies of Shakespeare and Middleton and to the mythic comedies of Chapman. The address to the 'Juditious Reader' claims that the merit of the play resides in the action, and, as in the early comedies, Webster is so greatly concerned with the unexpected twists and turns of the plot that they almost become an end in themselves. In the tragedies the tortuous actions, like the tortuous language, are a suitable vehicle for the torments of the spirit which we share with the characters. In *The Devil's Law Case* and *A Cure for a Cuckold* some element of this survives, enough to make the central characters of some interest, but the final impression is that the characters were made for the plot rather than the plot for the characters. Webster thereby surrenders his trump card. Yet it would be wrong to dismiss *The Devil's Law Case* as a mere indulgence in theatrical effects; the moral seriousness which provides the measure of the tragic characters' suffering, here assumes prominence for its own sake. The title rightly suggests the metaphysical interest of the play.

It seems likely that *The Devil's Law Case* was written for the coterie audience of Inigo Jones's new Cockpit Theatre in Drury Lane (where *Appius and Virginia* was also performed). Webster's two major tragedies had been written for public theatres, though the title page of *The Duchess* suggests it was designed for both the Globe and Blackfriars. In returning to the 'private' theatre Webster abandons the affective mode of the tragedies for theatrical virtuosity, but he was too much the bourgeois playwright-cartwright to be satisfied with theatricality for its own sake. The play abounds in surprising turns, the climax of which is reached when the unpleasant hero, Romelio, disguised as a Jew, goes to murder his sister's suitor Contarino but succeeds, in stabbing him, only in lancing an abscess and so inadvertently saves his life. The significance of this unexpected outcome is immediately made clear. Two surgeons catch the 'Jew' in the act of would-be murder and when he reveals his true identity tell him:

> Had you forborne this act, he had not liv'd
> This two hours.

> (III.ii.135–6)

The irony of this is partly lost on Romelio, who needs a revenge killing, not an accidental death, to satisfy him. The perversity of human nature (illustrated to overflowing throughout the play) is however constantly thwarted:

> The hand of heaven is in't,
> That his entent to kill him should become
> The very direct way to save his life.

> (III.ii.170–2)

This is the theme around which the surprising and unlikely events of the play revolve. The mercurial and irresponsible nature of human behaviour is constantly juxtaposed to a consistent Providence, which benevolently sees our desires are thwarted.

Contarino has in Ercole a rival suitor for the hand of Jolenta, Romelio's sister. The two suitors fight and apparently kill one another, though with unsurprising surprise we later discover that neither is in fact dead. This is, however, not before Webster has reinforced his moral, through the voice of Romelio's friend Prospero, that while God protects, man does his best to send himself to hell:

> Come, you doe ill to set the name of valour
> Upon a violent and mad despaire.
> Hence may all learne, that count such actions well,
> The roots of fury shoot themselves to hell.

(II.ii.50–3)

Romelio, who is a rich merchant, learns that his fleet has suffered substantial losses at sea and the lawyer Ariosto chides him on his presumption in calling the ships 'The Storms Defiance', 'The Scourge of the Sea' and 'The Great Leviathan' as 'very devilish names' (II.iii.65). The metaphysics of the play are nothing if not explicit. But Romelio (being human) is unmoved by these other-worldly considerations, which he describes as 'superstitious' (helping to throw light on that other figure of human presumption, the Duchess, when she rebukes her husband in similar terms[40]). We find Romelio entering into a complex intrigue with his sister in which she is to produce a child to father on to the pseudo-Ercole— the idea being to claim his fortune as well as the money Contarino has left to her in his will. As—to crown the picture of human fecklessness—Romelio has conveniently got a nun (no less) with child, a suitable bastard is shortly to be had (but not before in further twists and turns Jolenta has confessed and then unconfessed that she is and is not pregnant). All this intrigue, of course, is as futile and mistaken as *The White Devil*'s plot to send Camillo to the wars— Webster is consistent about human inconsequentiality.

Romelio's cynical response to the 'deaths' of the two suitors is highlighted when Bellman and Monk lament that the two noblemen cannot be given a Christian burial as they died in duelling. Romelio mocks the importance of Christian ceremony (in jingling octosyllabics):

> How then can any Monument say,
> Here rest these bones, till the last day,
> When time swift both of foot and feather,
> May beare them the Sexton kens not whither?
> What care I then, tho my last sleepe,
> Be in the Desart, or in the deepe . . .?

> (II.iii.137–42)

Romelio is of course wrong, and his wrongheadedness is incurable—being human. For all his losses Romelio remains as arrogant as ever:

> the more spatious that the Tennis court is,
> The more large is the Hazard.
> I dare the spitefull Fortune do her worst,
> I can now feare nothing.

> (II.iii.149–52)

the tennis court of chance (an image of chaos to the villainous Bosola) provides Romelio (and us) with a false perspective as he is immediately reminded by the Capuchin friar:

> Oh sir, yet consider,
> He that is without feare, is without hope,
> And sins from presumption: better thoughts attend you.

> (ll.153–5)

Providence treats us better than we deserve—else who should 'scape whipping?—and Romelio is no better at the end of the play than at the beginning, though it is not for want of instruction.

Before we reach the end we divagate via a trial scene in which Romelio's mother attempts to proclaim him a bastard and a second duel in which Romelio is to fight the revived Ercole. Ercole's name, incidentally, suggests that his role may be intended to be analogous to one of Chapman's Herculean figures. His rising from the dead in order to usher Contarino back to life would fit the part and he is instrumental in bringing Romelio to as near a sense of responsibility as he is ever likely to attain. That the role lacks the status that

Chapman gives his Herculean figures is a measure of the difference between the abilities of these two playwrights in this kind of play. Romelio's unrepentant nature is amply illustrated again in the penultimate scene of the play when he refuses to pray, as the Friar urges, before the duel:

FRIAR.   O, I tremble for you:
   For I doe know you have a storme within you,
   More terrible than a Sea-fight, and your soule
   Being heretofore drown'd in securitie,
   You know not how to live, nor how to dye . . .

                               (V.iv.121–5)

Wanting to be rid of the Friar and of his mother, Romelio changes tack and momentarily pretends to repentance as a ruse to enable him to lock them both up. In the locked room the Friar reveals to Leonora that Contarino is still living and that Romelio (accused of his murder by Ercole) need not fight the duel—though now, ironically, they cannot communicate the fact to him. He is to be (almost) hoist with his own petard. The lesson is again explicit:

FRIAR.   Oh looke upwards rather,
   Their deliverance must come thence: to see how heaven
   Can invert mans firmest purpose! his intent
   Of murthering Contarino, was a meane
   To work his safety, and my comming hither
   To save him, is his ruine: wretches turne
   The tide of their good fortune, and being drencht
   In some presumptuous and hidden sinnes,
   While they aspire to doe themselves most right,
   The devil that rules ith ayre, hangs in their light.

                               (V.iv.213–22)

Fashionable paradox and Christian doctrine are happily brought together. The Friar (being human) is of course wrong: he and Leonora appear, unexplained, to prevent the continuance of the duel, Jolenta appears, disguised as a blackamoor to discourse on the difference between appearance and reality and Ariosto distributes

justice by making Romelio agree to marry his nun and the various
participants pay reparations:

> That these so Comicall events be blasted
> With no severitie of sentence . . .

> (V.v.69–70)

Jolenta's gnomic, octosyllabic speech on the falsity of appearance
restates the play's theme of the difference between man's seeming
and God's being:

> Never mind the outward skin,
> But the Jewell that's within.

> (V.v.47–8)

In the tragedies the souls of the damned come to learn with
Flamineo too late that 'While we look up to heaven we confound /
Knowledge with knowledge', or with Bosola 'In what a shadow or
deep pit of darkness / Doth . . . mankind live'. In the comedy the
shadow is lifted so that knowledge can be revealed.

The sheer absurdity of the plot may suggest that Webster is, if
anything, supporting the cynicism of Romelio: but this would be to
mistake the tone of the play. *The Devil's Law Case* is an exercise in
mythic comedy, though it lacks the philosophical depths of
Chapman's exercises in the mode or the Shakespearean lyricism of
the mythic late romances. It is interesting that two themes of central
interest to Webster, the relation of merchant and courtier and of
men to women (the sub-title of the play is 'When women goe to Law
the Devill is full of Businesse, a new Tragecomoedy'), both figure
prominently, but are both subsumed in the overriding issue of
man's foolishness in the sight of God, and hence the farcical nature
of the action. The play shares its metaphysics with the great
tragedies, but now the message has become the *raison d'être* of the
play.

Webster's last play (seemingly) was the 'pleasant comedy' of *A
Cure for a Cuckold*, dating probably from 1624, perhaps for the Red
Bull.[41] Like *The Devil's Law Case* it abounds in surprising and
disconcerting changes of directions, which in this case put a
considerable strain on our belief in the characters who effect them.

The motto of the 1661 title page is 'Placere Cupio' ('I desire to please') and the seriousness of *The Devil's Law Case* and *Appius and Virginia* here give way to lighter entertainment, albeit of a sophisticated and complex kind. For this purpose Webster could not have chosen an apter partner than the competent and humane William Rowley who (if we accept Lucas's divisions of responsibilities[42]) seems to have been principally responsible for the Rochfield and Compass episodes in the plotting, leaving Webster responsible for the principal action, that concerning the friends Bonville and Lessingham, Bonville's wife Annabel and the mercurial Clare.

As Jacqueline Pearson has shown, in her excellent account of the play,[43] the sharing of responsibilities has not led to a loosely constructed play. Webster—following the manner of *The Devil's Law Case*—indulges us in constant surprises while Rowley steers a reassuringly humane course with his aptly named Compass. The play takes its title from the Rowley plot in which Captain Compass, arriving home from a long sea voyage ('new born indeed') discovers that his wife Urse has given birth to a child by another man. Instead of the expected repudiation (Rowley also being capable of surprising turns) Compass argues that he, not the natural father, should have the custody of the child and when he wins his case, he and his wife divorce and remarry so that he is saved from the stigma of cuckoldry. The steady and cheerful humanity of Compass provides a foil—and ultimately a direction (a 'compass') for the tortuous conduct of the characters of the main plot. Webster's characters (in contrast) are creatures who proceed crabwise, 'Which though't goes backward, thinks that it goes right'. Webster's plot, as Pearson argues, centres on the solving of a riddle delivered by Clare to her lover, Lessingham. She requires him to kill 'that Friend that loves thee dearest'. Lessingham assumes this means he must kill his best friend Bonville, but he is unsure whether he will win Clare's love by obeying her command. Lessingham tricks Bonville into travelling to Calais Sands with him on the pretence that he wishes Bonville to act as his second in a duel. On arriving at Calais he reveals that he must fight him on Clare's instruction. Bonville offers his life, but says 'all friendship dyes between us' (II.i.136). Lessingham cannot bring himself to take Bonville's life and they return, separately, to England.

Further surprises await us in England. Clare, thinking Bonville is dead, maintains her intentions have been misunderstood. She was seeking her own death, not Bonville's, because she had fallen hopelessly in love with him. Now he is dead she will marry Lessingham, but Lessingham, trying to outdo his erstwhile girlfriend in improbability, refuses (with a general statement on the unreliability of womanhood). Bonville returns, Clare confesses her love to him and receives another rebuff. Now Lessingham attempts to disrupt Bonville's marriage with Annabel. The play had started (unorthodoxly enough) with their wedding, which remained unconsummated because of Bonville's voyage to Calais. Lessingham's threat, however, is removed and the harmony of both couples is finally asserted. The play ends with Compass's reappearance to set the seal on the triumph of sanity and good nature.

Pearson argues ingeniously that the play presents us with a pattern of contrasts between comic sanity and tragic madness, but there is an uncomfortable sense in which the two plottings fail to engage at the same levels. Rowley's plots are primarily about characters—amusing people who have the illusion of reality about them—whereas Webster's characters have appearance but no substance. By comparison with Rowley's creations Webster's characters are wraith-like and incredible; conversely Rowley's characters simply do not fit into Webster's mannered and distorted world of appearances. In using dramatic techniques that depend for their ultimate meaning on a metaphysical world that is no longer adumbrated, Webster falls foul of that mere theatricality that he had so responsibly disciplined in his major works for purposes that transcended the theatre. In this play Webster finally succumbs to the enervating triumph of theatrical art over life. In his last comedy and his last tragedy it is as if those elements of theatricality and moral seriousness that had been in successful tension in his major plays have got separated out in different directions.

8

John Fletcher and his Collaborations

THE BEAUMONT PERIOD: 1606–13

Any attempt at a judicious appraisal of John Fletcher's contribution to Jacobean theatre bristles with difficulties. The sheer number of plays, whether of his own composition or whose composition he shared in, itself presents the critic with a daunting task of assessment. Over fifty plays still extant stand to his credit, either wholly or in part, dating from around 1606—the probable year of his collaboration with Beaumont in *The Woman Hater*—to his death (of the plague) in August 1625. Of these fifty-odd plays fifteen can be confidently ascribed to Fletcher unaided,[1] which means that for the greater part of his work the effects of his collaboration with colleagues, who included Beaumont, Shakespeare and Massinger, must be taken into account. This is not just a matter of distinguishing those parts of any collaboration that are Fletcher's from those of his colleagues (a task more or less satisfactorily accomplished by modern scholarship) but, more importantly, of assessing the effect of the collaboration itself on the dramatic texture. A yet further and more elusive problem lurks: Fletcher's impact on the Jacobean stage was that of an innovator. He and his closest colleague, Beaumont, set new fashions in the contemporary theatre and this provides the critic with a temptation both to overestimate the intrinsic value of the plays because of their historical importance and also to underestimate them by judging them too readily by the standards of the other Jacobean playwrights to whom Fletcher was reacting.

The sense of the originality of Fletcher's contribution to the Jacobean theatre—and that of his partner, Francis Beaumont, in the early years of Fletcher's career—is not easy to recapture, partly because, in some ways, their work, with its Sidneyan affinities, seems to be harking back to Elizabethan modes; partly because, from the vantage point of historical hindsight, their work seems like a half-way house to the more thorough-going neo-classical theatre of Dryden. Yet it is vital to assess their originality in order to prevent us judging their work inappropriately by the standards of what had gone before. This originality consists of freeing Jacobean theatre from religious and moral doctrines that are at once the guarantee of the high seriousness that made of the player Shakespeare a man of all seasons, and a restriction of theatrical vision. Shakespeare alone could sometimes transcend these limits in such extraordinary leaps of the imagination as we see in *Lear*, in *Coriolanus* and in *Antony and Cleopatra*. It is not that Beaumont and Fletcher's plays cease to reflect the simple Manichean divisions of popular Christianity, but that these moral considerations become subsumed in a more important aesthetic patterning. In Fletcher, at least in his best collaborations with Beaumont, beauty takes precedence over truth, or perhaps we should say that truth becomes admired primarily for its beauty— hence the characteristic preference of tragi-comedy, 'in respect it wants deaths',[2] over tragedy. For the moralist critic this change in emphasis looks like a betrayal, and has earned the playwrights the accusation of decadence, but this is simply to apply the wrong judgements, as misplaced as insisting on social relevance from classical ballet. Ironically, one of the consequences of this concern with the aesthetic is a markedly greater concern with propriety on the stage both in language and in the presentation of incident. The writers of the commendatory verses to the old folio editions were right to claim that Fletcher refined the stage. The change in tone that results, from the crabbed satiric realism of Marston, Middleton and Jonson to the purer air of heroic or Arcadian idealism is as remarkable as the determinedly secular insistence.

In Jacobean terms we can say—using the distinction J. V. Cunningham has so brilliantly examined[3]—that Beaumont and Fletcher's plays place primary emphasis on 'wonder' (*admiratio*) over the Shakespearean tendency to prefer 'woe' (*commiseratio*). As Cunningham explains it 'wonder' surprises us and is a source of knowledge and involves an element of distancing from the audience, an emphasis on the difference between the world of the play and the world of the audience, whereas 'woe' involves emotional identification: 'Such noble senses as draw the eye to flow' as Fletcher describes it in his prologue to the Shakespearean drama of *Henry VIII*.[4] Fletcher's own drama, while it frequently depicts strong emotions, does so at one remove from the audience, asking us to savour it with some philosophical, at times even ironical, detachment.

The earliest years of Fletcher's work for the theatre are dominated overwhelmingly by his collaboration with Francis Beaumont. Only one play, *The Faithful Shepherdess*, can be ascribed to Fletcher alone in the period 1606 to 1613 (the year in which Beaumont retired from theatrical work), while he collaborated in ten or eleven plays over these years with Beaumont. His initial impact on Jacobean theatre is therefore not only very much as a collaborator, but also in a collaboration where he tends to play a secondary role. The first collaboration, for instance, where seemingly both men made their debuts as playwrights, *The Woman Hater* (1606), was according to Professor Hoy a Beaumont play revised by Fletcher. Hoy estimates that Fletcher's contribution consists of two scenes in Act V (ii and iv) and two scenes substantially revised by Fletcher (III.i. and IV.ii.); the rest of the play is substantially Beaumont's.[5] The nature of their collaboration, however, differs from the usual Jacobean patterns in showing more thorough integration. Whereas in other collaborative efforts plots are assigned principally to one or other of the partners, Beaumont and Fletcher, as here, are willing to take shares in the same plot sequences, often involving them in collective work in creating the characters. This intimacy presumably reflects the intimacy of their personal relationship, described by Aubrey in his *Brief Lives*:

> They lived together on the Banke side, not far from the Play-house, both batchelors; lay together; had one Wench in the same house between them, which they did so admire; the same cloathes and cloake, etc between them.[6]

Sharing a bed with a friend (or often with strangers at an inn) was accepted practice in those days when space and bed-linen were costly, but there is more than a little in Fletcher's writing (especially) that suggests a homosexual's view of things.

The Woman Hater is not in itself a particularly original play. It is intrigue comedy with a certain amount of 'humours' comedy centred on the two eccentrics of the play, Lazarillo the gourmand, who will do anything (including marrying a whore) for a good meal, and Gondarino the woman-hater of the title. The 'humours', however, are not satiric portraits in the Jonsonian manner. There is no serious suggestion that either eccentric is morally reprehensible, even though Gondarino is punished for his treatment of the heroine Oriana by being subjected to some female petting—to his comic disgust. Gondarino is primarily Fletcher's creation and Gondarino's dislike of women is revealed in more depth and detail than is needed by his mere comic function. In Fletcher's first scene (III.i.) for instance, Oriana, finding herself accidentally at Gondarino's house, teases him into an outburst of misogynistic fury by pretending she likes him. The scene opens with Gondarino 'flying the Lady' and complaining of 'insatiate' woman, asking:

> Tell why thou followest me? I feare thee
> As I feare the place thou camst from: Hell.

$$(III.i.30-1)^7$$

Beaumont gives a rational explanation of this dislike earlier in the play when we are told Gondarino's marital experience has been unfortunate (II.i.16–17), but Fletcher prefers a psychotic explanation. In the later scene Oriana's effect on Gondarino is extraordinary; he reverts to baby-talk: 'Hearesta, and tha wants lodging, take my house . . . Shat have a Doctor too thou shatt . . .', and expresses the fear that if Oriana gets half a chance she will reduce him to abject dependency:

> To ha' my hare curl'd, by an idle finger,
> My cheekes turnd Tabers and be plaid upon,
> Mine eyes lookt babies in, and my nose blowd to
>   my hand . . .

$$(III.i.97-9)$$

Not surprisingly the play makes no attempt to cure Gondarino of his obsessive fears of women. At the end of the play, in another Fletcherian scene, he is incensed by being stroked and fondled by two women as his punishment for his treatment of Oriana, but is finally let off with a warning (which he gladly accepts) never to look on women again. The Gondarino scenes are more uncomfortable for the audience than entertaining.

This is clearly not satire, for there is no thought (or prospect) of cure. The purpose of the play, as the Prologue proclaims, is to 'make you laugh'; there is no malice and no attempt at the usual satire of 'Lordes, Courtiers and Citizens'. There is, in fact, some jesting at the expense of the citizen in the plot in which a mercer is deceived by his respect for learning into marrying a whore, but the generally benign tone of the laughter is both characteristic of the playwrights and suitable for the mixed class audience of Paul's, where it was one of the last plays to be put on before the theatre's closure in July 1606 (one notes, however, that the address of the Prologue is to 'Gentlemen' only). There is also some incidental satire on informers in the play, but in general the play reflects that concern with theatre as entertainment that is to be the hallmark of both dramatists throughout their careers.

Although there is not very much that is distinguished about this first venture of the two playwrights, there are (as we can see with hindsight) a number of pointers to the direction their work is to take. The comedy (as the Prologue tells us) is of a mixed kind ('I dare not call it Comedie, or Tragedie') that promiscuously mingles Dukes and dupes, prostitutes and courtly ladies, courtiers and citizens, comedy with a threat of tragedy; the comedy is to be polite ('If there be any amongst you that come to heare lascivious scenes, let them depart') and its setting in Italy without much more significance than if it were the coast of Bohemia. There is also a marked theatricality that is inward-looking (asking the audience to enjoy the dramatic artifice) expressed both in a fondness for linguistic parody—as for instance in the scene where Lazarillo is persuaded that he must address the Duke in absurdly circumlocutory courtly speech (II.i.236ff.—Beaumont) or when Lazarillo laments the loss of a fish-head in high astounding terms (III.ii.60ff.—Fletcher)—and in the depiction of character. It is to become a particular quality of Beaumont and Fletcher's work that character consistency is subordinated to theatrical impact. In this play we find this tendency not only in such scenes as that where Gondarino first rejects Oriana and then madly decides to head off the Duke's growing infatuation for the lady by pretending to be in love with her himself, while Oriana makes a complementary turn-around from liking to disliking (III.i.); there is also the sudden 'tragic' moment when Oriana is told that the Duke has condemned her to death; and the dramatic contrast of the chaste (but also wilful) Oriana locked up in a brothel. This delight in unexpected and often sudden contrasts is not sufficiently prominent here to prevent the play as a whole from seeming not so very different from the spate of City comedies that held the stage at that moment, but there is enough of these off-beat qualities to remind us of what was to come in future collaborations.

According to Dryden, none of the plays of these two dramatists, either written singly or in collaboration, was much of a success with its audiences before the tragi-comedy *Philaster* (1609).[8] If, as seems likely, *Cupid's Revenge* (c.1606)[9] was their next collaboration, then we need not be surprised that it failed to amuse its Blackfriars' audience. It does however mark a further step in the direction of the romantic theatricality characteristic of them. Here all interest in the psychology of the characters is completely undercut by their being puppets in the hands of a vengeful God (Cupid) whose rites the hero and heroine, Leucippus and Hidaspes try to suppress as superstitious. The relationship of hero to heroine unusually is the asexual one of brother and sister, a relationship that Beaumont exploits very differently in *A King and No King*. The most interesting thing about the play is what Beaumont and Fletcher do not do with this mythic material—in the hands of Chapman, or Shakespeare in his final phase, the story would have been exploited as myth, a foreshadowing of a world of psychic forces which humanity must learn to come to terms with. The material cries out to be allegorised as a whip for the puritanical, but the two playwrights turn their back on this and exploit the story more whimsically. We have, indeed, the opposite process at work from the late Shakespearean, where the secular material is mythologised. In Beaumont and Fletcher (and this is generally true of them) the myth becomes secularised, converted into terms of human emotion. The emotion, however, is characteristically kept at one remove from the audience, for it is impossible to take much interest in the emotions of characters who are so obviously puppets in the hands of an omnipotent deity.

About the time the two playwrights were collaborating in *Cupid's Revenge* they were each engaged with a production of an unaided play. Beaumont with the parodic *Knight of the Burning Pestle* and Fletcher with his pastoral play *The Faithful Shepherdess*. Both plays were performed by the Queen's Revels Children at Blackfriars and neither, apparently, was well received by its audience. Both plays give interesting insights into the essential nature of their dramatists' art.

However unlike the two plays are in terms of their genre, they reveal a similar attitude to theatre. Both are above all theatrical, exploiting theatrical artifice as a pleasure in its own right. Of course earlier dramatists had done this, notably Shakespeare in comedies like *Love's Labour's Lost* and *A Midsummer Night's Dream*, indeed the relishing of theatrical artifice is a feature of most of Shakespeare's work. But in Shakespeare the consciousness of theatre *in* the theatre always acts as a metaphor for something wider, for a disposition of mind through which we reaccommodate ourselves to the great world outside. Beaumont and Fletcher are the first of our dramatists to be more interested in the theatre than the world outside it; theatrical effectiveness is their primary purpose, not a means to some further end. With these two the play's the thing; for the first time its primary role is as aesthetic artifact.

This is just as true of the mildly satirical *Knight of the Burning Pestle* as of the more obviously ethereal world of the *Faithful Shepherdess*. In Beaumont's play, certainly, interests are aroused in the London of the Blackfriars' audience. The play continues that series of jocular parryings between citizen and courtier that we see in, for instance, the 'Ho' plays of Dekker and Webster, and Jonson, Chapman and Marston, and in some of Middleton's comedies. Beaumont's play, however, differs from these by making the subject of the parryings the drama itself. It is first and foremost a play about plays; for the first time we have a whole play (as opposed to plays-within-plays) that is primarily concerned to talk about itself. The intrusions of the Citizen and his wife and their apprentice Rafe on the stage is less the intrusion of London life into the theatre than the absorption of reality into the artificial world of the stage; here the audience literally gets absorbed in the fictional world.

As the irresponsible Wife organises on stage the action of the plot in which Rafe is to play his heroic part she not only reminds the audience of the fictional and collaborative nature of the whole theatrical enterprise and herself becomes the principal fictional character, but also reminds us of the fictional nature of the more orthodox plotting of the story of the two apprentices Jasper and Humphrey (itself a parodic echo of the apprentices' plot in *Eastward Ho*). If there is any satire here of the naivety of the Citizens' view of the theatre it is surely overborne by the implication that the audience is itself engaged in the demonstration that fiction has a reality of its own. The Citizen's response to Rafe's heroic death speech: 'Tis a pretty fiction i' faith' (V.313.),[10] is one that he shares with his sophisticated audience, though the values would no doubt differ. It is partly on the strength of this play that the plays of Beaumont and Fletcher have been dubbed 'Theatre-craft for the Gentry',[11] on the assumption that Beaumont is entertaining his elite audience at the expense of the citizenry. If Beaumont intended to flatter his audience in this way he failed, for—as the Q1 printer

(1613) tells us—the play was 'utterly rejected' by the public 'for
want of judgement, or not understanding the privy marke of *Ironie*
about it'.[12] There is nothing 'privy' about the irony at the citizens'
expense in the play and Burne was therefore presumably referring
to the more complex irony of the interplay of fiction and reality that
would have been a novelty to its Jacobean audience and which they
clearly failed to appreciate at first view. Beaumont and Fletcher's
reputation as 'elite' dramatists has unjustifiably coloured later
critical judgement, which overlooks the facts that Fletcher was the
principal playwright of the Globe as well as Blackfriars for a
generation and their three most successful collaborations were
Globe plays as well as Blackfriars' plays.[13] In fact, Beaumont's
treatment of the citizens in *Knight of the Burning Pestle* is more
affectionate than satirical, as is well illustrated by the play's
epilogue:

> CITIZEN. Come Nel, shall we go, the Plaies done.
> WIFE. Nay by my faith *George*, I have more manners then so, I'le
>   speake to these Gentlemen first: I thanke you all Gentlemen, for
>   your patience and countenance to Ralph, a poor fatherless
>   child, and if I might see you at my house, it should go hard, but I
>   would have a pottle of wine and a pipe of Tabacco for you, for
>   truely I hope you do like the Youth, but I would be glad to know
>   the truth: I referre it to your owne discretions, whether you will
>   applaud him or no, for I will winke, and whilst you shall do
>   what you will, I thanke you with all my heart, God give you
>   good night . . .

In all essentials the Citizen's wife shows here that she is shrewd
enough to know the difference between fiction and reality.
Beaumont, as the son of a country squire, has a great deal of fellow
feeling for these lower orders: it was a later, more political
generation that tarred his plays with a class consciousness that there
is no evidence his audience was aware of. Like Marston before them
Beaumont and Fletcher were members of the Gentry who made
money out of entertaining whoever was willing to pay to watch their
plays. The rumours of Charles II's dislike of *The Maid's Tragedy*, with
its strong criticism of royal immorality, as well as the suppression of
Fletcher's *Barnavelt*, suggest that neither dramatist was thought of
as an establishment toady in his own day.

Fletcher's *Faithful Shepherdess* is more obviously a rejection of the school of social relevance proclaimed by Jonson. Whether it preceded Shakespeare's return to the romantic mode in *Pericles* or followed it, like *Cupid's Revenge*, it heralds a change of fashion in the rejection of City comedy's 'image of the times', for a celebration of the illusory pastoral world where, as Fletcher explains in his address to the reader, we are not to expect real 'hirelings', but literary shepherds and shepherdesses as the ancient poets have depicted them. The literariness establishes—as in *The Knight of the Burning Pestle*—that here the emphasis is on the fictional. The play is not, however, any more than was Beaumont's play, an exercise in pure aesthetics; this is after all the seventeenth, not the nineteenth century: virtue is duly rewarded, vice repudiated. But the distribution of praise and blame provides the formal patterning rather than the substance of the drama, and this again becomes characteristic of Fletcher's (and Beaumont's) plays. Chapman felt the play too prelapsarian to be understood by a fallen generation:

> This iron age, that eats itself, will never
> Bite at your golden world . . .[14]

But the focus of the play is not on its Spenserean moral scheme, of true love and chastity in contrast to lust, but on the affections of the love-torn swains and responding or resisting shepherdesses.

Like *The Knight of the Burning Pestle*, *The Faithful Shepherdess* failed to please its first audience, as Fletcher himself hints in his address to the reader, because it failed to live up to their expectations of seeing hired shepherds 'sometimes laughing together and sometimes killing one another'. Clearly it was a bold step to attempt to adapt the Courtly pastoral for the commercial theatre.[15] Some of the commendatory verses confirm its initial failure. Nathanial Field, for instance, tells us the play failed to satisfy the demand for satire of an age 'that does despise / All innocent verse that lets alone her vice'. Shackerley Marmion confirms in the verses added for the third Quarto of 1634 that the original audience 'did not know its worth'. But the most interesting comment on this is Jonson's, who uses the opportunity of his commendation to engage in his customary attack on contemporary audiences:

The wise and many-headed bench, that sits
Upon the life and death of plays and wits,
(Compos'd of gamester, captain, Knight, Knight's man,
Lady or Pusil, that wears mask or fan,
Velvet or taffata-cap, rank'd in the dark
With the shop's foreman, or some brave spark
That may judge for his sixpence) had before
They saw it half, damn'd thy whole play and more:
Their motives were, since it had not to do
With vices, which they look'd for and came to.

Jonson's verse—full of substance as always—confirms Field's view
that the audience expected satire that (like his own comedies)
generally showed virtue by implication only. In place of this
boisterous, vicious, complex world of city life Fletcher gives his
audience an idealistic simplification of life, a golden world, in which
the characters represent somewhat disembodied passions—
faithfulness, love, lust and so on. Fletcher offers refinement of
morality, characterisation and language—in Field's words: 'Clad in
such elegant propriety / Of words, including a morality, / So sweet
and profitable . . .'. This is essentially what Beaumont and
Fletcher's successful plays were to offer, a paring-down of the gothic
exuberance of Elizabethan drama to an affective elegance, and it is
easy to understand its appeal as a novelty to an audience sated with
the boisterous and inelegant complexity of satirical comedy and the
tragedy of blood. The search for truth was to be made secondary to
the search for beauty. This stress on the aesthetic rather than the
moral Fletcher might equally have derived—along with his view of
tragi-comedy—from Italian theorising, for Castelvetro in his
commentary on the *Poetics* of Aristotle (1570) had insisted that
character in tragedy should be judged in primarily aesthetic terms
(see H. B. Charlton's *Castelvetro's Theory of Poetry* [1913], p. 105).

There were losses as well as gains in this shift of emphasis, and
subsequent criticism has largely concentrated on those losses.
Jonson's vivid picture of the sixpenny Blackfriars audience—though
obviously a partial one—gives us an excellent idea of the class mix
even in the 'private' theatre and suggests that Fletcher's work
involves a narrowing of appeal which had clearly alienated part of
that audience; but the evidence of Fletcher's later popularity

(admittedly after he had made some concessions) would indicate that the audience learned to like what they had at first rejected.

The four indisputably successful works of the Beaumont and Fletcher collaboration come hard on the heels of their individual failures: first *Philaster* (c.1609), then the comedy *The Scornful Lady* (c.1610), *The Maid's Tragedy* (1610?) and *A King and No King* (1611?). Fletcher had defined *The Faithful Shepherdess* as 'tragi-comedy' and two of these new plays belong to what the Italians had described as 'tragedia mista' or 'tragedia di lieto fin'—mixed tragedy or tragedy with a happy ending.[16] The attraction for our playwrights in this mixed kind was (as Fletcher explains in his account of *The Faithful Shepherdess*) that it avoided the ugliness of deaths while allowing free rein to the depiction of emotion under stress. The phenomenal success of *Philaster* throughout the seventeenth century is indicated by the nine quarto editions as well as its appearance in the second folio. The preface to the third edition (1628) tell us the play was 'affectionately taken and approved by the seeing auditors and hearing spectators' and goes on to compare the acting of plays to the mining of gold ore 'the actors being only the labouring miners'[17] while reading is the ore's refinement; a witness to the literary quality of the play, and also a useful reminder that a literary approach has its advantages. One of the important differences between the staging of *Philaster* and the earlier plays is that it was given by an adult company (at Blackfriars and the Globe) as opposed to the boy's company that played the earlier productions. Adult presentation would have the effect of strengthening the emotional impact of a drama that above all seeks to use emotion for aesthetic ends. Beaumont (the principal partner in this play) has in any case gone out of his way to present us with scenes of strong emotions, now not confined to love and hate but involving, in a secondary role, conflicts of power. The impression that these emotions are distanced somewhat from the kind of direct audience participation encouraged by much Shakespearean tragedy—where emotional involvement in Hamlet's or Othello's uncertainties is well-nigh inescapable—is corroborated by the play's choice, in the Restoration period, for representation by an all female cast.[18] In sexual matters, as in other sources of feeling, the impression the feeling creates is more important than the feeling itself. Generally Beaumont and Fletcher avoid the soul-revealing soliloquy of Shakesperean tragedy in preferring the theatrical 'aside'.

Like *The Faithful Shepherdess*, *Philaster* presents us with a world

that is abstracted from the real world. The setting is in a vaguely
classical Sicily, a courtly world where behaviour is pared down to
large gestures of conflict. There is a monolithic air about such
confrontations that anticipates the heroic drama of the Restoration
dramatists, who of course learnt much from these plays of
Beaumont and Fletcher. The principal actors—the King; the hero
Philaster, who has been denied his right to the throne; Arethusa,
betrothed to the Spanish Prince, but in love with Philaster; and the
devoted 'Bellario', whose real name is Euphrasia and who disguises
herself as a youth to be with her beloved Philaster—act in relation to
each other as if in a world apart, and this in spite of the occasional
intrusion of a lower world in the form of comic woodmen (IV.ii.) or
vindictive citizens (V.iv.) and the otherwise disembodied voice of
the people which comes to play a role in giving Philaster popular
support. There is nothing remotely akin to the intrusion of the
everyday world of Autolycus or the 'hireling' shepherds in
Shakespeare's Sicily, for Beaumont and Fletcher are not
concerned—as Shakespeare is—with reconciling the everyday with
myth, but in consistency of aesthetic pattern. Where they succeed
better than Dryden and his contemporaries is in engaging the
audience's emotion in the service of this aesthetic end.

A good example of the way the dramatists use emotion for
aesthetic effect can be seen, for instance, in the scene (by Beaumont)
where Philaster has been told by a courtier that Arethusa is being
unfaithful to him in favouring the youth 'Bellario'. Philaster,
enraged, confronts 'Bellario' and tries to get a confession from 'him':

BELLARIO.   Never my lord, by heaven.
PHILASTER. That's strange: I know she does.
BELLARIO.   No, by my life.
PHILASTER. Why then she does not love me; come, she does:
    I bad her doe it: I charg'd her by all charmes
    Of love between us, by the hope of peace
    We should enjoy, to yeelde thee all delights
    Naked, as to her bed: I took her oath
    Thou shouldst enjoy her: Tell me boy,
    Is she not parrallesse?

                                        (III.i.193–201)[19]

The superiority over Dryden's similar presentation of strong emotion is largely in the greater flexibility of the language for reflecting the nuances of feeling which range from the conversational to the ecstatically sensual, as we are asked to share in the delights of Arethusa abed. There is considerable psychological subtlety too—again a function of the flexible language—Philaster is of course trying to bait the hook that will catch the confession, but he is also succumbing to some emotional indulgence in the display of sensuality, an indulgence in which the audience is invited to share. It is sensuality at one remove (for both Philaster and audience) and reminds us that in a sense this emotional confrontation is a kind of shadow boxing, because both Philaster and 'Bellario' are not what they seem, they are playing roles; he to exact the confession, she in her disguise as the youth 'Bellario'. What further undercuts the straightforward impact of the emotional expression is our awareness that the accusation Philaster is levelling is sexually impossible and that 'Bellario' could readily reveal this if she were so minded. That she is willing to accept the death Philaster threatens her with rather than reveal who she is, only adds to the sense of theatricality of which we are conscious throughout. For all its psychological subtlety it is not, in depth, psychologically convincing. The effect is ultimately an aesthetic one, which has been achieved through its appeal to feeling. The technique is not dissimilar from that of such baroque painters as Guido Reni or Rubens, who engage our feelings in order to transmute them into aesthetic display. There is of course a moral connotation to the patterning, but it is again subservient to the aesthetic effect. Thus the King's periodic outbursts of remorse for his wickedness function not, as with Claudius, to suggest the moral *malaise* which is part of Hamlet's dilemma, but to lead to the climax of the King's renunciation of his ill-gotten kingdom in favour of the hero. The aesthetic enjoyment of this final moment of virtue's triumph is enriched by the sweet melancholy of Bellario-Euphrasia's disappointment. It has been suggested (by Andrew Gurr and others)[20] that Beaumont intended some specific parallels between the political situation in the play and James I's position, but such parallels as the fact that both kings rule over two countries merely highlights the difference, for no one seriously maintained that James had usurped the throne of England. Sicily in this play is surely as much a 'golden world' as the Thessaly of *The Faithful Shepherdess* and there could have been little problem in persuading the censors that the play held no political risks.

The metamorphosis of passion into art is a key feature of both the tragi-comedy *A King and No King* and *The Maid's Tragedy*. *A King and No King* is explicitly said to have been a Globe play on the title page of the first Quarto (1619), though subsequent editions change this to 'Acted at the Black-Fryers'—there were eight quarto editions in the seventeenth century as well as a printing in the second folio of 1679—as with *Philaster* attesting to the great popularity of Beaumont and Fletcher's plays. Presumably it came to be played at both theatres, but was perhaps designed with the larger (and more various) audience of the Globe principally in mind. There are a number of features of the play that may be accounted for in this way, notably the prominence given to the swashbuckling comic villain, Bessus. It has, too, a markedly simpler moral patterning compared to *Philaster*, though this as we have noticed, was a feature of Fletcher's *Faithful Shepherdess*. Arthur Mizener, in an important article,[21] pointed out that the moral pattern is essentially that of the old morality plays, with the king, Arbaces, as the 'mankind' figure torn between good council from his general, Mardonius, and evil council from the comic villain, Bessus—the very association of evil with the comic world also suggests an appeal to conventions of the popular theatre. Once again, however, the moral patterning merely provides the structure, not the substance, of the play. Indeed, the moral pattern is totally subverted at the end of the play for the sake of theatrical effect, when Arbaces, having finally succumbed to the sin of incest, discovers that the women he lusts after is not, after all, his sister. A simple moralistic reading of the play would force us to the conclusion that, for the fortunate, the gods are willing to reward evil.

The two playwrights (again, seemingly with Beaumont in the ascendant[22]) require a different response from their audience—as the audience by now had clearly learnt. We have only to compare the handling of the incest theme in this play with Webster's handling of the theme in the almost exactly contemporaneous *Duchess of Malfi* to see how revolutionary a change Beaumont and Fletcher had effected in audience expectation. Ferdinand's strange relationship with his twin sister in Webster's tragedy remains subterranean, finds its expression through the intensity of metaphors that reveal more than they say:

This was my Fathers poyniard: do you see
I'll'd be loth to see't looke rusty, 'cause 'twas his:
I would have you to give ore these chargeable Revels;
A Vizor, and a Masque are whispering roomes
That were nev'r built for goodnesse: fare ye well:
And women like that part, which (like the Lamprey)
Hath nev'r a bone in't.

(*Duchess*, I.i.370–6)

Ferdinand's lack of rational coherence allows the figures to coalesce with each other in multiple associations: their father's dagger made rusty by entry into his sister's body becomes infected with the obscene image of fornication and again sets up associations with the whispering rooms that house the evil (of dagger and lamprey?). Ferdinand's sexual obsessiveness is itself a sign of a world where evil is endemic and where one's best thoughts are those of leaving it. The language plays on the dark world of a natural corruption: nothing is said explicitly of incest, of sexual attraction between brother and sister, but there is a pervading sense of perversion that readily translates itself into such suggestions and infects brother and sister alike. The dislocated language is itself the sign of a disrupted world and the audience is assumed to recognise and share the feelings of a fallen state where none of us are free from taint.

By contrast, Arbaces inhabits a world not only where a sharp and easily recognised distinction is made between the good and bad, but where the assumption is that the bad can be resisted and overcome. Arbaces himself recognises the evil of his infatuation and struggles to resist it; the benevolent gods recognise the heroism of the failure by taking away the temptation. Nor are we, the audience, invited to share in the emotions of the struggle: the rhetorical orderliness of the language in which Arbaces finally declares his inability to resist his incestuous desires keeps the emotion at arms' length, presenting it as spectacle, as aesthetic rather than moral experience:

It is resolv'd, I bore it whilst I could;
I can no more, Hell open all thy gates,
And I will thorough them; if they be shut,
Ile batter um, but I will find the place

> Where the most damn'd have dwelling; ere I end,
> Amongst them all they shall not have a sinne,
> But I may call it mine: I must beginne
> With murder of my friend, and so goe on
> To an incestuous ravishing, and end
> My life and sinnes with a forbidden blow
> Upon my selfe.[23]

                                        (V.iv.1–11)

The speech is as significant for what it fails to say as for what it does say. For a speech about incest the language is noticeably unerotic, as indeed is the setting. Where the actor playing Ferdinand has all the opportunities of manipulating the dagger to heighten the erotic suggestiveness of the scene with his sister, Arbaces is on stage alone and the sword he carries is explicitly headed off from erotic association (as are such potentially erotic words as 'hell' and 'gates') by the reference to the murder of a friend—indeed the mention of incest comes only at the end of a list of hypothetical atrocities that succeed in blunting its impact. Here to name is to exorcise, more especially because the deed is cloaked in the decorousness of the poetic circumlocution 'incestuous ravishing'. In terms of the psychology of the character the speech is essentially confessional; this is not the vaunting of the Machiavel, but a decent (if volatile) man distraught and accepting the price of suicide he must pay as wages for his sin. The evasiveness of the language of course anticipates the evasiveness of the action. Arbaces does not sin and has no price to pay (as we know at least the second time round); we have been entertained with the spectacle of the dilemma without having to suffer any emotional consequences. But to charge Beaumont and Fletcher with moral irresponsibility (as for instance Robert Turner does in the Introduction to his edition of the play[24]) is to misunderstand the nature of their art. The engagement expected of the audience is no more moral identification than it is, say, in modern ballet; we are invited to watch the spectacle of Arbaces's emotional involvement for the aesthetic patterning it achieves. It is part of their dramatic skill that this patterning is expressed through a sufficiently convincing psychology that gives credence to the character's emotional responses.

Arbaces's and Panthea's inconsistencies, for instance, that Waith takes exception to,[25] are psychologically consistent with the effects of a passion that they both recognise to be evil. Arbaces's rapid swings from arrogance to reason are moreover those of a weak man supported by a strong creed of political absolutism (the combination was not unknown among the Stuarts) who might well be expected to lose control of strong passions. The characterisation is not an end in itself and the two playwrights are quite able to forgo psychological plausibility—as we have seen—if theatrical capital is to be made out of doing so, but generally their characterisation is plausible and consistent even in its inconsistencies. They are content, too, with broad strokes in painting character, as they are content with a single moral scheme, in order to shape the aesthetics of dramatic contrast. Bessus, the fool of the play, is perhaps a case where theatrical effectiveness overrules psychological probability. In order to achieve a single but effective dramatic contrast with the heroic Mardonius, we are asked to believe not only that Bessus is a coward of quite staggering proportions but that he has convinced many as a professional soldier.

The difference between Beaumont and Fletcher's tragi-comedies and their tragedies is the superficial one—as the Preface to *The Faithful Shepherdess* argues—that a tragi-comedy lacks deaths. That address to the reader also seems to imply that the difference is aesthetic rather than moral; in the tragedies we are not in a world of crime and punishment (as we mostly are in Jacobean tragedy) but a Manichean world divided by forces of dark and light that blends kaleidoscopically into colours where either light or dark might happen to prevail in the patterning. Just as the ending of *A King and No King* arbitrarily absolves all sin in the accident of birth, in *The Maid's Tragedy* (c.1610) human activity is presented as a result of powers ultimately out of human control. In the Masque in Act I that is produced to celebrate the wedding of Evadne with the hero Amintor, Night is called forth as the appropriate tutelary figure of the lovers' bedding: he in turn calls up the Goddess of the darkness, Cynthia, to preside over the pageant of Neptune, who is instructed to bring the winds of spring, inaugurating a theme of fecundity to grace the nuptials. The Masque, however, goes seriously wrong; Boreas, the North wind, inadvertently escapes and Neptune is forced to beat a hasty retreat to calm the sea storms that have arisen. Other elements of disruption appear throughout the Masque. Night arrives blind and groping and complains of her vulnerability to opposing day and even Cynthia grudges Phoebus his predominance:

> For almost all the world their service bend
> To *Phoebus*, and in vaine my light I lend,
> Gaz'd on unto my setting from my rise
> Almost of none, but of unquiet eyes.

(I.ii.146–9)[26]

The auguries are ominous, Cynthia is here the goddess of death, noticeably repudiating any association with her lover Endymion, and we are to understand that the marriage is doomed to sterility. The implications of the masque suggest that the colours of night are to prevail and that the human participants are doomed by the accidents of fate. Cynthia makes this explicit in reminding the Night: 'we may not break the Gods' decrees'. As with the tragi-comedies and with the earlier tragedy *Cupid's Revenge*, humans are seen controlled by a fate that might be good or bad according to the arbitrary decisions of the gods.

The effect of this sense of ineluctable fate is to make praise and blame largely irrelevant—as it did with Arbaces's uncontrollable passion. The dramatists are not concerned, however, to emphasise the metaphysical; the gods remain shadowy, ill-defined (in *Thierry and Theodoret*, for instance, set in early Christian France, they are a curious mixture of Christian and pagan) the focus is on the human suffering that results from divine decree. Although the masque directly introduces us to mythological figures these are presented at one remove, as it were, by being presented as a show in celebration of the marriage of the heroine Evadne to the man chosen for her by the King, Amintor. The play centres on the moral entanglement caused by the King's adulterous relationship with Evadne, which leads her to repudiate her husband Amintor on their marriage night. The plot does not evolve, however, primarily in terms of moral judgement, although Evadne expiates her crime of ambition finally by murdering the King; instead we watch the spectacle of this entanglement, sharing with the gods the pleasures of the tragic patterning. For this purpose the playwrights keep the world of the play in a remote country (Rhodes) at a remote—and unspecified—time. The King is not given a personal name and this is indicative of the characterisation generally—it remains only broadly individualised in spite of such acutely conceived psychological encounters as that between Evadne and her new husband on their wedding night (II.i.). The play moves by a series of subtle emotional contrasts: the wilful and ambitious, but not unsympathetic, Evadne in aesthetic contrast with the pathetic, largely passive figure of Aspatia, to whom Amintor was betrothed; the contrast between the blustering but impotent Calianax, Aspatia's father, and the forceful heroic figure of Melantius, Evadne's brother, whose honour has been betrayed by the King's whoring of his sister; and the bold honesty of Melantius in contrast to the devious King and the well-meaning but weak Amintor.

The playwrights' concern for theatrical effectiveness above all else, is seen most clearly in their handling of Melantius. He is the dominating heroic figure of the play, a successful soldier whom we see welcomed home from his victories at the beginning of the play. The play revolves around Melantius's concern to avenge his family honour, but in one of the most effective scenes of the play (IV.ii.) he indulges in a series of barefaced lies that would grace any Machiavel. Amintor discloses the state of his marriage relationship with Evadne to Melantius, who swears to kill the King. This is overheard by Calianax, who promptly turns informer. Interrogated by the King in Calianax's presence, Melantius denies the intention and outfaces the old man:

> Pardon me Sir,
> My bluntness will be pardoned, you preserve
> A race of idle people here about you,
> Eaters, and talkers to defame the worth
> Of those that doe things worthy, the man that uttered this
> Had perisht without food, bee't who it will,
> But for this arme, that fenst him from the Foe . . .

(IV.ii.121-7)

In Shakespearean tragedy such duplicity would imply a moral rebuke, but Melantius is no Machiavel; what impresses us here is not his duplicity, but the strength of character that can unflinchingly brazen out a lie to avenge his honour. No clearer example could be given of the triumph of aesthetics over morality.

The underlying ideological basis for this preference for the comely over the virtuous is revealed in one of the most successful of the two playwrights' joint plays, *The Scornful Lady* (1610)—it had run into eleven editions by the end of the seventeenth century. Choosing a Middletonian theme of spendthrift gentleman rake (Young Lovelesse) in conflict with City usurer (Moorecraft), Beaumont and Fletcher celebrate the triumph of gentlemanly trickery by marrying off their rake hero to a rich widow, after he has been readily forgiven by his elder brother for the attempt to sell off the family estate to further his carousings. The triumph is completed by the conversion of Moorecraft into a hard drinking and whoring gallant at the end of the play. Add to this the acquisition of a rich wife by the young Welford (the Elder Lovelesse's rival) by disguising himself as a woman to sleep with the unsuspecting gentlewoman, Martha, and the triumph of gentlemanly trickery is complete. There is of course some class bias throughout, but the key to the success of all three young men (the Elder Lovelesse's task is to trick the scornful Lady into marriage) is that they are young, handsome, and pleasure-loving and this is emphasised by a contrasting courtship between the threadbare clergyman Roger and the 50-year-old and lecherous serving woman, Abigail. Much comedy is made of her hideousness in contrast to the gentlefolks' comeliness. This is the only fundamental division that is not healed in the final moments of the play. Handsome does as handsome is.

FLETCHER WITHOUT BEAUMONT

The Maid's Tragedy was—seemingly—not the last of Beaumont's collaborations with Fletcher, but from 1613 (the date of his marriage) Beaumont seems to have withdrawn into the background while Fletcher looked around for other collaborators: Shakespeare (himself in semi-retirement) in *Two Noble Kinsmen, Henry VIII,* and the lost *Cardenio;* and such newcomers as the actor Nathan Field and Philip Massinger. In *Beggar's Bush* and *Thierry and Theodoret,* Beaumont and Fletcher divide their work with Massinger, who is gradually inducted into the art of the playwright to become first Fletcher's major partner after Beaumont's death in 1616 and eventually a major playwright in his own right. The fact that the collaborations included the elderly Shakespeare for a short time should remind us that the Beaumont and Fletcher manner developed out of Shakespeare's, emphasising those tendencies towards a drama of aesthetic effect that was always an important tendency in Shakespeare's work, especially in the later 1590s, before Shakespeare shifted ground to accommodate the moral bias of the Jonsonian revolution. One suspects that Shakespeare was not averse to returning to a less acerbic manner in his old age.

We need to remind ourselves of what Fletcher and Shakespeare have in common in a play like *Two Noble Kinsmen* before turning to the much more obvious differences that the play reveals— differences so acute that the opening and closing acts of the play (principally Shakespeare's) and the three central acts seem almost (apart from their use of the same Chaucerian story from the *Knight's Tale*) to be completely independent plays. The most striking difference is in the tone of awe and reverence that Shakespeare infuses into the dialogue, even when the subject would hardly seem to warrant it. The sense of awe is not only produced by the extraordinarily convoluted language of Shakespeare's last phase, though that plays an important part in conveying a ceremonious solemnity to even trivial proceedings; it stems above all from his awareness of the metaphysical implications of human action. This is most obvious in the final act, where the tutelary gods speak directly to their votaries, but it is equally present in the earlier Shakespearean passages where merely human affairs are concerned. A case in point is the one Shakespearean scene of Act III, where Arcite meets his rival Palamon for the first time after they have left prison and agree to fight for Emilia's love. Shakespeare begins this scene by giving Arcite a soliloquy of thirty lines which is an invocation to Emilia:

> This is a solemn rite
> They owe bloomed May and the Athenians pay it
> To th'heart of ceremony. O Queen Emilia,
> Fresher than May, sweeter
> Than her gold buttons on the boughs or all
> Th' enameled knacks o' th' mead or garden—Yea,
> We challenge too the bank of any nymph
> That makes the stream seem flowers! Thou, O jewel
> O' th' wood, o' th' world, hast likewise blest a place
> With thy sole presence, in thy rumination,
> That I, poor man, might eftsoons come between
> And chop on some cold thought.

(III.i.2–13)[27]

It is not only the context of the 'solemn rite' of May and the identification of Emilia with the personified Spring month, the very quality of the words gives the impression of ritual enactment, in which literal meaning is of secondary importance to incantation: 'Thou, O jewel / O' th' wood, o' th' world . . .'. Mere literality is giving way to a striving for ecstatic union with qualities unseen, intangible otherworldy presences. Shakespeare has lost interest in human activity for its own sake, hence what we might think of as an un-Shakespearean unconcern for characterisation or action—for the actual world is seen as a mere shadow of what it conceals.

In contrast Fletcher, as always, is irremediably secular. The Chaucerian material is 'demythologised' in this play as it is in the later play based on the *Wife of Bath's Tale*, *Women Pleas'd*. Fletcher was no doubt fascinated by the eerie effects the Shakespearean language creates, for it gives a feeling of wonder that Fletcherian drama constantly strives to achieve for its own theatrical ends. But Fletcher's own contribution to the play is to bring the characters down to earth in ways that present us with a ludicrous contrast with the Shakespearean solemnities. This can be seen most obviously in the sub-plot of the Jailor's Daughter, initially introduced by Shakespeare at the opening of Act II, but thereafter left largely to Fletcher. The jailor's daughter falls hopelessly in love with Palamon, allows him to escape from her custody and follows him on his wanderings. In the scene immediately after Arcites' incantation to Emilia, Fletcher shows us the jailor's daughter, having failed to find Palamon, imagining he has been eaten by wolves and contemplating her own death. The scene has its own pathos, but the pathos is undercut by the ludicrousness of the girl's aspirations, a ludicrousness that is further realised in later scenes when it becomes increasingly clear that she is suffering from acute sexual frustration. In subsequent scenes she becomes deranged and harps on her would-be lover's sexual prowess: 'There is at least two hundred now with child by him' (IV.i.128). She is finally cured of her madness by a doctor who organises a session of sexual therapy for her that would be at home in the world of *Jake's Thing*. All this might be merely comic contrast were it either, for, of course, the Jailor's Daughter exemplifies the sexual madness that prompts the characters of the main plot and acts as a paradigm of Fletcher's comic view of the general predicament.

In the third scene of Act III—a scene following the Shakespearean invocation to Emilia and the lament of the Jailor's Daughter—

Fletcher gives us a scene between Palamon and Arcite in which the comic parallels become inescapable. Arcite, as he has promised in the Shakespearean scene (III.i.) brings food and armour to Palamon as he lies in hiding in preparation for their epic fight over Emilia. As they eat and drink their wine the two friends and enemies reminisce over their previous amatory conquests:

> PALAMON.   She met him in an arbor:
> What did she there, coz? Play o' the' virginals?
> ARCITE. Something she did, sir.
> PALAMON.   Made her groan a month for 't',
> Or two, or three, or ten.
> ARCITE.   The Marshall's sister
> Had her share too, as I remember cousin . . .
>
>   (III.iii.33–7)

There is clearly an unbridgeable gap between the Arcite of Shakespeare's scene and the cynical libertine of these prosy lines, and the comic cynicism is turned against him when immediately afterwards Palamon and Arcite begin quarrelling vehemently over Emilia. 'What fools these mortals be' becomes not just the partial comment of a mischievous fairy, as in the old play, but the very ground of Fletcher's action.

I am not intending to draw this contrast between Shakespeare's otherworldly vision and the starkly secular nature of Fletcher's outlook in deprecation of the younger playwright—on the contrary, I am suggesting that the criteria for judging two such opposed attitudes must be totally different. Fletcher's insistence on judging his characters in secular terms as products of their circumstances and impulses implies the psychological and physiological determinism that we have already noted in his earlier collaborations with Beaumont. In some of Fletcher's unaided plays a shift away from the purely aesthetic towards a greater concern with ideas, is evident, but even when his theme is explicitly Christian, as it is in the *Island Princess* (1621), the interest is much more on the affective clash of Mohammedan and Christian cultures than on Christian doctrine.

Fletcher's increasing preference for comedy over tragedy in his career after 1613 is a consequence of his tendency, again noted earlier, of standing somewhat aloof from his creations in an attitude of mildly cynical amusement. Fletcher draws no metaphysical conclusion from contemplating the quirkiness his theatricality illustrates and herein he differs markedly from someone like Middleton whose cynical view of humanity he largely shares. The difference is between the *sprezzatura*, the calm aloofness of the gentleman in contrast to the Calvinistic moralist of the City. This contrast comes out vividly in a comedy like *Wit Without Money*, of some time between 1614 and 1620. The play has the typically Middletonian theme of an impecunious young man, Valentine, who has had to mortgage his estate to an enterprising merchant (called simply 'Merchant' throughout). The romantic name of the hero immediately points to a difference in attitude from Middleton towards his Easys and Witgoods, for Valentine is not in a world of Middletonian sharkers, but is a romantic eccentric who wants to free himself, quixotically, from the shackles of property and live by his wits. Fletcher's Merchant, indeed, is a tolerant, even benevolent, figure, who simply wants to bring Valentine to his senses. Fletcher is not at all interested in illustrating the depravity of a world given over to such materialistic concerns, but in relishing wryly the quirkiness of human conduct through the unexpected outcome of the action. For Valentine's refusal to obey the normal rules of self-interest, especially his refusal to intrigue in the hope of catching the rich widow Lady Heartwell, leads unexpectedly to her falling in love with his aggressive independence and granting him all the benefits he has refused to strive for. The perversity of human response is equally illustrated through the parallel relationship that develops between Valentine's brother Francisco and Lady Heartwell's sister Isabella, but while Lady Heartwell is drawn to Valentine's outspoken independence, the less assertive Isabella is attracted by Francisco's modesty. Fletcher is concerned with patterns of contrast and similarity, but his purpose goes beyond the confines of the theatre here to a comic delight in overturning conventional wisdom. The gentlemen in the audience would no doubt draw comfort from the defeat of bourgeois caution, but the concern is less to win a round in the class war (the Merchant, as I say, comes out of the encounter with honour) than to enjoy the spectacle of the eruption of the unexpected in human conduct.

It is often difficult to say whether the search for theatrical novelty or the need to dramatise a novel idea is the primary motivation. Fletcher's lively riposte to *The Taming of the Shrew* in *The Woman's Prize* (1611) has, the epilogue tells us, the intent 'To teach both sexes due equality', a novel enough idea for a generation brought up to blame Eve for all human woes. The play deals with Petruchio's second marriage where the new wife, Maria, uses Lysistratan tactics to bring her husband to heel. Fletcher manages a convincing account both of macho assumptions failing the test of the real psychological world and of a feminine determination that remains as charming as it is firm. It is noticeable that Fletcher is more concerned with convincing psychology here and less with thematic patterning than Shakespeare is in his play, and if the later play is not as vigorous, it has more psychological subtlety. It is a measure of the modern professional stage's unadventurousness that the Royal Shakespeare Company chose *The Roaring Girl* to 'answer' the 1982 production of *Taming of the Shrew*, rather than Fletcher's play. The Court in 1633, having 'likt' Shakespeare's play on 26 November found that on the 28th *The Woman's Prize* was 'very well likt'.

The defence of woman's independence in *The Woman's Prize*, like the triumph of romantic over libertine values in the late comedy *The Wild Goose Chase* (c.1621) should make us hesitate to accept the charge of 'decadence' levelled so frequently at Fletcher. It is true that Fletcher's themes show a narrowing of focus compared to his great predecessors, and it is vain to deny that the sensational or the bizarre is sometimes made the opportunity for a theatricality that lacks the aesthetic poise that renders the best of the Beaumont collaborations so impressive. A play like *The Mad Lover* (1616), for instance, where the central character, the General, anxiously pleads that his heart should be ripped out and presented as a token of his love to the Princess Calis, manages to combine psychological implausibility with bad taste, as do the venereal and homosexual elements in *The Humorous Lieutenant* (c.1619). Though the distinction between comedy and tragi-comedy favoured by the second folio of 1679 is often a fine one it is generally in the latter that the temptations to sudden and spectacular reversals of expectation or of indulgence in the bizarre prove debilitating, though in a tragi-comedy such as *The Loyal Subject* Fletcher uses the serious theme of political obedience for a display of balanced and convincing dramatic patterning.

Fletcher's two unaided tragedies, *Valentinian* (?1612) and *Bonduca*, also show some shift towards the thematic concern we have already remarked on. Here too the distinction between these plays and the more sombre tragi-comedies is not clear-cut: *Bonduca* especially might equally well be seen as the most sombre of the tragi-comedies.

Apart from these two plays there are a number—*The Double Marriage*, *The Prophetess*, *Rollo*, *The False One*, *The Lover's Progress* and *Sir John Van Olden Barnavelt*—where Massinger and occasionally others shared in the composition. *Valentinian* is perhaps the most discursive of all Fletcher's plays, its central theme being the limits of obedience—a subject of Jacobean topicality. The theme is presented in both political and personal terms. Lucina, the wife of the Roman General Maximus, is raped by the Emperor Valentinian, leaving the husband with the political dilemma central to Jacobean political debate, the right of the individual to oppose the monarch and seek redress for a tyrannical act. As Ian Donaldson has shown in his study of Renaissance responses to the Lucrece story,[28] the moral dilemma of the rape victim was of great fascination to the period. The debate is made explicit in *Valentinian*, where Aecius argues eloquently that Lucina should not commit suicide (as does Lucrece) for that is to take the law into her own hands; her living presence will remind Valentinian of his wickedness and might lead to repentance. In any case it is the duty of the individual to abide the will of heaven.

> . . . compeld and forcd with violence
> To what ye have done, the deed is none of yours,
> No nor the justice neither; ye may live,
> And still a worthier woman, still more honoured:
> For are those trees the worse we teare the fruits from?
> Or should the eternall Gods desire to perish,
> Because we daily violate their truths,
> Which is the chastitie of heaven?

> (III.i.220–7)[29]

This is essentially a Christian argument for it assumes the doctrine of original sin: we are all guilty of sin and only God can free us from it, therefore God must be allowed to decide where ultimate responsibility lies, the individual should not take the law into his or her own hands. The doctrine of absolute obedience to God's will is reflected in political terms in the doctrine of absolute obedience to the King's will, for the king is God's surrogate. Aecius is perfectly consistent, therefore, in arguing throughout the play for obedience to Valentinian, however perverse and tyrannical the Emperor's demands. From the opening act—that is, well before Valentinian has committed his crime of rape—Aecius is concerned to persuade Maximus that their duty is to suffer the Emperor's will:

> We are but subjects *Maximus*; obedience
> To what is done, and griefe for what is ill done,
> Is all we can call ours; the hearts of Princes
> Are like the Temples of the Gods; pure incense,
> Untill unhallowed hands defile those offrings,
> Burns ever there; we must not put 'em out,
> Because the Priests that touch those sweetes are wicked;
> We dare not deerest friend, nay more we cannot,
> (While we consider why we are, and how,
> To what lawes bound, much more to what Law giver) . . .
> Like desperate and unseason'd fooles let fly
> Our killing angers, and forsake our honors.

> (I.iii.17–26, 30–1)

Again this is Christian argument, so familiar among the most conforming during the Stuart period. Critics have found Maximus's change from loyal general to Machiavellian revenger inconsistent,[30] but his rejection of Aecius's loyalism is itself a sign of his moral instability. This point is nicely made when the Emperor achieves access to Lucina as a result of winning Maximus's wedding ring in a game of chance. For the admirable Aecius is presented (though not unequivocally) as the measure of moral excellence in the play, as is the loyalist Archas in *The Loyal Subject*. Though the subject is Roman decadence, the play, as Wallis points out, is 'unsympathetic to a corrupt, lascivious court';[31] it also presents a more-or-less approving view of passive obedience that we might now find quaint and outmoded (which may well be a measure of a refusal to notice its pervasiveness) but which is a perfectly viable and logical moral viewpoint.

Insisting on the thematic coherence of the play, however, is not to argue that *Valentinian* is essentially a drama à thèse. Clifford Leech is clearly right to stress the 'coldness' of the play;[32] Aecius's loyalty is not so much advocated by the play as stated as a ground for interpreting the action. The overall effect of the play is not of advocacy but of wry observation. The assumptions of Fletcherian drama, as we have already noted, are comic, involving distancing and detachment. Aecius may be thought to believe in divine justice, but his death at his own hand is only one of the many ironies of a play which abounds in ironies. Maximus, seeking to avenge his wife's honour, ends by posthumuously prostituting his wife for his own political advancement: 'If I rise / My wife was ravish'd well'; while the revenge he seeks is taken out of his hands by the unexpected intervention of two protégés of Aecius, the apostle of non-resistance, Phidias and Aretus. The crowing irony perhaps is that the play ends with the crowd's acclamation of Valentinian's Empress, Eudoxia, as she announces the revenge of her unfaithful husband in Maximus's death by poison.

The pervasive irony of the play, however, is not so much a moral comment on human affairs as an aesthetic device—a device, like the occurence of the key events off-stage that Leech has remarked as characteristic,[33] which asks us to look on the action from an emotional distance. It is the pattern in the carpet that intrigues, not the use to which the carpet is put. Just how carefully patterned the carpet is, is shown in Wallis's excellent scene-by-scene analysis of the play.[34] Fletcher's aesthetic concerns are well illustrated in the intrusion of two short comic scenes immediately before the climax in which Maximus is crowned and murdered. In the comic scenes the pageant-makers discuss their artistic task for the inauguration ceremony entirely in terms of its aesthetic effectiveness. The purpose of these scenes is not comic relief in the Shakespearean manner—to throw light on the significance of the main action—but rather to draw our attention to the theatrical viewpoint which is a premise of the main action.

Bonduca has frequently been compared by critics with Shakespeare's *Cymbeline*:[35] both use Holinshed for a source and both deal with Romano-British history. But, unusually for Shakespeare, *Cymbeline* is markedly ahistorical, Shakespeare giving his play an otherworldly air that explains its usual inclusion in the group of late romances. *Bonduca*, on the other hand, again unusually for its author, has the feel of Renaissance history about it. Both it and *Valentinian* indeed might best be thought of as part of that attempt to represent the new heroic view of Rome on the stage that Jonson initiated and to which Chapman and Shakespeare contributed.[36] The picture of the Romans given in *Bonduca* is highly favourable and, rather surprisingly, the eponymous British heroine is contrasted unfavourably with her Roman opponents. Like such near-contemporary Roman plays as *Coriolanus* and Chapman's *Caesar and Pompey*, moreover, the play deals with the clash of equally balanced antagonists and the tragedy stems not from individual delinquency but from opposing principles that are regarded as equally laudable—in this case the Roman desire for martial conquest against the British desire for independence. The play is less about Bonduca (she is in fact killed in the fourth act) than about two opposing societies. The two chief protagonists indeed are Suetonius, the Roman general, and Caratach, whose uncommon heroic qualities are emphasised in his opening reproof to Bonduca in praise of his enemies:

> And still to try these *Romanes*, whom I found
> (And if I lye, my wounds be henceforth backward,
> And be you witnesse, gods, and all my dangers)
> As ready, and as full of that I brought
> (Which was not fear nor flight) as valiant,
> As vigilant, as wise, to do and suffer,
> Ever advanced as forward as the *Britains*,
> Their sleeps as short, their hopes as high as ours,
> I, and as subtil, Lady.

> (I.i.74–82)[37]

Bonduca indeed provides a partly hidden counter-theme which appears quite frequently in Fletcher's works, of women as threat to the world of heroic male values—a more unequivocal example is Brunhalt of *Thierry and Theodoret*. Caratach makes this theme explicit in his outburst of anger against Bonduca after the defeat of the Britains:

> The woman fool. Why did you give the word
> Unto the carts to charge down, and our people
> In grosse before the Enemie? We pay for't,
> Our own swords cut our throats: why?—on't,
> Why do you offer to command? The divell,
> The divell, and his dam too, who bid you
> Meddle in mens affaires?

> (III.v.128–34)

This is not the usual Jacobean anti-feminism, with its justification in Christian doctrine, but a deep-seated feeling of woman's 'otherness' which portrays them as both incompetent (at men's things) and yet a genuine threat. Bonduca is rather oddly cast as both villainess and heroine: 'She was truely noble, and a queen' says Suetonius after her death. In an earlier scene, however, Bonduca is shown in barbaric mood instructing her willing daughters to torture their Roman prisoners: 'Torment 'em wenches . . . then hang 'em' (II.iii.19). One suspects that this anti-feminist element in the play is out of control, that Fletcher has in this instance lost his habitual detachment, distorting the neo-classical intentions which would seem to be to depict two societies of equal merit in conflict and where the tragedy resides not in the death of the supernumerary heroine, but of the innocent and brave Hengo, Caratach's nephew.

The dramatic patterning of *Bonduca* therefore turns out to be unsatisfactory because, for once, Fletcher has allowed thematic considerations to intrude too far and inconsistently. His best work is where theme is subservient to dramatic impact, where the pattern in the carpet is more interesting than the use to which the carpet can be put.

Notes and References

(Note: Place of publication of all titles cited is London unless stated otherwise.)

1 INTRODUCTION: JACOBEAN PROFESSIONAL THEATRE AND SHAKESPEARE

1. *Wit Without Money* I.i.102; *Bartholomew Fair*, Introduction, 89–90.
2. See Harbage, *Shakespeare's Audience* (1941), p. 56, for excellent detailed discussions of Jacobean audiences; see also Ann J. Cook, *The Privileged Playgoers of London 1576–1642* (Princeton, 1981) and Michael Hattaway, *Elizabethan Popular Theatre* (1982).
3. John Stow, *The Survey of London*, Everyman edition, p. 399.
4. The phrase occurs in Harvey's annotation of a copy of Chaucer's works: 'his *Lucrece* and his tragedie of Hamlet, Prince of Denmark, have it in them to please the wiser sort', *Marginalia* edited Moore Smith (1913), p. 232.
5. *Malcontent*, Introduction, 68–9.
6. The Oxford English Dictionary interpretation of 'clapper-claw' in this passage is: 'To claw or scratch with the open hand or nails: to beat, thrash, drub' and this interpretation has led modern commentators to assume the passage means that the play was never *presented* to the public, but this would make the repetition of 'palms' redundant. It is surely more likely that a pun is intended on 'clapper-claw' meaning that it was not applauded in its brief appearance at The Globe. This would explain why the title page of the Quarto was changed from announcing the play as 'acted by the Kings Majesties Servants at The Globe'—not because it was untrue but because it was unwise to advertise it.
7. References are to G. K. Hunter's Arden edition, 1959.
8. For a detailed discussion of the plays see Chapter 5. Uncertainty about dates makes it difficult to judge whether Shakespeare's play comes after or during Chapman's sequence. *All's Well* certainly post-dates *Gentleman Usher*, and may well be later than the date 1603 often assigned to it.
9. E. M. W. Tillyard, *Shakespeare's Problem Plays* (1950), p. 91.

2 JOURNEYMEN AND GENTLEMEN

1. 'Address to the Reader', *The English Traveller* (1633).
2. G. E. Bentley, *The Jacobean and Caroline Stage* (1956) I, p. 161.
3. 'Address', *English Traveller*.
4. See, for instance, title pages of *Iron Age*, *Wise Woman of Hogsdon*, *Troia Britannica*.
5. Edition of M. H. Leonard (Garland Series, 1980).
6. T. S. Eliot, *Selected Essays* (3rd edn; 1951), p. 175.
7. Edition of R. W. Van Fossen (Revels Plays; 1961).

8. For the success of this play see introduction to *The Iron Age* edited A. W. Weiner (Garland Series; 1979), p. xxxii. Shakespeare's play was advertised in the Quarto (1609) as 'never clapper-clawd with the palmes of the vulgar', which is usually taken to mean 'the play had never been acted in a public theatre' (Arden edn, introduction, p. 2) but could as well mean that it was never popular as a stage play, a possible selling point in an address to 'an ever reader'.

9. M. Grivelet, *Thomas Heywood et le drame domestique Elizabéthain* (Paris, 1957), p. 51: 'monstre dramatique, qui allie les couleurs sombres d'une sorte de "revenge-play" aux gaietés incongrues de chansons grivoises, pourrait traduire le déssaroi d'un esprit qui essaie malgré lui de s'adapter au pessimisme en vogue'.

10. References are to F. T. Bower's edition, *Dramatic Works of Dekker* (Cambridge, 1955–61).

11. *The Comic in Renaissance Comedy* (1981), ch. 4.

12. Cyrus Hoy, Introduction to Bowers' *Dramatic Works of Dekker* (1980) III, p. 81.

13. G. R. Price, *Thomas Dekker* (New York, 1969), p. 30.

14. 'Conversations with Drummond', Herford and Simpson, I, pp. 133, 137.

15. *Hierarchy of the Blessed Angels* (1635), p. 205.

16. Leslie Hotson, *Shakespeare's Sonnets Dated* (1949), pp. 198–9.

17. Quotations are from the edition of R. S. Burns (Garland), 1980.

18. Burns, Introduction, pp. 36–7.

19. Ibid., pp. 15–27.

20. Ibid., pp. 2–3.

21. References are to the edition of A. H. Bullen, *The Works of John Day* (1881), reprinted with introduction by R. Jeffs, 1963.

22. The details of Rowley's career are taken from E. K. Chambers, *The Elizabethan Stage* (1923), III, pp. 473–5 and G. E. Bentley, *Jacobean and Caroline Stage* (1956), V, pp. 1014–27.

23. Details of Tourneur's life are from E. K. Chambers, *The Elizabethan Stage*, III, p. 499.

24. Ibid., p. 500.

25. Quotations are from the edition of Gill and Morris, 1976.

3 BEN JONSON

1. Quotations are from Herford and Simpson, *Ben Jonson*, Oxford 1925–1950.

2. *Volpone*, 'Address', 108–9.

3. C. G. Thayer, *Ben Jonson, Studies in the Plays* (Oklahoma 1963), pp. 221–3.

4 JOHN MARSTON

1. W. R. Gair, *The Children of Paul's 1553–1608* (Cambridge, 1982), p. 118.

2. W. R. Gair, Introduction to *Antonio's Revenge* (Revels Plays; 1978), p. 30.

3. A. Davenport, *Poems of John Marston* (Liverpool, 1961), references are to this edition.
4. See Oxford English Dictionary under 'Kinsing'.
5. P. J. Finkelpearl, 'John Marston's "Histriomastix" as an Inns of Court Play', *Huntington Library Quarterly*, 29 (1966).
6. *Plays of John Marston*, edited H. Harvey Wood, III, p. 301.
7. See Frances Yates, 'Queen Elizabeth as Astraea', *Journal of Warburg Institute*, 10, (1947).
8. *Plays*, ed. Wood, p. 288.
9. Ibid. p. 295.
10. George Geckle, *John Marston's Drama* (1980), p. 34.
11. *Plays*, ed. Wood, p. 260.
12. *Antonio and Mellida*, edited G. K. Hunter (Regents Renaissance Drama, 1965), Induction, 136.
13. Hunter, Introduction, p. ix.
14. P. J. Finkelpearl, *John Marston of the Inner Temple* (1969), p. 140, refers to them as 'a unique comic-tragic diptych'; Gair (Introduction, p. 22, *Antonio's Revenge*) refers to the second part as 'exceptional in that it is ostensibly the second part of a play which began as a comedy'. Hunter (p. xv) refers to 'the volte-face between part 1 and part 2'.
15. See Mervin Herrick, *Tragicomedy* (Urbana, 1962), pp. 67ff.
16. Ibid., p. 90: 'Cinthio's conception of the *tragedia mista* . . . remained firmly rooted in Seneca.'
17. Plautus's *Amphitryo*, however, is defined by Giraldi as 'mixed tragedy', in spite of its comic elements, because it dealt with 'noble persons' (Herrick, *Tragicomedy*, p. 67).
18. Herrick, *Tragicomedy*, p. 68.
19. Galeatzo may also be referring to *Isaiah*, 58:5.
20. For example, Geckle, *John Marston's Drama*, p. 71.
21. Hunter (ed.), *Antonio and Mellida*, p. 2.
22. R. A. Foakes, PQ, 41 (1962).
23. *Antonio and Mellida*, II.i.191–5.
24. Quotations are from edition of Reavely Gair (Revels Plays, Manchester, 1978).
25. George Gascoique's translation of Pope Innocent III, 'De Contemptu Mundi', I.
26. 'Works' edited G. Ponte (Milan, 1968), p. 494, 'superbientem inter miserias suas et fragilitatis sibi conscium; vilissimis vermibus imparem, vite brevis, etatis ambigue, fati inevitabilis, ac mille generibus mortis expositum'.
27. 'Death's Duel', 1630.
28. Thomas Newton, 'Dedicatory to The Tenne Tragedies of Seneca', 1581.
29. Herrick, *Tragicomedy*, p. 74.
30. *Le tragedie di m Gio. Battista Giraldi Cinthio . . . appresso Giulio Cesare Cagnacini* (1583), vol 2: V.iii.156–8.
31. V.v.415–16, 420–6: Ben è vana, e fugace / questa felicità nostra mortale . . . Dunque a quella immortale, / ch'è là dov'è il signor che'l ciel governa, / chiunque il ver discerna, / del veloce pensier spiegar dee

l'ale, / e lasciar questa frale / qui godere a gli sciocchi, / cui le cose terrene appannangli occhi.

32. For a discussion of sixteenth-century attitudes, see H. J. Laski's introduction to *A Defence of Liberty against Tyrants* (1964).
33. Ed. cit., p. 39.
34. Quoted by F. L. Lucas, *Seneca and Elizabethan Tragedy* (1922), p. 58.
35. Finkelpearl, *John Marston*, pp.154–7.
36. Arden edition of *Hamlet* (1982), p. 9.
37. References are to H. Harvey Wood, *Plays of John Marston*, vol. III.
38. References are to M. R. Woodhead's edition (Nottingham Drama Texts, 1980).
39. Gair, *Children of Paul's*, p. 147.
40. *Cynthia's Revels*, V.viii.33.
41. *Volpone*, Prologue 32.
42. As by E. K. Chambers, *Elizabethan Stage*, vol. IV, p. 21.
43. Finkelpearl, *John Marston*, p. 135.
44. Woodhead, Introduction, p. iii.
45. Finkelpearl, *John Marston*, p. 173.
46. *Malcontent*, edited Martin Wine (Regents Renaissance Drama, 1965).
47. M. Scott, *John Marston's Plays* (1978), pp. 29–31.
48. R. Hosley, 'The Playhouses', *Revels History of Drama in English* (1975), p. 123.
49. Francis Bacon, 'Of a King', *Works* (1879), vol. I, p. 308.
50. *The Fawn* edited Gerald A. Smith (Regents Renaissance Drama, 1965).
51. Finkelpearl, *John Marston*, p. 202.
52. R. K. Presson, 'Marston's Dutch Courtesan: the study of an attitude in adaptation', *JEGP*, 55 (1956), pp. 405–13.
53. Geckle, *John Marston's Drama*, ch. 9.
54. Scott, *John Marston's Plays*, pp. 38–47.

5 GEORGE CHAPMAN

1. Appendix IV of Herbage's *Shakespeare's Audience* (1941), p. 178 shows two of Chapman's plays in the top ten of Henslowe's plays for June 1594 to July 1597. *Humorous Day's Mirth* comes only slightly below *Dr Faustus* as Henslowe's most successful play in these years.
2. Edited F. Manley (Regents Renaissance Drama Series), (1968).
3. *Elizabethan Critical Essays*, edited Gregory Smith (Oxford, 1904), vol. II, pp. 319–20.
4. *The Plays of George Chapman (The Comedies)*, edited T. M. Parrott (reprint, 1961), vol. I.
5. *The Gentleman Usher*, edited J. H. Smith (1970), p. 3. Quotations are from this edition.
6. *Poems*, edited Bartlett, p. 49. II, 33–7.
7. 'A Free and Offenceless Justification of . . . Andromeda Liberata', *Poems* (Bartlett), p. 327, II, 5–8.
8. *Poems*, p. 328, I, 72.
9. See Smith's Introduction, pp. xx, 3.

10. An interesting reading of the play in terms of these 'hieroglyphics' is to be found in Jackson Cope, *The Theatre and the Dream* (1973), pp. 32–52.
11. *Poems*, p. 224, II, 188–91.
12. *The Works of George Chapman: Poems and Minor Translations* with an introduction by Algernon Charles Swinburne (1875), p. xxx.
13. *Poems*, pp. 224–5.
14. For a somewhat different account of Vandome's Herculean role compare A. P. Hogan's article 'Thematic Unity in Chapman's *Monsieur D'Olive*', *Studies in English Literature*, II (1971) pp. 304–5. Vaumont also compares Vandome at this point in the play with Hermes the messenger of the Gods; in Neoplatonic thought, the 'guide of souls' who 'calls the mind back to heavenly things' (Edgar Wind, 'Botticelli's Allegory of the Seasons', *Pagan Mysteries of the Renaissance* [1967], pp. 121–4). References to *Monsieur D'Olive* are to Parrott's edition.
15. [les Chrétiens] de la Renaissance . . . ont assigné à Hercule un rôle dans le plan providential', Marcel Simon, *Hercule et le Christianisme*, Paris, 1955, p. 195. 'Hercule fut, dès Moyen Age, entendu comme l'équivalent païen du Sauveur', Raymond Trousson, *Le Thème de Prométhée dans la Littérature Européenne*, Geneva (1964), I, p. 123. Alexander Ross writes in *Mystagogus Poeticus* (1648), p. 171: 'our blessed Saviour is the true Hercules' and Spenser makes use of the analogy: *Faerie Queen*, I.xi.27. Ronsard draws a parallel between Hercules's descents into the underworld with Christ's in his poem *Hercule Chrestien* (1555):

> Hercule ayant une masse de boys
> Vint aux Enfers, Jesus ayant sa Croix
> Y vint aussi. Hercule osta Thesée
> Hors des Enfers, et son cher Pirrithée,
> Trainant par force à reculons le Chien
> Fortier d'Enfer, attaché d'un lien:
> Et Jesus Christ, ayant donté le Diable,
> Rompit l'Enfer de sa Croix admirable,
> Et ses amys hors de Lymbes getta.

Hymnes edited A. Py, Geneva (1978), p. 272. The parallel between Christ and Hercules as redeemer figures is present in Dante's *Inferno*, ix, 97–9 (cf. *Inferno*, viii, 124–6).
16. See Parrott's notes, *Comedies*, II, 787–8.
17. *Petrarch's Secret* translated . . . by William Draper (1911), p. 138.
18. Ibid., p. 132.
19. Ibid., p. 139.
20. Ibid., p. 84. The original reads: 'Habet te funnesta quedam pestis animi, quam accidiam moderni, veteres egritudinem dixerunt', *Opere*, ed. G. Ponte (Milan, 1968), p. 504.
21. *Opere*, pp. 534–6.
22. Ibid., p. 554.
23. M. MacLure, *George Chapman, a critical study* (Toronto, 1966), p. 102.
24. Ibid., p. 101.

25. P. V. Kreider, *Elizabethan Comic Character Convention in . . . Chapman*, (1935), p. 86
26. MacLure, *George Chapman*, p. 103.
27. Swinburne, *The Works of George Chapman*, p. xxxi.
28. References are to the edition of Akihiro Yamada (Revels Plays), 1975.
29. E. M. Smeak, p. xix.
30. Ibid. The Italian text reads: Ma sendo l'intento mio scrivere cosa utile a chi la intende, mi è parso più conveniente andare drieto alla verità effectuale della cosa, che alla immaginazione di essa.
31. Alexandra Ross, for instance, identifies Apollo and Christ: 'He is immortal and "the good shepherd who hath laid down his life for his sheep", having for his sheep's sake forsaken his Father's glory', *Mystagogus Poeticus* (1648) p. 28.
32. *Bussy D'Ambois* edited Nicholas Brooke (Revels Plays, 1964).
33. Ed. cit. note to II.i.190–204; p. 39.
34. References to all the later tragedies are to Parrott, *The Plays of George Chapman, The Tragedies* (reprint, 1961).
35. Dedication of *The Revenge of Bussy D'Ambois*, Parrott, I, p. 77.
36. See A. H. Tricomi, 'The Revised version of Chapman's *Bussy D'Ambois* and the *Revenge*', *English Language Notes*, 9 (1972), pp. 253–62.
37. Rees, *The Tragedies of George Chapman* (1954), argues convincingly for an earlier date for *Caesar and Pompey* 'at least as early as 1605, and perhaps several years earlier', p. 129. If it is as early as this it might be seen as inaugurating the distinctive move towards a more 'correct' classic style on the public stage.

6 THOMAS MIDDLETON

1. Margot Heinemann, *Puritanism and Theatre, Thomas Middleton and Opposition Drama under the early Stuarts* (1980), p. 50.
2. Herford and Simpson, I, p. 137.
3. *Michaelmas Term* edited R. Levin (Regents Renaissance Drama), p. xii.
4. For example, St. Augustine, *City of God* translated H. Bettenson (1972), pp. xiv, 28.
5. *Romans*, 7:14 (Geneva Bible, 1560).
6. Thomas Middleton and William Rowley, *The Changeling* edited G. W. Williams (Regents Renaissance Drama, 1967).
7. *The Revenger's Tragedy*, edited R. A. Foakes (Revels Plays, Manchester, 1966).
8. *A Chaste Maid in Cheapside*, edited R. B. Parker (Revels Plays, Manchester, 1969).
9. *A Trick to Catch the Old One*, edited G. J. Watson (New Mermaids, 1968).
10. *The Works of Thomas Middleton* edited A. H. Bullen (1885), IV.
11. To such an extent that G. E. Rowe in an interesting analysis sees the play as a deliberate parody of benevolent comedy: *Thomas Middleton and the New Comedy Tradition* (1979), pp. 114–30. Rowe, however, ignores the religious element altogether.

12. See Parker's Introduction, p. xxix.
13. *Works* edited A. H. Bullen, vol. VII, p. 214.
14. This is not the place for detailed arguments concerning Middleton's authorship of these plays, but merely to register the present writer's opinion that the case for Middleton's authorship of *Revenger's Tragedy* and *Second Maiden's Tragedy* has been placed beyond reasonable doubt by the work of David Lake, *The Canon of Thomas Middleton's Plays* (Cambridge 1975). See also the discussion of authorship in Anne Lancashire's edition of *Second Maiden* (Manchester, 1978); G. R. Price, 'The authorship and the Bibliography of Revenger's Tragedy', *The Library*, 5th series, xv (1960), pp. 262–77; and P. B. Murray, 'The Authorship of the Revenger's Tragedy', *Papers of the Bibliographical Society of America*, 56 (1962), pp. 195–218. Both the arguments against Tourneur's authorship and for Middleton's authorship of *Revenger's Tragedy* are particularly strong. The attribution to Tourneur rests almost entirely on a list of plays, known to be faulty, dating from 1656, almost fifty years after the play's first publication. There is no evidence that Tourneur had contributed anything to the theatre before his one surviving play *Atheist's Tragedy* (1611), which is markedly different from and inferior to *Revenger's Tragedy* in style and philosophy. Apart from the close stylistic corroboration of *Revenger's Tragedy* with Middleton's acknowledged plays, dealt with by Lake and others there is important external evidence that he was the author

(a) in the coupling of the play with *A Trick to Catch the Old One* in the Stationers' Register under the name of the printer George Elde (7 October 1607);
(b) an allusion to the play in Nathanial Richards' commendatory verses for *Women Beware Women*.

The main argument against Middleton's authorship is that the play was performed by the King's Men at the Globe, whereas Middleton was primarily writing for the Boys' companies. There are plenty of examples, however, of playwrights who wrote for both kinds of theatre more or less contemporaneously (for example Jonson, Chapman, Day, Dekker and Webster) and—as I have argued—tragedy was more suitable for adult companies.

15. *The Second Maiden's Tragedy*, edited Anne Lancashire (Revels Plays, Manchester, 1978).
16. *Works*, vol. II edited Bullen (1885).
17. *Women Beware Women* edited J. R. Mulryne (Revels Plays, 1975) pp. xxxii–xxxviii.
18. References are to the edition of G. W. Williams (Regents Renaissance Drama, 1966).
19. *City of God*, translated Betterson, pp. xiv, 11–13.
20. *Women Beware Women*, ed. Mulryne, pp. lxiv–lxxii.
21. Ibid., pp. lxix–lxx.
22. Ibid., p. lvii.

7 JOHN WEBSTER

1. *The White Devil* edited E. M. Brennan (New Mermaids, 1966), 'To the Reader'.
2. The attributions are those of Murray and Lake, see D. Lake, *The Canon of Middleton's Plays* (1975), p. 48.
3. References are to F. Bowers, *Dramatic Works of Dekker*, vol. II (1955).
4. See III.iii.40f.
5. Allardyce Nicoll, 'The Dramatic Portrait of George Chapman', PQ 41 (1962).
6. For biographical details see M. C. Bradbrook, *John Webster* (1980).
7. 'A Cunning piece of wrought perspective', *John Webster*, Mermaid Critical Commentaries, edited Brian Morris (1970, p. 174.
8. IV.i.40.
9. Charles Lamb, *Specimen of English Dramatic Poets*, *Works*, ed. E. V. Lucas (1904) vol. IV, p. 179.
10. Ibid., IV, p. 190.
11. L. L. Brodwin, *Elizabethan Love Tragedy* (1972), p. 279.
12. J. R. Mulryne, 'Webster and the Uses of Tragicomedy', *John Webster*, edited Morris (1970), p. 13.
13. Pp. 135–6.
14. Commendatory verse prefacing the 1623 edition of *Duchess of Malfi*.
15. Edited E. V. Lucas, *The Complete Works of John Webster*, vol. I, p. 128.
16. *Webster, the Critical Heritage* ed. D. D. Moore (1981), p. 35.
17. Ibid., p. 33.
18. *Duchess*, ed. Lucas, I.i.317.
19. See R. W. Dent, *John Webster's Borrowing* (1960), pp. 87–8.
20. QI, sig.L4^r.
21. Jeremy Taylor, *The Rule and Excercises of Holy Dying*, 1650 (1838), pp. 73–4.
22. Dent, *John Webster's Borrowing*, p. 147.
23. See my chapter on Middleton in *The Comic in Renaissance Comedy* (1981).
24. See D. C. Gunby, *Webster, The White Devil*, pp. 48–9.
25. M. C. Bradbrook, *John Webster*, 'from Marston he took most', p. 137.
26. A. J. Smith, 'The Power of the White Devil', *John Webster*, ed. Morris (1970). p. 74.
27. There are explicit references to predestination in the play, notably Flamineo's 'Man may his Fate foresee, but not prevent' (V.vi.181).
28. For a useful summary of modern critical attitudes to the play see Joyce Peterson, *Curs'd Example*, *The Duchess of Malfi and Commonwealth Tragedy* (1978), pp. 1–13.
29. J. W. Lever, *Tragedies of State* (1971), p. 94 (quoted by Peterson).
30. *John Webster*, ed. Morris (1970), pp. 181–204, 207–28.
31. Peterson, *Curs'd Example*, p. 110.
32. Bradbrook, *John Webster*, p. 150.
33. 'A vertuous Widdow' and 'An ordinarie Widdow', 'Characters', *Complete Works of Webster*, ed. Lucas, vol. IV, pp. 38–9.
34. 'A Monumental Column', 220; *Works*, ed. Lucas, vol. III, p. 280.

35. *Anatomy of the World*, ll.155–7; *Works*, ed. Lucas, vol. ɪ, p. 176.
36. *Romans*, 7:19 (Geneva version).
37. *Works*, ed. Lucas, vol. ɪɪɪ.
38. Bradbrook, *John Webster*, pp. 178–9.
39. *Works*, ed. Lucas, vols. ɪɪ, ɪɪɪ.
40. *Duchess*, III.ii.367.
41. Bradbrook, *John Webster*, p. 176.
42. *Works*, ɪɪɪ, p. 10–18.
43. Jacqueline Pearson, *Tragedy and Tragicomedy in the Plays of John Webster* (Manchester, 1980), ch. 8.

8 JOHN FLETCHER AND HIS COLLABORATIONS

1. For a discussion of the evidence see Cyrus Hoy, 'Fletcher and His Collaborators', *Studies in Bibliography*, vɪɪɪ (1956), ɪx (1957), xɪ (1958), xɪɪ (1959), xɪɪɪ (1960), xɪv (1961), xv (1962). I have accepted Hoy's divisions between the various collaborators as a basis of my critical discussion.
2. 'To the Reader', *The Faithful Shepherdess*, ed. Hoy (1976). (Bowers, ɪɪɪ). Where possible quotations will be taken from the Bowers' edition of the *Dramatic Works* throughout the chapter.
3. J. V. Cunningham, *Woe or Wonder* (Denver, 1957).
4. *King Henry VIII*, ed. R. A. Foakes (1957), Prologue, 4.
5. Hoy, *Studies in Bibliography*, ɪx (1958), 85.
6. Aubrey, *Brief Lives* ed. O. L. Dick, (1962), p. 128.
7. Ed. G. W. Williams, *Bowers*, ɪ, pp. 145–259.
8. John Dryden, 'Of Dramatic Poesy', ed. G. Watson (1962), ɪ, 68.
9. The dating of *Cupid's Revenge* is usually given, as by the *Bowers* editor, Bowers himself, as 'about 1607–8' (p. 331). The title page of the first Quarto (1615), however, refers to the play's performance by 'the Children of Her Majesty's Revels', a title lost by the company (after the fracas over Day's *Isle of Gulls*) in 1606.
10. Ed. cit.
11. The phrase is from L. B. Wallis's *Fletcher, Beaumont and Company* (New York, 1947), ch. 7.
12. 'WB' (Walter Burne), 'To his many waies endeered friend Maister Robert Keysar', *Bowers*, ɪ, 7, 6, 4–5.
13. The Q1 title page of *A King and No King* refers to it as 'Acted at the Globe', with no mention of Blackfriars.
14. *Bowers*, ɪɪɪ, p. 493; G. Chapman, 'To his loving friend M. Jo. Fletcher concerning his Pastorall'.
15. Samuel Daniel had introduced pastoral drama to the Court at Oxford with *The Queen's Arcadia* (1605).
16. See M. T. Herrick, *Tragicomedy* (1955), pp. 93ff.
17. Dyce's edition (1843), ɪ, p. 206.
18. Dyce, ɪ, p. 203 (quoting Langbaine).
19. Ed. R. K. Turner, *Bowers*, ɪ.
20. Edition of *Philaster* (Revels Plays) (1969), pp. liii–lviii.

21. 'The High Design of *A King and No King'. Modern Philology* (1940), pp. xxxviii.
22. Hoy, *Studies in Bibliography*, xi, p. 91.
23. Ed. G. W. Williams, *Bowers*, ii.
24. *A King and No King* (Regents Renaissance Drama, 1964), p. xxv.
25. Eugene Waith, *The Pattern of Tragicomedy in Beaumont and Fletcher* (1952), p. 34.
26. R. K. Turner's edition, *Bowers*, ii.
27. Quotations are from the edition of Clifford Leech (Signet, 1966).
28. Ian Donaldson, *The Rape of Lucretia, a myth and its transformations* (Oxford, 1982).
29. R. K. Turner's edition, *Bowers*, iv.
30. See W. W. Appleton, *Beaumont and Fletcher, A Critical Study* (1956), p. 58.
31. Wallis, *Fletcher, Beaumont and Company*, p. 216.
32. Clifford Leech, *The John Fletcher Plays* (1962), p. 130.
33. Ibid., p. 129.
34. Wallis, *Fletcher, Beaumont and Company*, pp. 210–18.
35. See, for instance, Leech, *The John Fletcher Plays*, pp. 163–8, Appleton, *Beaumont and Fletcher*, p. 54.
36. For the distinction between the earlier and later Elizabethan view of the Romans see T. J. B. Spencer's article, 'Shakespeare and the Elizabethan Romans', *Shakespeare Survey*, x (1957), pp. 27–38.
37. Cyrus Hoy's edition, *Bowers*, iv.

Index

203